CROSSES OF IRON

COLFAX COUNTY, 1912

Map
Area

NEW
MEXICO

RAILROADS OF NEW MEXICO AND COLORADO

1 **Atchison, Topeka and Santa Fe** (branch lines to Van Houten and Blossburg)

2 **El Paso and Southwestern** (terminus at Dawson)

3 **St. Louis, Rocky Mountain and Pacific** (branch lines to Koehler and Raton)

4 **Cimarron and Northwestern**

5 **Santa Fe, Raton and Eastern**

6 **Colorado and Southern** (branch line to Sopris)

7 **Denver and Rio Grande**

8 **Colorado and Wyoming** (branch line to Primero)

Map by Jim Frost; Source: Rand McNally Library Atlas of the World, 1912

Map 1. Colfax County, New Mexico, 1912. (Map by Jim Frost)

CROSSES OF IRON

The Tragic Story of Dawson, New Mexico, and Its Twin Mining Disasters

Nick Pappas

Foreword by Richard Melzer

UNIVERSITY OF NEW MEXICO PRESS   ALBUQUERQUE

ISBN 978-0-8263-6528-6 (paper)
ISBN 978-0-8263-6529-3 (electronic)

Library of Congress Control Number: 2023940430

Founded in 1889, the University of New Mexico sits
on the traditional homelands of the Pueblo of Sandia.
The original peoples of New Mexico—Pueblo, Navajo,
and Apache—since time immemorial have deep
connections to the land and have made significant
contributions to the broader community statewide.
We honor the land itself and those who remain
stewards of this land throughout the generations
and also acknowledge our committed relationship
to Indigenous peoples. We gratefully recognize our
history.

Cover photograph by Roberto Rosales
Designed by Isaac Morris
Composed in Alegreya, Copperplate, and Ms Eaves.

To the lost miners of Dawson,

their families,

and all who remember them

✦

In the foothills of some mountains,
There's a little camp where I was raised.
This camp witnessed my birth,
It is where I lived a happy life.

The years passed me by
as though it was a dream in a night.
It was the most wonderful dream,
which I have ever dreamed.
While I live, I will never forget.

Oh, my beloved Dawson,
when will I ever see you again.
You were my loving cradle;
Which gave me my life,
Which brought me enchantment,
and gave me my existence.

Wherever I will go,
I will tell this story to the world:
You were a beloved camp,
and because of my love for you,
I shall never forget you.

—Augustine Hernandez
Farewell to Dawson! / *¡Adiós a Dawson!*
Lyrics provided by Roberta Hernandez Perez

Allá en las faldas de unas montañas,
está un campito donde me crié.
Ese campito me vio nacer
y en el mi vida feliz pasé.

Ahi los años se me pasaron,
como una noche y un sueño fue,
Sueño tan lindo que yo he soñado,
nunca en mi vida lo olvidaré.

¡Ay! Mi Dawson tan querido,
cuando te volveré a ver.
Fuiste mi cuna querida,
que me dio la vida,
que me dio el encanto,
que me dio mi ser.

Por donde quiera, que yo camino,
Al mundo le he de contar,
que fuiste un campo querido,
y por lo tanto que te quiero,
nunca, nunca te olvidaré.

CONTENTS

FOREWORD   xi
Richard Melzer

PREFACE   xiii

CHAPTER 1.   Entombed   1

CHAPTER 2.   The Birth of Dawson   7

CHAPTER 3.   The Early Years   16

CHAPTER 4.   A Model Community   22

CHAPTER 5.   The Immigrants   29

CHAPTER 6.   Danger in the Mines   37

CHAPTER 7.   October 22, 1913   44

CHAPTER 8.   The Burials   56

CHAPTER 9.   The Sorrow   61

CHAPTER 10.   The Cause   68

CHAPTER 11.   The Inquest   76

CHAPTER 12.   Back to Normal   86

CHAPTER 13.   Oh, No, Not Again!   93

CHAPTER 14.   What Happened This Time?   105

CHAPTER 15.   Writing on the Wall   115

CHAPTER 16.   Closing Time   124

CHAPTER 17.   Dawson Cemetery   134

CHAPTER 18.   Down Memory Lane   143

EPILOGUE   157

ACKNOWLEDGMENTS   160

KILLED IN THE EXPLOSION OF OCTOBER 22, 1913   165

KILLED IN THE EXPLOSION OF FEBRUARY 8, 1923   173

NOTES   177

BIBLIOGRAPHY   211

INDEX   219

FOREWORD

Richard Melzer

Long before there were oil wells, gas lines, uranium mines, wind farms, or solar panels, coal was the number one source of energy in New Mexico. The coal industry helped produce energy for homes, factories, and railroads not only in the state, but far beyond.

Companies as small as the Albuquerque and Cerillos Coal Company and as large as the Phelps Dodge Corporation built whole communities to facilitate the mining of their coal and provided housing of various quality for their workers. Company towns dotted the New Mexico landscape in McKinley County to the west, Colfax County in the northeast, and Santa Fe County in the north-central region of the state.

With time, each company town enjoyed its own identity and sources of pride. Madrid was known for its spectacular Christmas displays. Many camps held extravagant Fourth of July celebrations. Some fielded fine athletic teams. Most towns were proud of the children their citizens raised and the successful careers they pursued, from judges and engineers to army colonels and Catholic priests.

Dawson is remembered as the largest, most modern of New Mexico's many company towns. Owned and operated by Phelps Dodge, Dawson's coal mines served as the major supplier of coking fuel for the corporation's valuable copper smelting plants in southern Arizona. With good housing, reputable schools, a large mercantile store, a popular amusement hall, a hospital, a bank, and amicable labor–management relations, most employees were proud of their model town and to be residents of it. A mixture of nationalities and ethnicities learned to appreciate and respect each other's cultures as fellow workers and neighbors. Dawson was a highly desirable place to live, especially compared to many less-appealing towns in New Mexico and the rest of the country.

But like all coal towns, Dawson was also a place of extreme potential danger. No matter its location, coal mining remained among the most dangerous jobs of the late nineteenth and early twentieth centuries. The best most miners could hope for was that their companies maintained strict safety regulations, provided modern safety equipment, and conducted regular safety drills.

With narrow profit margins, small companies were less able to invest in such protective measures. Statistically, the odds of experiencing a major mining disaster were therefore highest when working for small, money-strapped companies and lowest when employed by large, profitable operations.

Knowing that it was advantageous for both its business and its workers, companies like Phelps Dodge took pride in protecting the safety of their mines and their miners. Phelps Dodge's interest in safety became a major benefit in recruiting and retaining good miners. Aging photographs show Dawson's miners attending safety classes and participating in drills, using the most modern procedures and equipment.

It therefore came as a terrible shock when the Phelps Dodge operation in Dawson faced not one but two major catastrophes in the course of ten years. How could a corporation and work force so well prepared suffer some of the worst mining disasters in New Mexico history? What caused the 1913 and 1923 mine explosions, leaving 383 men dead? How did the company, the industry, the town, and New Mexico react to the crises at the moments they occurred and in their aftermath? What impact did the explosions have on individual lives and on Dawson as a whole, particularly as the town faced other challenges, from the ravages of the Great Depression to competition with more modern fuels?

These are the questions that journalist Nick Pappas answers in one of the best-written, most thoroughly researched histories ever published on mining disasters in American history. As a prize-winning veteran newspaper writer and editor, Pappas is the ideal author to tell this story with precision, compassion, and engaging prose.

Dawson is now a ghost town. But unlike most ghost towns, it has no old buildings or abandoned streets to explore. All that remains is the town's cemetery, filled with hundreds of identical metal crosses, each marking the grave of a brave miner who perished in the town's two tragedies. The crosses are sad reminders of what took place a century and more ago.

Like these crosses, Nick Pappas's compelling new book will serve as a reminder for those who seek to learn how the strong, determined residents of a New Mexico community coped with recurring catastrophes, somehow recovering and managing to thrive for years to come.

—*Richard Melzer*
coauthor of A History of New Mexico Since Statehood

The bumpy road leading into Dawson, New Mexico, is pretty desolate, to say the least. No homes. No businesses. No people.

That doesn't change at the end of this unpaved five-and-a-half-mile byway, where a metal gate with a "No Trespassing" sign blocks entrance into a fifty-thousand-acre tract of land that in its heyday was home to the largest company-owned town in the Southwest.

And one with as macabre a history as the writings of Edgar Allan Poe. Consider:

- On October 22, 1913, 261 coal miners and two outside rescue men were killed in an explosion that stands today as the nation's second-deadliest mine disaster. Some of the bodies were recovered in such a mangled state that they were buried—unidentified by colleagues or next of kin—in unmarked graves.
- A decade later, on February 8, 1923, another blast—the sixteenth-worst mine disaster based on loss of life—claimed the lives of 120 men, some related by blood to men killed in 1913.
- All told, 521 men died from work-related injuries in the Dawson mines during the town's forty-nine-year history. That figure doesn't include countless others who were disfigured or maimed in accidents that were far too common in US mines in the early to mid-twentieth century.

Today, the only hint of this forgotten place can be found a short walk from the locked gate in historic Dawson Cemetery, where rows of white iron crosses memorialize the nearly four hundred miners killed in the 1913 and 1923 explosions.

At its core, then, *Crosses of Iron* is a narrative recounting of the twin tragedies to befall Dawson, the only mining town in America to suffer two mishaps of this magnitude. Yet, the story involves so much more.

It's the story of John Barkley Dawson, the fearless pioneer, rancher, and trailblazer who put down stakes on the land that years later would bear his name.

It's the story of the model mining town that Phelps, Dodge & Company built there, a cosmopolitan community of roughly six thousand souls that boasted a one-thousand-seat opera house, excellent schools, two churches, a huge mercantile store that hosted fashion shows, a state-of-the-art hospital, and, at 6,774 feet, the highest-elevation golf course in the country at that time.

It's the story of European immigrants—from Austria, Finland, France, Germany, Great Britain, Greece, Ireland, Italy, Poland, Sweden, and other countries—who came to Dawson in the early 1900s to seek better lives for themselves and their families.

It's the story of the American labor movement and its at-times bloody crusade to secure better working conditions for the nation's mine workers. US labor organizer Dolores Huerta was born in Dawson. In the aftermath of the 1913 mine explosion, Louis Tikas, the Colorado labor leader who would be killed six months later in the Ludlow Massacre, sneaked into Dawson to commiserate with his fellow Greeks.

It's the story of the closing of the last mine in 1950, when Dawson residents were given only a few months' notice to pack up their possessions. With few exceptions, all of the buildings, homes, and equipment were sold for parts, moved, or bulldozed into oblivion.

It's the story of the rediscovery of Dawson Cemetery, courtesy of two brothers who stumbled upon the deteriorating graveyard while metal detecting decades later. One of the men made it his mission to work hand in hand with New Mexico officials to get the cemetery listed on the National Register of Historical Places and succeeded in 1992.

And it's the story of thousands of folks who have kept the memory of Dawson alive through generations, reuniting every other Labor Day weekend to share stories, display mementos, exchange photographs, and relive memories of what it once meant to be a Dawsonite. For some families, it's not unusual to use these biennial visits to bury the cremated remains of their newly departed loved ones in the historic cemetery.

So why is Dawson, New Mexico, relevant today? Why spend four years researching and writing a book about a mining town that hasn't existed for more than half a century?

Because Dawson *still* has an important tale to tell, one perhaps unmatched in breadth and scope by any other mining town in America. What's more, the themes of mining life that surfaced in the shadows of the Sangre de Cristo Mountains are as pertinent today as they were when Dawsonites faced not one but two of the greatest calamities in the West's young history.

Despair. Faith. Courage. Fortitude. Resilience.

And a love of community unbroken to this very day.

Crosses of Iron is that story.

CHAPTER 1

ENTOMBED

*It was the impossible that happened. Just another case of the unloaded
gun which discharged.*
—J. C. Roberts
US Bureau of Mines
October 24, 1913

✦

If the Dawson mines were ocean liners, they would have been
deemed unsinkable.

High-capacity fans chased out poisonous and explosive gases. A sophis-
ticated fire-protection system circulated water through miles of underground
pipes to sprinklers and hoses. A state-of-the-art rescue station housed oxygen
helmets, resuscitation devices, safety lamps, and other equipment. First-aid
teams drilled regularly and competed for prizes and medals in company-run
competitions.

Such was the reputation in 1913 of the Stag Cañon Fuel Company, which
operated five coal mines tucked into the northeastern corner of New Mexico
not far from the Colorado border. Phelps, Dodge & Company of New York had
purchased the fledgling mining community eight years earlier from the Dawson
Fuel Company—the first mining firm to punch ground-level tunnels into the
spur of a mountain—to ensure a steady stream of fuel for its copper-smelting
plants six hundred miles to the west in southern Arizona.

On the afternoon of October 22, 1913, Thomas "T. H." O'Brien was in his
office a mile from Mine No. 2, the company's most productive coal source a year
earlier. The New York native looked more like a bank executive than the general
manager of a Western coal company, with his slight build, boyish face, and round
rimless glasses. Yet, here he was, after cutting his teeth in the sooty mines of
neighboring Colorado, presiding over what would soon become the largest company-owned town in the Southwest.

Around 3:00 p.m., what sounded like the high-pitched crack of a rifle rattled
O'Brien's eardrums. A muffled roar shook the floor beneath his feet. Outside his

window, from the mouth of No. 2, a dragon-like tongue of flame spewed hundreds of feet into the sky before giving way to billowing clouds of dense black smoke.

O'Brien activated the emergency siren, prompting workers from the adjacent mines to rush hell-bent toward the smoldering No. 2. Much to their horror, they found the main entrance clogged with tons of debris. O'Brien ordered them to clear a path through the entryway. Then he and his crew made a beeline toward the air shaft, one mile north of the entrance and 250 feet deep, which contained a ladder and steps for such emergencies. But the air there was already saturated with poisonous gases, a surefire sign that the fan had been silenced by the ferocious force of the explosion.

Undeterred, O'Brien and his men donned oxygen helmets and rushed inside Mine No. 5, which shared a tunnel with the wrecked mine. Here, too, they found the passageway blocked. For O'Brien, the urgency became crystal clear: Unless rescue crews were able to break through the debris-filled entrance—and quickly—the death toll would be incomprehensible.

Time was not on their side. The explosion had flattened the timber frames used to buttress the roof and sides of the mine, so rescue teams had to replace them as they went, step by step, piece by piece, lest they be crushed themselves. And that tedious work could be done only after clearing the avalanche of debris—coal, earth, rock, and timber—that stretched from the entryway thousands of feet underground into the belly of the mine. Still, the rescuers persevered. By 10:00 p.m., seven hours after the explosion, they had penetrated roughly one hundred feet into the mine. Deep enough to rescue five entombed miners.

O'Brien was a beacon of hope and inspiration through it all. He recruited help from mining camps near and far, supervised the entrance work, even led rescue crews in the frantic search for the nearly three hundred trapped miners. Until he couldn't. Some twenty-four hours after the explosion, having never paused to eat, at the brink of exhaustion, he collapsed while raising an oxygen helmet to his head to lead yet another rescue team into the mine.

✦

James "J. C." Roberts, chief of the US Bureau of Mines rescue station in the Denver-based Rocky Mountain District, learned of the Dawson incident from the Associated Press news service at 8:30 p.m., some five and a half hours after the explosion. He made plans to leave that night with a rescue car, one of the bureau's fleet of converted Pullmans containing trained rescue crews and the finest equipment. Before departing, Roberts telegraphed for additional help from rescue cars stationed in Pittsburg, Kansas, and Rock Springs, Wyoming.

Rushing to a mine disaster was not new to Roberts, a forty-seven-year-old former metallurgy professor at the Colorado School of Mines in Golden. When Congress established the bureau in 1910 in response to a barrage of mine disasters, he became the district's go-to guy to lead the government's first response teams. In this role, Roberts already had witnessed enough heartache to last a lifetime: Seventy-nine bodies in Delagua, Colorado, in 1910. Seventeen in Cokedale, Colorado, in 1911. Seven in Kemmerer, Wyoming, in 1912. Now this.

Roberts and his team took command upon their arrival the next afternoon, but it wasn't long before he grasped the hopelessness of the rescue mission. One glimpse at the first bodies showed that they had been killed instantly by the violence of the explosion or moments later by inhaling the dreaded black damp, a deadly mixture of carbon dioxide and nitrogen that permeated the mine after the fan was rendered inoperable by the blast. Roberts found one dead miner leaning against a wall, both hands raised as if trying to block a punch to the jaw. Another was standing, pick in hand, as if he had "struck his last blow into the coal."

For some families, the procedure for identifying the dead—or what remained of them—only deepened their anguish. If a deceased miner could not be identified with certainty by mine officials, wives and relatives were ushered into an old company store converted by grim necessity into a makeshift morgue. Here, amid the eye-watering stench of decomposition, they were given mere seconds to determine if the disfigured or mutilated body lying before them was a father, a husband, a son, a brother, an uncle, a cousin. The corpses that defied identification would be buried in the town cemetery under nameless iron crosses.

✦

Dr. James Douglas, president of Phelps Dodge, was six hundred miles away in his namesake town of Douglas, Arizona. He boarded a special train with Walter Douglas, his elder son and the company's general manager, and arrived on the morning of October 24, two days after the incident.

Douglas was no bean-counting figurehead. A brilliant metallurgist and mining engineer by trade, this Canadian-born son of a prominent Scottish surgeon had been recruited by Phelps Dodge as a consultant in 1881 after he earned national acclaim for his pioneering work in the extraction of copper from its ores. By the time Douglas became president in 1908, Phelps Dodge was well into its transformation from an old New York–based mercantile company into a copper-mining juggernaut of international renown.

Still, the long train ride could not have prepared father and son for what awaited them: Helmeted rescue men, in regular shifts of fifteen, trudging out of the mine with stretchers bearing the hidden remains of miners. Mothers and wives, only yards from the charred entrance, pressed up against hastily erected ropes to prevent them from interfering with rescuers. A steady stream of empty coffins, arriving by the trainload from as far away as Colorado and Texas, ticketed for the morgue.

This wasn't the first visit to Dawson for the seventy-five-year-old Douglas, who was called "Dr." out of respect even though he had never completed his medical degree. He had spent many days here negotiating the purchase of the mines in 1905 and had made frequent trips in the ensuing years, even journeying deep inside the tunnels despite his advancing age. This time, he kept to administrative work, sparing no expense to procure the best rescue equipment available. His son, meanwhile, spent much of his time inside the mine, aiding the rescue work and leading efforts to clear the air of dangerous gases.

Both arrived just in time for the first funerals.

✦

Town Supervisor Thaddeus "T. L." Kinney was quick to set up a relief camp a few yards from the mine entrance, where survivors and overextended rescuers could find rest and medical care. But the forty-year-old Indiana native had another critical assignment: in keeping with Phelps Dodge's strict anti-union philosophy, he was charged with making sure labor agitators from nearby coal camps did not gain entry into Dawson under any circumstances—even to assist in the rescue of their fellow miners.

That's precisely what happened to Edward L. Doyle, secretary–treasurer of the Colorado-based District 15 of the United Mine Workers of America. Doyle was so irate over his treatment at the railyard that he fired off an angry telegram to US Rep. Edward E. Keating of Colorado two days later. "Went to Dawson to offer financial assistance to those in distress and was driven out by coal company's mounted police," he wrote. "Hundreds of miners still entombed. Action a disgrace to civilization."

Later, the *United Mine Workers Journal* published a more colorful account of the incident: "Men from the neighboring mines came to this privately-owned town, intending to render what assistance they could, by aiding in the work of rescue, and to proffer financial assistance to the families of the victims. But they were met at the railroad station by the camp marshals and forced to walk, at the muzzle of a rifle, six miles, to the end of the private holdings of this company."

In Dawson-speak, they were "kicked down the canyon."

+

Rees H. Beddow, New Mexico's first mine inspector after its admission into the union in 1912, knew the Stag Cañon mines well. In fact, he had left Dawson just days before the explosion after wrapping up his inspection of all five mines. During his two-day examination of Mine No. 2, conducted on October 15 and 16, he took a head count of workers underground, examined the ventilation system, and sent an air sample to the US Bureau of Mines to test for levels of methane, which can be deadly in high concentrations in coal mines.

The fifty-four-year-old inspector found little to dispute the conventional wisdom of the day among mining experts: the Dawson mines were among the safest in the country. In his annual report to the governor, submitted six weeks after the explosion, Beddow wrote that the mine was "a modern one in every respect," its ventilation system was "well planned," its equipment was "first class," and the company's shot-firing system, used to dislodge coal inside the mines, "can not be beaten."

Beddow did flag the presence of highly flammable coal dust, the fine powder generated by the crushing or grinding of coal. The dust had already played a major role in coal mine disasters around the world, including the second-worst on record, at Courrières in northern France in 1906, which claimed the lives of 1,099 miners. While Beddow acknowledged that the amount of coal dust necessary to feed an explosion was open to debate, he found a worrisome amount throughout the mine, due, in part, to New Mexico's dry climate. "[I]n this dust lies the greatest danger to the operation of mines," he wrote, "and there is no doubt in my mind that the dust problem will be given more serious consideration, and that the most approved remedies for this danger will be applied." If not, he warned, he would push for stricter laws to help him deal with the problem.

Beddow was 150 miles away in the capital city of Santa Fe on the afternoon of the explosion. After conferring with the governor, he left for Dawson at 9:00 p.m. and arrived the next morning. By 7:00 a.m., he was inside the corpse-filled mine.

+

Governor William C. McDonald was no stranger to coal mines, having worked as a mining engineer in White Oaks, New Mexico, before entering state politics thirty years earlier. The fifty-five-year-old Democrat made it known that the state was prepared to offer assistance—financial or otherwise—to aid the victims' families.

The American Red Cross reached out, too. By noon the day after the explosion, Dr. S. P. Morris, a representative from the district office, had arrived in Dawson to help. National Director General Ernest P. Bicknell also informed McDonald that he could count on a donation of $1,000 to help ease the suffering of the miners' families.

Both offers were appreciated but declined by Phelps Dodge officials, who assured the governor and the relief agency that the company would take care of its own. It would make good on that promise, paying for the burials and making lump sum payments of roughly $1,000—the equivalent of about $30,000 today—to each widow and $100 to each child of the deceased miners.

✦

Mine Superintendent William McDermott was riding toward the mines on horseback two hours before the explosion when he spotted Tim Tinsley up ahead. Tinsley, a veteran coal miner, had come out of retirement in neighboring Colorado three years earlier to become foreman of the Dawson mines. Tinsley told McDermott he was on his way to Mine No. 2 to check on an injured worker. McDermott, well into his first year as superintendent, said he wanted to speak to the pit boss about the accident, so he instructed Tinsley to take care of some business in the No. 1 mine instead.

McDermott was still in the mine when it exploded.

Ultimately, the official death toll was set at 263—261 trapped miners and two rescue men from an outside coal camp—making it the second-deadliest mine disaster in US history. Two-thirds of the dead were recent immigrants from Italy and Greece. Only twenty-three men survived.

Three weeks after the explosion, Kinney, the town supervisor who doubled as a judge, swore in the six men chosen to participate in the coroner's inquest.

Their charge?

To determine, in the words of County Attorney George E. Remley, "whether or not [the victims'] death was caused by a crime of any person or persons."

And, if so, by whom?

CHAPTER 2

THE BIRTH OF DAWSON

I went sometimes without the necessaries of life. I used my rifle and fish hook many times to keep from going hungry. The blazed trail is nearly finished. I hewed the way for my children. The way has much improved. I shall leave it to you to see the improvement. I will not attempt to describe it.
—John Barkley Dawson
Autobiographical notes, 1912

✦

There would have been no Dawson—at least in name—without John Barkley Dawson. Cattle driver. Farmer. Pioneer. Rancher. Texas Ranger. Trail blazer.

Coal baron? Hardly. Dawson's primary use for the surface coal scattered about his ranch was to keep his family comfortable during those frosty New Mexico winters. The coal, it turned out, burned longer than wood inside his woodstove.

J. B. Dawson was born on November 10, 1830, in Grayson County, Kentucky, the only son of Thomas and Letitia de Graffenried Dawson. His grandfather served in the 1st Virginia Regiment during the American Revolution and married Mary Ann Clay, a relative of American statesman Henry Clay.

Dawson grew up to be a man of indisputable character, a trait that would serve him well years later when he was the defendant in a land eviction proceeding that reached the US Supreme Court. Based on a story he was fond of reciting to his children and grandchildren, that character was put to the test at an early age. As recounted by his granddaughter, Delphine Dawson Wilson, Dawson's parents sent him out to hunt wild game to put some food on the table, not an uncommon chore for a nine-year-old of that day. But poor John got lost. Tracking the sound of ax striking wood, he spied a cabin where a father and son were chopping down trees. As the story goes, John arrived around mealtime, and the man invited him to stay. Inside, John counted ten children around the table, each with an eye on some small baked potatoes, roughly eighteen in all. It didn't take long for him to do the math. Even though he had yet to eat that day, a famished John chose only two tiny ones for his plate.

"Take three, stranger, take dang-nigh all of them, stranger!" the man shouted at him.

John started to reach for another until he caught the anxious look on the children's faces. Recognizing that this family was more destitute than his own, he pulled back. John was "shown the way home," where he not only found himself hungry but with nothing to feed his family. Whether he got a good whippin' when he got home is open to conjecture.

✦

After spending six or seven years in southwestern Missouri, in 1840 the Dawson family moved near Fort Smith, Arkansas, nestled along the Arkansas River near the Oklahoma border. Since its founding in 1817, Fort Smith had developed into a key supply post for US soldiers, and before long John's father had secured a government contract to furnish hay to the military men stationed there. These were prosperous times for the Dawson family, which by now had expanded to include kinfolk and friends.

Near the end of the decade, however, Fort Smith underwent a historic transformation, kick-started by the discovery of gold at the base of California's Sierra Nevada Mountains. Within a year, it became a popular supply center not just for the military, but also for "forty-niners" lured westward by the promise of riches.

These prospectors did not include the Dawson family, at least not at first. It would be another four years before Thomas, Letitia, John, and his younger sister Henrietta left Fort Smith behind to travel by ox team to California. While their precise route is not known, John's brief account suggests they crossed the Platte River in Colorado, hoofed it through what is now Denver, then passed through Salt Lake City on their way to their final destination.

That turned out to be Rough and Ready, a scrappy mining town that had wasted no time in carving out a permanent—if somewhat dubious—place in US history. Furious over California's imposition of a mining tax, townspeople voted in 1850 to secede and form the Great Republic of Rough and Ready, complete with constitution, president, and cabinet. That early experiment in self-governance lasted less than three months, ending, appropriately enough, on the Fourth of July. By at least one account, the townsfolk scrambled to rejoin the union after several residents were denied the purchase of celebratory alcohol in nearby Nevada City because they were "foreigners."

The Dawson family's stay in Rough and Ready was less dramatic. In fact, after only two years out West, they pulled up stakes and headed back to Arkansas. For John, now twenty-five, that experience proved to be life-changing. By the time the family reached home, he knew what he wanted to do: return to California, not in search of gold, but as a driver of cattle.

✦

The California Gold Rush had taken a toll on the wild game on which miners in the Sierra Nevada foothills relied for food. In this, Dawson saw opportunity. In 1855, he set off on another journey across the continent, this time with an estimated four hundred head of cattle. He was accompanied by relatives and friends and secure in his knowledge of the trail.

Few details exist about Dawson's maiden cattle drive: Not the route. Not the breed of cattle. Not the length of his trip. Not any close calls with bandits or Natives. In Dawson's typical understated way, this is how he described that experience thirty years later: "I returned to California in the fall of 1855. I drove a herd of cattle from Arkansas to California and located at the Butte Mountains, near Marysville. I remained there until the fall of 1857. I sold out my stock and returned to Arkansas where my parents were."

That the trip was a financial success is beyond dispute. A year later, on the recommendation of legendary frontiersman Kit Carson, Dawson and his father obtained one thousand acres of prime cattle-grazing land about four hundred miles to the west in Fort Belknap, Texas. It would be here that Dawson would establish himself as one of the premier cattle drivers of his generation.

By this time, Dawson had learned that gold had been discovered in the Rocky Mountains of Colorado, sparking what would become known as the Colorado Gold Rush. Between 1858 and 1861, an estimated one hundred thousand people flocked to Pikes Peak, roughly halfway between present-day Pueblo and Denver. While these "fifty-niners" dreamed of lining their pockets with gold, Dawson was more interested in stuffing their bellies with beef. He headed north with a herd of cattle, sticking closely to the trail he had blazed years earlier on his way to California. In time, a version of this route would become known as the Dawson Trail.

That cattle drive would be the first of many Dawson would lead—either on his own or with partners—into the wilderness of Colorado, New Mexico, and Wyoming. At times, he trailed as many as six thousand head to sell to miners, government outposts, and even random travelers along the way. These drives, coupled with some shrewd investments in cattle companies in New Mexico in the early 1880s, would go a long way toward making Dawson a wealthy man.

✦

This is not to say that his life was without hardship. Nowhere was that more evident than in his love life.

Dawson met the woman who would become his first wife in 1861. As the story goes, he and his best friend, Tom Stockton, were walking the streets of San Antonio, Texas, when Dawson was struck by "the prettiest music I'd ever heard" coming from a nearby balcony. Reaching for his boot, Dawson pulled out his knife and jimmied the corner of a shuttered window to see who was responsible for the piano playing and song. She turned out to be Tom's half-sister, Edwena Stockton. The two were married months later.

John was thirty years old, ten years older than his new bride, when the newlyweds settled in Fort Belknap. Edwena bore him a child, a son named Augustus Green Dawson, in December 1862, but she fell ill and died a year later, possibly from complications related to the birth.

✦

In the aftermath of Edwena's death, Dawson's life, in the words of his granddaughter, was "thrown out of focus." This may explain why he and Stockton, Edwena's half-brother, joined the Texas Rangers in 1864, three years after Texas seceded to join the Confederate States of America. Dawson's only written account isn't much help: "My wife died December 1st, 1863. I joined the Texas Rangers where we had to serve one fourth of our time. We were organized to protect the frontier of Texas. The service was exclusively for the state in watching and keeping the bands of wandering Indians and Mexicans out. . . . I remained a member of the Rangers for four years."

The only record of this service is a story he shared through the years with family and friends. One retelling came some forty years later, in 1906, in the presence of Charles Goodnight, a fellow cattle rancher and close friend, and journalist Hatton W. Sumners. Goodnight cajoled Dawson into telling Sumners about "the fight on Paint Creek."

Based on Sumners's published account, Natives raided Dawson's Fort Belknap neighborhood and killed a young boy. Dawson, Stockton, and four others tracked them on horseback for 125 miles, killing one before the rest escaped. On their return home the next day, just before sundown, they came across another six Natives on horseback, one a boy of about seventeen, driving a team of what they surmised to be stolen horses. The ensuing confrontation left four

Natives dead and another badly wounded. When the teenaged boy realized he could do nothing to help his wounded companion, he headed straight toward Dawson, bow and arrow in hand, to avenge his death:

> He was coming straight for me. I shot him with a rifle. Tom Stockton and Elias Hale were shooting at him with six shooters. The boy had on a loose shirt and I could see the pistol bullets drive the shirt into his body as the bullets went true.
>
> But they could not stop him. The men who were shooting at him with their pistols were kneeling down. The Indian was coming erect, straight for me.
>
> He got so close to us that Stockton and Hale moved back and I started to mount my horse.
>
> When he saw me doing this, he mounted one of our horses and met me face to face about ten steps apart.
>
> We both started to shoot almost at the same time, I with my pistol, he with his bow. He was a little quicker than I was and his arrow went into my right hand as I was aiming my pistol at him, and into the lock on my pistol, disabling it and rendering me helpless.
>
> Just as he was getting another arrow with which he would no doubt have killed me, George Baylor shot him with a shotgun and he fell from the horse, dead.
>
> When we looked at his body, we found he had one rifle wound and nine pistol wounds, besides the wound made by the shotgun. There were no wounds in his arms or legs. His shirt was as bloody as if it had been dipped in blood.

Sumners's account of Dawson's near brush with death ends here, though family members say Dawson invariably ended his telling of this story by heaping praise on the young Native as "the bravest man I ever met."

✦

Shortly after partnering with a few men to purchase ranchland along the Vermejo River in New Mexico, Dawson met schoolteacher Laura Stout in Veal's Station, Texas. They married in September 1868. This marriage, too, would end in hardship. Shortly after giving birth to his third son, while her husband was away on business, Laura came down with a fever and died, less than four years after their wedding day. John was now in his early forties and, with the arrival of sons Siria Milton and Abner Bruce, the father of three motherless boys.

The search for wife No. 3 turned out to be no less adventurous than one of Dawson's patented cattle drives. Eager to find a new mother for his three boys—now nine, two, and two months in age—Dawson turned to family and friends for some matchmaking. After someone spoke highly of a widow in Trinidad, Colorado, Dawson boarded a stagecoach to go and meet her. He didn't get far.

Dawson picked up a Baptist magazine left onboard and noticed an article written by a Lavinia Jefferson of Middletown, Iowa. At the next stop, a mere twenty-five miles into the journey, Dawson stepped off and caught the next stagecoach home. Using his rudimentary writing skills, perhaps with some assistance, he crafted a letter to the next Mrs. John Barkley Dawson—or so he hoped. He told her he liked her article. He told her he was forty-two years old and in good health. He told her about his "motherless children." And he told her he would like to meet. With that, he mailed the letter to the magazine, hoping that someone would forward it to her.

No doubt many women would have crumpled the stranger's letter and tossed it into the nearest trash heap. Not Lavinia. There was something about it that persuaded this unmarried thirty-one-year-old schoolteacher to reply. She would be willing to meet with him, she wrote, but only if he waited a year—after all, his second wife had died only months earlier.

Still, they corresponded for a time. Before long, Dawson was on his way to Iowa to meet her. When he got off the train that night, the station agent asked him if he was the person who had been writing to "the widow Jefferson's daughter." When Dawson acknowledged he was the one, the agent told him: "You know, you couldn't do better'n marry that girl. Her mother has an acre of good pasture land and a fine Jersey cow." With that, Dawson checked into a hotel for the night.

The pair's morning visit was cut short because Lavinia wasn't feeling well. After this forgettable first meeting, Dawson returned a second time to find her in much better health. A whirlwind courtship culminated in her walking down the aisle of her Baptist church accompanied by this "handsome well-set-up man with neatly trimmed beard and moustache." The wedding took place on March 28, 1873, less than a year after the death of Dawson's second wife, Laura.

"I went as did Rebecca of old, nothing doubting," she wrote years later. "We were married. I bade farewell to home, sister, friends and went to that far-away-land I thought so little of a few months before."

✦

Once Lavinia reached the Dawson ranch, no one would have blamed her if she had climbed back onto the buckboard wagon and headed home to Iowa. It was not long before she had her first taste of what her life was about to become as a member of the Dawson "family." She met John's parents. She met the parents of John's second wife. She met two brothers of John's first wife, one of whom was married to the sister of John's second wife. She met John's partners in the cattle business, one of whom was married to John's cousin. And so on . . . all living on the sprawling Dawson ranch.

Lavinia not only stayed but did her part to expand the family even more. Manley Mortimer, Dawson's fourth son, was born the next year, 1874, followed by another boy, Jefferson Leo, in 1876, and yet another, John Barkley II, in 1878. The run of boys ended with the arrival of Edwena in 1880 and Laura in 1882—both named by John after his first wives without seeking Lavinia's consent. Henry Miller Dawson became the last of John's nine children upon his birth in 1886.

But Lavinia did much more than help populate the ranch with little Dawsons. With her husband away much of the time on business and cattle drives, she became a key partner and administrator, starting with the introduction of her Jersey cow and fresh milk for family and neighbors.

Life was good for this frontier family—until it wasn't.

✦

Dawson was just a boy in 1841 when the Mexican government bestowed a leaf-shaped, 1.7-million-acre tract of land to Mexican citizens Carlos Beaubien and Guadalupe Miranda, the largest such grant in US history. After a series of legal disputes over the legitimacy and boundaries of the grant—the majority in what is now northeastern New Mexico—the property found its way into the hands of Lucien Maxwell, Beaubien's son-in-law. In 1870, he became the sole owner of what became known as the Maxwell Land Grant.

Enter Dawson, brother-in-law Joel Curtis, cousin Dick Miller, and business partner Taylor Maulding. In 1869, they reached an agreement with Maxwell to purchase a loosely defined tract of land along the Vermejo River for $3,700. Prior to signing the deed, Dawson met with Maxwell on the property, pointed out the boundaries of the parcel as he understood them, and sealed the deal with a handshake. The purchase became official on January 7, 1869, clearing the way for Dawson and his family to move from Texas to their new home in the New Mexico territory.

Fifteen months later, Maxwell sold the remainder of the land grant to a Colorado senator and his partners, backed by an English syndicate, for $1.35

million. One of the first acts of the Maxwell Land Grant and Railway Company was to order the settlers whom Maxwell had permitted to occupy the property to pay for the privilege or be evicted, which led to armed conflicts and what became known as the Colfax County War. After that company went bankrupt, the property was acquired by the Holland-chartered Maxwell Land Grant Company in 1880.

By this time, businessmen were well aware of the vast deposits of coal underlying the property—and, in particular, the portion claimed by J. B. Dawson and his family. It also became clear that the deed executed among Maxwell, Dawson and his partners twenty-three years earlier was so vague that relying on it to define the exact boundaries of Dawson's land was a fool's errand. Consider:

> All the land or ground now suitable for farming or cultivating purposes in the valley or drainage of the Vermejo River, County of Mora, Territory of New Mexico, within the following boundaries, to-wit: beginning at a certain dam at the head of a certain ditch at the right-hand point of rocks, from thence running down on the north side of said river to a certain other pile of rocks, on a knoll or elevation, with some bushes near thereto; thence running very near southward across said river to a pinon tree to the right of a ridge, near a wash, which tree is marked with the letter 'L;' thence running up said river on the south side to the place of beginning; containing about [blank] acres, more or less.

The company had no issue with Dawson's use of his 1,200-acre ranch, consisting of his home, barns, fields, orchards, and the like. What it wanted—and what it claimed Dawson had no legal right to—were the twenty thousand acres encompassing the five canyons farther down the river that he had claimed over the years as his own.

In 1892, the Maxwell Land Grant Company filed an ejectment suit against Dawson in Colfax County District Court. After a change of venue, however, a jury in San Miguel County found in favor of Dawson; so did the Supreme Court of the Territory of New Mexico upon appeal. Undeterred, the company filed an appeal with the US Supreme Court, claiming the San Miguel judge had erred in admitting some of Dawson's testimony. On this point, the court found in favor of the company and reversed and remanded the case back to San Miguel District Court for a new trial. No matter. On May 26, 1896, after a ten-day trial, a jury again found in Dawson's favor, and the Supreme Court of the Territory of New Mexico declined to consider another appeal. After four years of legal wrangling, Dawson had won clear title to more than twenty thousand acres, indecipherable deed and all.

He now had a much better understanding of the lengths some people would go to acquire the valuable coal seams running through his property.

+

Dawson retained ownership until 1901, when he sold nearly all of his property and mineral rights for $450,000 to a group of businessmen led by railroad promoter Charles B. Eddy, though not without concessions. Dawson kept the 1,200 acres for his ranch, and his wife secured an exclusive ten-year deal to sell milk to the coal camp. The new owners, now incorporated under the name Dawson Fuel Company, also agreed to name the new town in Dawson's honor.

For Dawson and his family, life never would be the same. Coal dust. Noise. And far too many people. Within a year of consummating the deal, and thirty years after escorting his third wife, Lavinia, to his New Mexico ranch, the now seventy-two-year-old patriarch relocated his family to a spot along the Yampa River in northwestern Colorado, roughly twenty miles west of Steamboat Springs. Here, in Routt County, he accumulated enough land to build a 2,400-acre ranch, where the family raised cattle, horses, and mules for a dozen years.

Ironically, Dawson soon realized he had again been blessed—or was it cursed?—to have settled on valuable coal land. In 1912, he and Lavinia moved to the warmer climes of southern California, returning to spend summers on their Colorado ranch. Three years later, Dawson sold the ranch to the Victor American Fuel Company, which by that time was operating dozens of coal camps in Colorado.

John and Lavinia were living in Ocean Park, California, when the New Mexico town named after him made international news following the mine explosion of October 22, 1913. "I have been greatly distressed and shocked by the news of the accident at the Dawson mine," Dawson told the *Los Angeles Times*. "It appealed to me especially for I know every inch of the property, as I worked and lived there for thirty-five years. . . . I am greatly distressed over the widows and orphans that have been made by the disaster, and since it occurred have scarcely been able to sleep."

On December 27, 1918, at the age of eighty-eight, John died, just as he had lived, surrounded by family in Los Angeles. Lavinia passed away four and a half years later at age eighty-one. Both were buried at Woodlawn Cemetery in Santa Monica.

By the time Lavinia died, the town named after her husband would be known around the world for more than the 1913 mine disaster.

CHAPTER 3

THE EARLY YEARS

This property at Dawson is going to be one of the greatest coal properties in the country. Thousands of dollars have been spent there in betterments about the mine and development work is going right ahead so that it will soon be one of the greatest producers in the country.
—Jo E. Sheridan, US mine inspector
March 14, 1904

✦

Even before Phelps, Dodge & Company acquired the Dawson mines in 1905, it was clear that this would be no run-of-the-mill mining town. Credit the Dawson Fuel Company, which was incorporated on June 12, 1901, after businessman Charles B. Eddy and his partners acquired all mineral rights and about twenty thousand acres from J. B. Dawson. Eddy, founder of the El Paso & Northeastern Railroad, then formed the Dawson Railway Company to build a 132-mile line to connect the coalfields of Dawson to Tucumcari, New Mexico, where the Chicago, Rock Island & Pacific Railroad provided direct access to markets in the Midwest.

Dawson Fuel dumped its first car of coal at the tipple in May 1902. Eight months later, the first shipment over the Dawson Railway—twenty-nine carloads in all—reached Tucumcari, at which point the cars were turned over to the Rock Island line. By the end of June, Dawson's three fledgling mines had produced 240,000 tons of coal, the second-highest output in the territory.

Something else was taking root in Dawson beyond the nuts and bolts of excavating, loading, weighing, washing, marketing, selling, and transporting coal: a sense of community. In four years, Dawson Fuel had built hundreds of homes and boardinghouses for its workers—many recent arrivals from eastern and southern Europe—in a suburban-type style described as "pleasing to the eye." The homes blended nicely with the scenic Vermejo River, which flowed in serpentine fashion through the town. Even Jo E. Sheridan, the US mine inspector for the territory of New Mexico, couldn't help but wax poetic about the picturesque landscape. He wrote: "On either hand are seen orchards which in spring fill the air with the fragrance of their blossoms and in fall are laden with luscious fruits, while the prevailing gentle winds come down the canyon pregnant with the perfume of pines which adorn the eroded canyons and the table-topped sandstone hills upon all sides."

Sheridan may have missed his true calling as a man of letters, but he knew mining. Based on what he had witnessed, coupled with the acquisition that year by Phelps Dodge, he was convinced that Dawson would be home to the "greatest producing coal mines of any single camp in the Western States or Territories."

By 1905, 125 ovens converted Dawson's coal into coke for smelting, two hundred more were under construction, and another three hundred were planned for "as fast as the work can be done." A power plant delivered electricity inside the mines to motorized cars used to haul coal directly to the tipple for sorting and weighing. A washery cleaned up to one thousand tons of coal a day prior to loading for transport. A waterworks plant pumped the pristine waters of the Vermejo River into the mines for fire protection and to homes for domestic use. A general store operated by the Southwestern Mercantile Company served the day-to-day needs of miners, their families, and other residents. By the time Phelps Dodge acquired the mines and the associated railroads in a package deal that year, Dawson was the top-producing coal mine in the top-producing county in the territory.

✦

This is not to say that all went without a hitch during Dawson Fuel's four-year run.

On September 4, 1903, after ending work for the day at 6:45 p.m., several miners spotted fire coming from curtains used to control the flow of air within Mine No. 1. They quickly extinguished it and alerted the pit boss, who checked to ensure that everything was secure before exiting the mine. Twenty minutes later, a second curtain fire broke out, roughly two thousand feet into the mine.

For the next twelve hours, men worked nonstop to douse the flames, with little success. Then, at 6:40 a.m., an explosion shook the mine, demolishing the fan house and sending the men scurrying for safety. All were "scorched and scratched" and some "badly hurt," according to one news report.

After the explosion, crews struggled to erect partitions behind which they could battle the blaze. But with the fan inoperable, the accumulating deadly gases rendered that plan unworkable. Instead, near the mouth of the mine, the men erected an eight-foot-thick barrier of wood, rocks, dirt, and mud to smother the fire. A similar scheme was employed at the other two openings. That was how the mine would remain for the next several weeks.

W. R. Martin, general manager of the El Paso & Northeastern Railroad, told reporters that sealing the mine was the best approach. He was confident that no bodies would be found inside the mine despite early reports to the contrary. That would turn out to be wishful thinking.

On September 17, with the blessing of the territorial mine inspector, company officials attempted to reopen the mine. But soon after breaking down the barrier, the men were overcome by carbon monoxide. Many had to be resuscitated after being carried out by their colleagues, some "more than once." Crews made repeated bids to penetrate the gas-filled mine in the ensuing weeks, but it wasn't until October 14—forty days after the explosion—that they met with some success. At 6:00 p.m., officials started up the new replacement fan, and within ninety minutes crews were in the burning section of the mine, bringing the first of many fires under control.

The next morning, men discovered the bodies of D. P. Jones, age forty-five, and Serapio Rengal, thirty-eight, in separate rooms off the second south entry. Jones, an African American, was married and had been with the company for a year. Rengal, an unmarried Mexican miner, had started on the job at about the same time. A third body was later identified as Miguel M. Salazar, twenty-four, whose closest relatives lived in Mexico.

By the time Sheridan filed his report, he suspected the explosion had been caused when the fire ignited carbon monoxide and coal dust inside the mine. But what of the fire that sparked it, the second to break out within twenty minutes? Company officials speculated that it started when the flame of a miner's lamp accidentally came into contact with a ventilation curtain. Gossip making the rounds blamed it on a careless miner using his lamp to light his pipe.

Sheridan didn't buy either story. "From the testimony adduced the fire was of incendiary origin," he wrote in his report, "the curtains in the mine being fired twice within an hour." Despite his conclusion, there appears to be no surviving record of an investigation into who set the fire or why.

✦

Dawson Fuel's emergence as a major player came half a century after the first organized attempts to mine the territory's coal in the 1850s, though the coalfields around Madrid in Santa Fe County may have been tapped two decades earlier. In 1861, US Army soldiers assigned to Fort Craig excavated coal for heating and blacksmithing about twenty miles southeast of Socorro at the Carthage coalfield, which would remain in operation for about one hundred years.

But it wasn't until the expansion of railroads into New Mexico a decade after the 1869 completion of the transcontinental railroad that coal mining began to take off in the territory. In 1878, the Atchison, Topeka and Santa Fe Railway was the first to enter New Mexico, extending its track southward from Trinidad, Colorado, after negotiating a right-of-way deal with Richens Lacy "Uncle Dick" Wootton—frontiersman, mountain man, trapper, Army scout, trader with Native tribes, friend of Kit Carson, and one of the most colorful characters of the American West.

In 1865, Wootton secured permission from the territorial legislatures in Colorado and New Mexico to build a twenty-seven-mile toll road over the Raton Pass of the Sangre de Cristo Mountains. At the toll gate, he erected a combination two-story inn and general store, where he began charging one dollar and fifty cents for passage of a wagon, twenty-five cents for horsemen, and five cents apiece for loose sheep or swine. "Sometimes I adjusted these matters through diplomacy," he said, "and sometimes I did it with a club." Either way, Natives and lawmen chasing outlaws crossed for free. Because Wootton's toll road was the most direct way to traverse the rugged Colorado–New Mexico border, AT&SF officials in 1879 offered him $50,000 to run their tracks over his road.

Wootton turned them down.

Instead, he asked for and received one dollar, a lifetime railway pass for his family, jobs with the railroad for all of his descendants, and a twenty-five-dollar-a-month grocery stipend for his wife, Maria Paulina. After his death, the stipend was raised to fifty dollars and later to seventy-five. When Maria Paulina died in 1935, four decades after her husband, the grocery stipend was passed on to their "invalid daughter" Mary Fidelis until her death at the age of eighty-five in 1957. The stipend originally negotiated between Wootton and the AT&SF in 1878, then, lasted seventy-nine years.

The AT&SF, which barely beat the Denver and Rio Grande Railroad Company to the punch for the rights to Raton Pass, wasn't the only railroad with an interest in the territory and its coal. Soon the Chicago, Rock Island & Pacific, the El Paso & Northeastern, the El Paso & Southwestern, the St. Louis, Rocky Mountain & Pacific, the Southern Pacific, and other lines would be active in transporting coal.

For some, hauling coal was only part of the business. In 1907, the St. Louis, Rocky Mountain & Pacific Company owned two hundred thousand acres of coal lands and mining rights to about three hundred thousand more, making it one of the largest coalfield owners in the nation. In Colfax County, their holdings included coal properties previously owned by the Maxwell Land Grant Company and the Raton Coal and Coke Company. No longer content to rely on outsiders to transport its coal and coke, the company entered the railroad business, which in time gave it access to markets stretching from California to Texas, as well as Mexico. With its Colfax County mines in Brilliant, Blossburg, Gardiner, Koehler, and Van Houten, this firm, along with Phelps Dodge, would dominate New Mexico's coal industry for years to come.

✦

Charles B. Eddy's successful Dawson venture came on the heels of one that didn't work out quite as planned: the El Paso & Northeastern Railroad. Incorporated as the El Paso & Northeastern Railway Company in 1897, with the backing of deep-pocketed investors from New York and Pennsylvania, its original goal was to build a rail line connecting El Paso to the coalfields near White Oaks, 150 miles away. Instead, a dozen miles before reaching its planned New Mexico destination, Eddy diverted the route southeast toward the coal mines near Capitan, where he began mining in 1899. There was one problem: The coal in this area was so difficult to reach that it was soon evident the mines would be unable to produce enough. "It was not long until the limitations of the Capitan mines became painfully apparent," railroad historian Vernon J. Glover wrote years later. "Cut and broken by volcanic intrusions and slate, the coal veins could not be efficiently worked to produce the amount of coal needed for the railroad and other customers."

While Eddy had better luck at a nearby mine in Coalara, his economic disaster at Capitan prompted him to look farther north toward the more accessible and untapped coal mines owned by J. B. Dawson. And untapped they were. Dawson's interest in mining the property was so limited—three hundred tons in the sale year of 1901—that the territory's mine inspector didn't even bother to visit. That changed quickly under Eddy's Dawson Fuel. By 1904, more than 450 workers in five mines were producing 443,000 tons of coal.

For Eddy, never shy about pursuing new opportunities, it was time to find a buyer.

✦

Enter Phelps, Dodge & Company, founded in 1834 as an import–export business specializing in cotton and metals. By the end of the nineteenth century, the New York–based firm owned railroads and operated several major copper mines in Arizona that were dependent on huge amounts of coke—the purer version of coal—to fuel its smelting operations. To ensure a steady supply, Phelps Dodge entered into a five-year contract in 1901 with the Colorado Fuel and Iron Company, which by 1903 was under the control of American industrialist John D. Rockefeller. But periodic strikes by workers at CF&I's Colorado mines, coupled with occasional shortages of railroad cars, convinced Phelps Dodge officials that they could no longer rely on outside sources for the supply and transport of coke for its smelters and coal for its steam locomotives.

When Charles Eddy approached Phelps Dodge officials about making a deal, they were all ears—until they learned of Eddy's asking price. The company balked at what it believed to be an exorbitant amount, broke off negotiations, and turned its sights to coalfields in the northwestern part of the territory. But Eddy knew something Phelps Dodge didn't: that the northwestern coal, unlike Dawson's, made for poor coke. After arranging for tests to prove his point, Eddy and Phelps Dodge resumed talks, and on May 19, 1905, Eddy announced that the two sides had reached an agreement. "I have officially announced today the sale of all the New Mexico Railway and Coal Company properties to Phelps Dodge and Company of New York," he said in a written statement, "and while we may all regret any change of ownership yet if it had to be there is certainly no one so acceptable as these purchasers."

When the sale closed on July 1, Phelps Dodge became the new owner of all the properties previously held by Eddy's holding company: the Dawson Fuel Company, Dawson Railway, El Paso & Northeastern Railroad, El Paso & Rock Island Railroad, Alamogordo & Sacramento Mountain Railway, and Alamogordo Lumber Company. The purchase price was $16 million, or roughly $500 million in today's inflation-adjusted dollars.

Phelps Dodge could not have been happier. "The coal mine itself can supply all the coal needed for the next hundred years. . . . We have a blanket of coal at least five feet thick extending in one direction for ten miles and in the other, eight miles," said Dr. James Douglas, who helped negotiate the purchase.

Three years later, Douglas would become the first president of a reorganized Phelps, Dodge & Company.

A MODEL COMMUNITY

Dawson now has a splendid hotel and club house, churches, flourishing schools and
every earmark of a prosperous town. . . . The workmen are paid good wages and the
utmost harmony prevails between the employes [sic] *and the company . . . Dawson is*
one of the coming cities of the territory.
—*Albuquerque Morning Journal*
December 23, 1906

✦

To call Dawson a "coal camp" would be a misnomer or, as someone once wrote, doing so in the presence of a Dawsonite would assure "trouble a-plenty." After all, how many camps in the early 1900s could lay claim to a thousand-seat opera house—the largest theater in New Mexico at the time? Or a mercantile store that hosted fashion shows, stocked furs, and could boast it sold everything from "mouse traps to tractors"? A state-of-the-art hospital? A full-service bank that handled money transfers to the immigrant workers' home countries and paid 4 percent interest on savings accounts? An outdoor swimming pool for temporary relief from the scorching desert sun? Or a golf course to match Dawson's, at 6,774 feet then the highest-elevation course in the country?

None of this was by accident. To understand the rise of Dawson as a model company town—one created by and for the sole purpose of supporting a single company—it helps to go back a few decades to Phelps Dodge's baby steps into the copper-mining business in the untamed camps of Arizona.

✦

While Phelps Dodge knew little about mining when it first purchased stock in the Detroit Copper Mining Company in Morenci in 1881, it did know a thing or two about copper. Founded in New York by Anson Green Phelps and several relatives as an import–export business in 1834, the company had already made an international name for itself in the metals trade by shipping Southern cotton to Britain in exchange for copper, iron, and tin. In 1844, Phelps established the

Ansonia Brass and Battery Company in Ansonia, Connecticut, which special-ized in the manufacture of copper kettles and other metal products. By 1869, the renamed Ansonia Brass and Copper Company consumed more copper than any other mill of its type in the nation, employing 1,500 workers with an annual payroll of $900,000.

Still, it would be a dozen years before Phelps Dodge invested in copper mining, thanks by and large to its future president James Douglas. After study-ing in Edinburgh to become a Presbyterian minister—he passed the exam but never pursued ordination—he teamed with geochemist Thomas Sterry Hunt in Canada to patent a revolutionary procedure for extracting copper from its ore in 1869. The discovery of the Hunt-Douglas electrolytic method was life-altering for the thirty-one-year-old Douglas, starting with a contract to incorporate this new process at a Chilean copper mine. Upon his return to the United States, he was asked to do the same at the Chemical Copper Company's refinery in Phoenixville, Pennsylvania, making it the first plant in the country to utilize the Hunt-Douglas method. Chemical Copper shut down in 1881 for reasons unrelated to the new technology, but not before Douglas—now the company's superintendent—made a visit to the Arizona territory's copper fields at the behest of some Eastern money men seeking his expertise. It was in that role, as a respected mining con-sultant, that he was asked to go to New York the next year to meet with Phelps Dodge executives.

At that time, William E. Dodge Jr., who had risen to senior partner upon the death of founder Anson Phelps, was contemplating building a copper smelter on an island his family owned in Long Island Sound. Dodge saw this as a cheaper alternative to shipping the company's domestic ore overseas to Swansea, Wales, then the world leader in smelting and refining. Before reaching a final decision, however, he wanted to know what Douglas thought of his idea. Douglas advised Dodge that his money would be better spent investing in smelters closer to the source of the copper.

Coincidentally, shortly before Douglas's visit, a man named William Church had walked unannounced into Phelps Dodge's New York offices to ask for a loan of between $30,000 and $50,000 to build a smelter to service his new cop-per claims in southeastern Arizona. Church, a Colorado mining engineer, had acquired a controlling interest in the Clifton-Morenci properties a year earlier and promptly began construction of a mill, a boardinghouse/general store, and several cottages. Now, however, his Detroit Copper Mining Company needed an infusion of cash to finish the job. With that unexpected visit fresh in his mind, and aware that Douglas was already planning a second trip to Arizona, Dodge asked him to check out this new investment opportunity and report back to him. After an adventurous trip—Apache raiding parties were common in the region— Douglas recommended that Phelps Dodge help bankroll Church's investment in Morenci, which the company did in 1881 in return for a "substantial block" of stock.

+

The company's introduction to the copper-mining business was not seamless. For the stodgy New York investors, Morenci, Arizona, was a brave new world, aptly described as "a howling mixture of bad men, gambling dives, bad whisky and dance-houses." Indeed, the Morenci of this era was a rough-and-tumble settlement broken into two distinct sections, one no less seedy than the other. The residential district, fittingly known as "Hell Town," consisted of homes made of "adobe, tin cans, dry goods boxes, barrel staves, and anything else that could be nailed or plastered." The commercial district? Predominantly brothels, dance halls, gambling houses, and saloons. In fact, outside of Tombstone of O.K. Corral fame, Morenci was considered the "toughest camp in Arizona." As a case in point, Phelps Dodge geologist John Boutwell, perhaps prone to hyperbole, once wrote that "very few mornings passed that a corpse was not found down the canyon in the days of 'Old Town.'"

Not long after Phelps Dodge installed Charles E. Mills to serve as super- intendent of Morenci, a major fire broke out that proved to be a blessing in disguise. Dwight E. Woodbridge, a Minnesota mining engineer, recounted the impact years later: "The ashes were hardly cool before Superintendent Mills posted notices of eviction; the next morning men were grading the old site for company purposes. A new town arose. All gambling dens and evil resorts have vanished to Newtown, over the hill; and Morenci itself is clean."

Embellished? Perhaps. But what is not in dispute is that Phelps Dodge was handed a golden opportunity to remake Morenci in its own image. In 1899, the company built the Morenci Club—a precursor to the Dawson Opera House—con- taining billiard rooms, bowling alleys, a gymnasium, a library, meeting rooms, and other amenities. A few years later, it completed work on a new company store, a four-story structure that was considered the "finest in the territory." The steel-and-stone building housed a post office and train depot, offered a delivery service by mule, and became a popular gathering spot.

Phelps Dodge adhered to this same formula when, again acting on Douglas's recommendation, it acquired a stake in some yet-undeveloped mining lands nearly two hundred miles south in Bisbee. After assuming full ownership of the initial claim and the adjacent Copper Queen mine in 1885, the company built a school, library, and hospital, the first of more than a dozen new buildings in the commercial district. Prime among them was the Copper Queen Hotel, a grandiose structure of Mediterranean style with seventy-five rooms to serve traveling company officials, copper buyers, mining experts, and the like. The company was no less attentive to quality-of-life issues for its workers, introducing electricity, sewers, streetlights, and telephone service.

✦

Phelps Dodge didn't have to wait for a fortuitous fire to begin building a model community in Dawson. The Dawson Fuel Company had laid the foundation for that work during its four years of ownership. Over the next decade, Phelps Dodge would take what it had learned in Bisbee and Morenci and do it one better. Historian Ralph Emerson Twitchell put it this way: "The new owners opened more mines, improved the equipment, installed more efficient apparatus, and particularly improved the status of the workers and created an *esprit de corps*, installing many and splendid improvements in all departments."

Perhaps nowhere was this *esprit de corps* reflected more than in Phelps Dodge's early push to build a multipurpose opera house in the center of town for its five thousand residents. In 1906, the company set aside $25,000 to build the facility—with its billiards room, bowling alleys, dance hall, meeting rooms, reading rooms stocked with magazines and newspapers, and other amenities— as part of its plan to make Dawson "as nearly a model camp as there is in the southwest."

On September 28, 1907, one thousand people, roughly one-fifth of the town's population, waited in line to patronize this new venture in downtown Dawson. On that night, the opera house kicked off its season with the Boston Ideal Opera Company's performance of Edmond Audran's comic opera *La Mascotte*. Patrons paid as much as one dollar and fifty cents for an orchestra seat in a theater "crowded from pit to its fullest capacity."

✦

Phelps Dodge didn't move as quickly to build its own mercantile store, perhaps because it had inherited one "of more than ordinary architectural beauty" opened by Dawson Fuel in 1903 and operated by the Southwestern Mercantile Company.

In 1911, however, the company reorganized and created the Phelps Dodge Mercantile Company to manage all of its mining community stores, which at the time included those in Bisbee, Dawson, Morenci, and Sonora, Mexico.

Two years later, the firm built a new company store in Dawson, converting the original into a gymnasium and dance hall. "Company store" hardly did it justice. The three-story brick structure, measuring fifteen thousand square feet, supplied everything a Dawsonite might need: bakery goods, clothing, drugstore items, fresh meats, groceries, furniture, hardware, shoes, and more. It was common for its buyers to travel East to purchase the latest men's and women's fashions—"Our New York buyers are constantly combing the markets for new merchandise and always shipping us the cream of the market," according to one advertisement—which the store would showcase at periodic fashion displays and revues "with living models." In between shows, when they weren't being recognized in national contests, professional decorators displayed these cutting-edge fashions in the store's windows.

For Amelia Lopez García, the mercantile store was much more than a job: it was a major part of her life. She began working for Phelps Dodge after her high school graduation in 1927 and didn't stop until the store shut down in 1950. Among her many memories were the store's fashion shows—"I didn't make it as a model, but I didn't mind. I was too busy with my work," she said—and its participation in an annual company-sponsored outing.

"The manager of Dawson would give the Dawson people a picnic," she said. "We had the P.D. Store prepare all the food. It was held at the swimming pool location, even before the pool was constructed. The P.D. Store cooked and prepared everything . . . beans, hams, weiners [sic] and plenty of buns [and] watermelon."

✦

One of the first things Phelps Dodge did upon acquiring the Dawson mines, even before constructing the opera house and the mercantile store, was to build a new hospital and dispensary. This was consistent with the company's practice in all of its mining towns, starting with the Copper Queen Hospital in Bisbee in 1902. When the Dawson facility opened in 1906, it was said that "there is not a more modern and up-to-date institution of this class to be found in the West." The thirty-two-bed hospital had two wards—one surgical, one medical—a well-equipped operating room, the latest in X-ray equipment, and a trained staff of doctors and nurses. It also offered an ambulance service, and "saddle horses are at hand for the use of the physicians in responding to emergency calls."

Under the direction of chief surgeon Frank C. Diver, a company transfer from Bisbee, the hospital adopted a proactive role in the health and safety of the community. "The chief surgeon and his assistants give frequent lectures on first aid, not only to the organized first aid crews but to all who care to be present," a historian wrote years later. "The attendance at these lectures is quite large. The work taught is so efficient that to wear a 'Dawson First Aid' button is considered a distinction in any coal camp of the country, as it is proof of careful and effective training."

✦

In time, this model company town would grow to support four schools and two churches, one Catholic, one nondenominational. A bakery, bank, barber shop, confectionary and ice cream parlor, hotel, garage, photo studio, restaurants, tailor shop, and other businesses soon filled out Dawson's growing business district. For recreation, residents could choose among athletic fields, a gymnasium, a golf course, an outdoor swimming pool, and tennis courts, in addition to the offerings of the opera house.

Little of this would have mattered if Dawsonites were living in squalor in the ramshackle tarpaper huts once common to Morenci and other mining towns in the Southwest. It was not so here. By 1909, the town consisted of nearly six hundred comfortable homes, ranging from four to eight rooms, in addition to boarding and lodging houses. The white frame houses—with their quaint yards and nice gardens—cost miners two dollars per room each month for rent and twenty-five or fifty cents for electricity, depending on the candlepower. In return, the company handled all necessary maintenance and repairs. Water was provided for free.

✦

None of this would have been possible, of course, if Phelps Dodge was not on its way to making Dawson a force to reckoned with in the coal industry. By 1913, the company's Stag Cañon branch was running five mines and producing 1.37 million tons of coal annually, a close second in the state that year to the 1.41 million tons coming out of the twelve mines owned by the St. Louis, Rocky Mountain & Pacific Company. Combined, the two Colfax County heavyweights accounted for roughly three-quarters of all the coal mined that year in New Mexico. For Dawson, however, coal was only part of the equation. The mines also generated

294,715 tons of coke—nearly two-thirds of the state's total output that year—for shipment over the company-owned El Paso & Southwestern Railroad for sale and to fuel its copper smelters in Arizona. By this point, the Dawson workforce had grown to roughly 1,600 workers, who were being paid as well as or better than their counterparts in other parts of the state.

+

One other development sheds some light on Phelps Dodge's approach to worker safety in Dawson. In 1910, three years before the devastating mine disaster, the company finished construction of a "second to none" rescue station, consisting of a basement and upper floor of stone and concrete wedged into a hill. The top floor led to two airtight tunnels, nine feet apart, driven thirty-two feet into the hill and connected in the rear. Here, in an 8' × 8' indentation, trainers set fires and released noxious fumes to simulate what helmeted rescue men would encounter upon entering a burning mine. Men practiced maneuvering through the smoky tunnels with their oxygen-filled breathing apparatuses while their colleagues observed through three large windows. The upstairs also housed a library and meeting room where miners could attend lectures on rescue work or twice-weekly night classes.

Word of the rescue station and training traveled quickly in mining circles—so quickly, in fact, that Dawson miners played a prominent role a year later when the US Bureau of Mines staged a controlled detonation at its Experimental Mine outside of Pittsburgh to test the explosiveness of coal dust. Afterward, two pre-selected rescue teams entered the mine to inspect the impact of the blast, one a seven-member contingent from Dawson. The crew was also on hand the next day at Forbes Field when President William Howard Taft handed out American Red Cross medals and first-aid packages to the captains of the forty rescue teams in attendance.

Nearly two years later to the day, that training would be put to the ultimate test.

CHAPTER 5

THE IMMIGRANTS

*"So and so from such and such village sent home so many dollars within a year" is
heard in a certain village, and the report, flashed from village to village and growing
from mouth to mouth, causes the farmer to desert his plow, the shepherd to sell his
sheep, the artisan to throw away his tools . . . and all set aside the passage money so
that they can take the first possible ship for America and gather up the dollars in the
streets before they are all gone.*
—Seraphim G. Canoutas

✦

Eugene Santi must have been one funny guy. Perhaps the first
Santi to emigrate from Italy to the United States, he listed "Comedian" as his
occupation on the ship manifest that would take him to New York City on New
Year's Day in 1839. Other than his age—forty-five—not much is known about
Santi. Unlike ships' manifests in later years, there were no boxes to fill out for
birthplace, last place of residence, marital status, final destination, the name and
home address of the person you intended to meet, or other details.

What is known is that Eugene wasn't the last Santi to travel to America.
Between 1895 and 1913, roughly 140 people of that name left their homes in Italy for
the New World, more than half from the northern mountain village of Fiumalbo.
Others came from the nearby municipalities of Modena and Pievepelago. Nearly
three dozen—most of them from Fiumalbo—would make their way to the
Dawson mines and help populate the town with what would become its dominant nationality. By 1910, when the Dawson workforce numbered more than
eight hundred, Italians made up 40 percent of the underground workers and 32
percent of those employed outside the mines.

"Italian immigrants in search of work or adventure fanned out across the
country," writes historian Vincenza Scarpaci. "Over time, some Italian immigrants who read or heard about opportunities in the American West traveled
directly to places like Albuquerque, New Mexico. Most of this fanning-out
resulted from the location of work. Labor agents, operating in Italy, New York,
Chicago, and Montreal, and in small mining, railroad, and factory towns across

North America, channeled this human stream to work sites." The Santis of Fiumalbo navigated this "human stream" from Ellis Island to the coalfields of Colorado and New Mexico. By 1910, nearly two dozen of them, many related by blood or marriage, identified themselves as coal miners in Dawson; others would follow over the next few years.

Nine Santis would be inside Mine No. 2 on October 22, 1913.

✦

What motivated these Europeans to bid farewell to their ancestral homes, leaving their loved ones behind? The answer is, in short, poor economic conditions in their home countries coupled with the prospect of higher-paying jobs and a better quality of life in the rapidly industrializing United States.

In Italy, the unification of the country in the mid-1800s had little immediate impact on the broad economic disparities between the more industrial north and the largely agrarian provinces to the south. Overpopulation, soil erosion, and rising taxes introduced additional roadblocks to the economic advancement of the poor, many of whom worked the land as sharecroppers. Southern Italy also suffered two natural disasters around this time: the massive Messina earthquake and tsunami of 1908 that claimed the lives of between sixty thousand and one hundred and twenty thousand people; and a tiny aphid that wreaked havoc on vineyards and the wine industry in the late 1800s. All contributed to the great exodus of Italians to America during this period. Many immigrants found work in coal camps in the Western states and territories of Colorado, New Mexico, Utah, and Wyoming.

✦

Like its European neighbor, Greece was a strong candidate to join the migration to the West. Christos Tsakonas is credited with sparking a wave of immigration that brought four hundred thousand Greeks to America between 1880 and 1920. Tsakonas, dubbed by his countrymen the "Columbus of Sparta," was in his mid-twenties when he made a solo trip to America in 1873. Impressed by what he saw, he returned to his home country before leading a party of five Spartans back to the United States in 1875, where they found work as fruit peddlers in Chicago.

Two thousand Greeks, mostly from Sparta, chose to follow Tsakonas' footsteps during the 1880s, a figure that grew to more than fifteen thousand in the next decade. This time, the driving force behind the exodus was economic, when Greece faced the catastrophic loss of France as a trading partner for its wine-making raisins, which represented 70 percent of the Aegean country's exports. The dispute crippled the raisin trade and contributed to the Greek government's filing for bankruptcy in 1893. By 1907, as many as forty thousand Greeks were working in the American West, like the Italians, many in the region's mines or on the railroads.

Seraphim G. Canoutas, perhaps best known in Greek circles for his book claiming Christopher Columbus was of Greek origin, took a dim view of the latter. While traveling through the region by rail in 1911, the sight of Greeks laboring with picks and shovels prompted this entry in his diary: "All these have left their beloved fatherland, their families, their fellow countrymen, and their lands, and come here to build and repair railroads in the hope of acquiring a few thousand francs—instead of which they acquire rheumatism, tuberculosis, venereal diseases, and those other ills, while others are deprived of feet, hands, eyes, and some their lives!"

While each European nation has its own immigration tale to tell, historians generally cite crop failure, disease, famine, land shortages, low-paying jobs, overpopulation, rising taxes, and war among the principal drivers. In some cases, ethnic, political, and religious persecution played a role, too. Still, it's doubtful that migration of this magnitude could have occurred without technological advancements in the steamship industry, which over time shortened the Atlantic crossing to a week or less. That was a far cry from the maiden voyage of the *Sirius* in 1838—considered the first transatlantic crossing to be powered entirely by steam—which took eighteen days, fourteen hours, and twenty-two minutes to transport forty-two passengers from Cobh, Ireland, to New York.

✦

The long ocean voyage from Greece, Italy, and other European nations was not for the faint of heart. Most immigrants, unless they had the financial wherewithal, traveled below deck alongside the ship's cargo in what was known euphemistically as "steerage." Here, passengers—at least those who didn't succumb to infectious diseases along the way—would spend weeks packed like sardines in the most wretched living quarters imaginable. Sickness and disease were everyone's companions.

Morris Abraham Schneider was ten years old when he and his family emigrated from Poland on the steamship *Rotterdam* in 1920. The fourteen-day voyage made such an impression that he was able to recount his experience in painstaking detail more than seventy years later:

The stench, it was the summer, in August, the humidity, the heat, having no air conditioning, having [no] cooling facilities, it was very hot, compounded by the fact that there must have been anywhere from two to three hundred people in that huge cavernous area. The body smells, the body odors, the lack of sanitation, the lack of any kind of facilities, washing, there was no such thing as washing or bathing. The stench, the vermin, it was rat infested. But, being children, I guess, had its advantages, in this case because we always tried to get out of there. We tried to go, get out of the steerage, get out of the babble of voices, get out of the heat and the stench and get on the main deck. We all were permitted to stay there for a little while but we were constantly chased.

Stories such as this could perhaps be dismissed as the active imaginations of the young, embellished with the passage of time, if not for corroboration by the US government. In December 1910, the Immigration Commission—more popularly known as the Dillingham Commission after its Republican chairman, Vermont Sen. William P. Dillingham—issued a report to Congress based on its investigation of steerage conditions on passenger ships. The report was based on eyewitness accounts and interviews conducted by the commission's special agents while sailing on twelve different steamships "in the guise of immigrants." The report was prepared by Anna Herkner, an agent of the commission who made three such trips.

While conditions varied from ship to ship, one unnamed female agent's summary of her days in steerage gave credence to the horror stories recounted by immigrants years later. "During these twelve days in the steerage I lived in a disorder and in surroundings that offended every sense," she wrote. "Only the fresh breeze from the sea overcame the sickening odors. The vile language of the men, the screams of the women defending themselves, the crying of children, wretched because of their surroundings, and practically every sound that reached the ear, irritated beyond endurance. There was no sight before which the eye did not prefer to close. Everything was dirty, sticky, and disagreeable to the touch. Every impression was offensive."

Yet, despite these abhorrent conditions, immigrants came by the millions, year after year, decade after decade, from countries large and small, many already bound for manufacturing jobs in America's industrializing cities or the more back-breaking work of railroading or mining the coal that would power the steam engines to keep the factories running. Many found work in the coal mines of the American West. In Dawson, that meant Germans, Greeks, and Italians.

Brits, Irish, and Scots. Austrians, Hungarians, and Slavs. Finns and Swedes. French and Poles. Others came from as nearby as Mexico and from as far away as China and Russia.

◆

Georgios V. Makris was one of those Greeks. In January of 1913, he bid goodbye to his wife, Stamatina, and his two-month-old son, Vasilios, to begin a long, perilous voyage to America. Once there, the twenty-eight-year-old planned to travel west to Dawson to join his younger brother, Constantine, who had reached New York four years earlier as a steerage passenger out of the Peloponnesian port city of Patras.

The Makris brothers were natives of Karpathos, a picture-postcard island located roughly halfway between Crete and Rhodes in the southeastern Aegean Sea. Shaped like an upright, long-eared rabbit, the mountainous island is known for its countless beaches and coves that dot miles of coastline. A dozen colorful villages rise up amphitheater-style from the slopes of rocky hills or set back along the pristine green-blue sea. Byzantine churches scattered throughout the island boast histories that stretch back to the fifth and sixth centuries, and archaeological digs have found evidence of inhabitants as far back as the fourteenth century BCE. In the late 1800s, Karpathians began heading to America for economic and political reasons, lured in part by glowing advertisements placed in Greek newspapers by US companies in search of labor. When Constantine and Georgios left at the turn of the twentieth century, most of the island's 7,500 inhabitants were farmers, masons, or shepherds.

What we know about Georgios's trip to America is based on four letters he wrote to his wife after leaving home, two from mainland Greece and two from Dawson. In the first, dated January 19, Georgios wrote that he had arrived in Athens "healthy" the previous day but didn't know when he would be boarding a ship for departure. That information was contained in a second letter written five days later from the port city of Piraeus. He was leaving that day for the United States with a stop in Naples, Italy, but not before he arranged for the shipment to his wife of a backpack containing several pairs of slippers, a head of cheese, the Greek delicacy *loukoumi*, and four small religious icons to be shared by his family.

Stamatina didn't hear from her husband again until she received a letter dated March 7, nearly six weeks after he wrote from Piraeus. In it, Georgios wrote that he had "arrived well" in Dawson after a nerve-wracking five weeks at sea: "Our trip through the ocean was a little rough and, on the 8th, and 9th of

February we were in danger because during these two days we had very rough seas and the waves came crashing into the ship, but praise the Lord we survived," he wrote. "Our whole trip from Karpathos to here was 37 days on the ocean."

Georgios' fourth and final letter was dated September 18, six months after he arrived and roughly a month before the mine explosion. Curiously, he shared nothing about his life in Dawson, other than to say "I am well." Similar to his earlier letters, Georgios closed with: "I hug and kiss you."

There were other Karpathians in Dawson besides the Makris boys. By 1911, an estimated 140 Greek islanders called the New Mexico mining town home, eclipsing the population of the first US Karpathian settlement in Canonsburg, Pennsylvania. Nor were they the only residents from their home village of Volada. On the night before the explosion, Constantine and Georgios shared a room with Alexis Kritikos, age twenty-six; Vasilios Ladis, thirty-six; Vasilios Maglis, twenty-five, and Polichronis Stavrakis, thirty-five. Ladis was the newest arrival to Da1wson, having joined his fellow villagers just two weeks earlier.

✦

Phelps Dodge depended heavily on European immigrants to excavate coal in those early years. By 1910, three-quarters of the men working underground came from Italy (40 percent), Slavic countries (16 percent), Greece (10 percent), Austria (6 percent), Hungary (2 percent), France (1 percent), Germany (1 percent), and Finland and Sweden (1 percent). Spanish-speaking natives of Mexico and New Mexico made up another 9 percent of the coal diggers.

This is not to say that native-born Americans played a minor role in the operation of the Dawson mines. While they represented only 13 percent of the underground miners in 1910, they made up nearly half the men (44 percent) employed outside the mine.

Perhaps no American miner's journey to the coalfields of Dawson was more peculiar than the one traveled by Lloyd Peter Upton: Ivy League graduate, Phi Kappa Psi, postgraduate medical student.

Upton, the second-oldest of six children, was born to Hiram D. Upton and the former Annie E. Perkins on December 10, 1883, in Jaffrey, New Hampshire, a tiny town of 1,300 people situated at the base of Mount Monadnock. Hiram, a Dartmouth College graduate, rose to prominence in banking and real estate circles, earning a reputation for generosity, integrity, and a "wonderful capacity for dealing with figures or intricate questions of finance." He also enjoyed a short but memorable stint in New Hampshire politics, representing his Manchester ward in the House of Representatives in 1889–1890 while serving as its speaker—at twenty-nine, then the second-youngest ever to be elected to that prestigious post.

Three years later, Hiram Upton lost everything in the Panic of 1893: his bank was among nearly six hundred across the country that failed or suspended operations. Always known for his affable nature, he was never the same after that devastating blow, though a newspaper account of his death noted that "throughout all of his reverses," it was believed he kept up payments on his $50,000 life insurance policy.

By the time his forty-one-year-old father died of apoplexy on December 1, 1900, Lloyd Upton was well on his way to being, in the terminology of the day, "fitted for college" at Manchester High School. Though prone to absences and tardiness in his early years, Upton was a good student, popular enough to be elected vice president of his sixty-two-member graduating class in 1902. Then, like his father before him, Upton was accepted to an Ivy League college—Brown University in Providence, Rhode Island—to begin his studies toward becoming a physician or, in the words of his yearbook editor, to "powder and pill a helpless public."

But a whiff of phosgene gas in a chemistry lab accident his junior year derailed Upton's medical career. The phosgene, a highly toxic gas that would be weaponized during World War I, damaged Upton's lungs severely enough that remaining on the East Coast was no longer feasible. While he took his diploma from Brown in the spring of 1906 and returned for graduate classes in the fall, he only lasted a month—the university blamed it on a case of tuberculosis—before packing up and heading toward the healthier climes of the Southwest.

When Upton arrived in northeastern New Mexico that fall, the chances are that he couldn't tell the difference between coal dust and pixie dust. Still, for a born and bred New Englander, he adjusted quickly to a life of homesteading. Using his share of his late father's life insurance policy, he built a two-room rock house in what would become the town of Solano. Here, he started a new life of self-sufficiency as a rancher and christened his new home Upton Ranch.

As at Brown, it didn't take long for the young man to distinguish himself. Within a year, he was appointed to serve as a deputy sheriff for Mora County. Later, he became a livestock commission agent, buying and selling on behalf of other ranchers. And, in 1912, he was appointed by the chief judge of the district court to be a US commissioner, a position established in the late 1700s to help judges administer federal law.

Life out West was not without its adventures. Once, as his family tells it, after being bitten by a snake while working away from home, he had to walk five or six miles on his injured foot before running into a railroad section crew, one of whom was kind enough to take him on a twenty-mile journey for medical treatment—on a handcar.

A different encounter had a much happier ending. It took place at a dance, possibly in Solano, where Upton met Alice Estella Hepburn. Before the night was over, Upton wrapped his arms around the eighteen-year-old girl and boasted that he was going to marry her. Sure enough, the couple were married in Solano on January 7, 1913.

Nine months later, the happy couple would leave the ranching life behind for a fresh start in the coal town of Dawson.

CHAPTER 6

DANGER IN THE MINES

The leading mining experts both of America and Europe tell us that it is perfectly practicable to prevent most of this loss of life. . . . In view of these facts it becomes a question whether these fatalities which can be so readily foreseen and so easily prevented ought to be called accidents; some day we may come to regard them as little better than murders.

—John Randolph Haynes

December 30, 1911

✦

The first recorded fatal mine accident in the New Mexico territory occurred on August 13, 1894. On that day, a falling rock crushed the back of Clovis Deboute while he was digging coal at the White Ash Mine in Cerrillos. He succumbed to his injuries sixteen days later.

The White Ash Mine was also the setting six months later for the territory's first full-fledged mine "disaster," defined by the federal government as any incident that resulted in the death of five or more workers. In what was dubbed by one newspaper the "White Ash Mine Horror," twenty-four men died in a gas explosion on February 27, 1895.

Newspaper reports sketched a scene worthy of that description. "When the news of the disaster spread to the mountain houses the frantic wives, many of them carrying babies in their arms and having children clinging to their skirts or following them, came rushing to the entrance of the mine, and there they stood for hours, amid tears and prayers, watching and waiting, while hundreds of men were vainly struggling to gain an entrance farther into the mine," the *Albuquerque Morning Journal* reported under a twelve-deck headline topped by a succinct "Killed!"

Coincidentally, John W. Fleming, US mine inspector for the territory of New Mexico, had arrived in Cerrillos the previous night as part of his mine inspection tour. That morning, he met with James Duggan, superintendent of the Cerrillos Coal Railroad Company-owned mine, and asked about its condition. Duggan told him "it was never better," that he had taken air measurements for the previous eight or ten days and found the ventilation to be "better than ever before." When Fleming asked that the superintendent accompany him into the mine for his inspection, Duggan told him he had a commitment a few miles away but would be back by noon.

Before Duggan returned, there was an explosion. Fleming rushed to the mine and made two attempts to enter but was driven back by poisonous gases. Three hours would pass before the air was safe enough for rescue parties to enter. By 11:00 p.m., twenty-two bodies had been carried to the surface. Two more would be found later. Roughly one hundred men survived.

Fleming wasted little time investigating the cause of the explosion separate from the coroner's inquest. Though there was a slight difference in their findings, he concluded that the tragedy occurred when two miners crossed a "danger line" with an open lamp, igniting a patch of standing gas in a room that had not been worked the previous two nights.

✦

While mine explosions would continue to make headlines, coal miners at the turn of the twentieth century were far more likely to die under much less newsworthy circumstances. Consider: Of the 41,746 US miners killed while working underground between 1870 and 1912, only 7,502, fewer than one in five, died in accidents resulting from gas explosions, coal-dust blasts, or fires. Three times as many (26,480) were crushed by falling coal or rock, often one or two men at a time, while others met their deaths by being struck or run over by mine cars (5,676), electrocution (589), suffocation (216), animals (207), mining machines (85), or other causes (1,874). This would continue throughout the century.

Why did so many men breathe their last in the coal mines of America? First and foremost, it was dangerous work. In the early 1900s, there weren't many more hazardous jobs than toiling underground amid unstable roofs, explosives, and deadly gases. Even if a miner was fortunate enough to dodge those obstacles, plenty of other slipups could lead to serious injury, disfigurement, or death. Consider the final moments of these New Mexico miners at the cusp of the century:

- Antone Zucca, thirty years old, skull crushed when his blasting powder ignited prematurely. The Italian immigrant was dead within the hour.
- John Fahey, twenty-three, an Ohio native, run over by a mine car, breaking his neck. Died instantly.

- Tranquilino Martinez, a twelve-year-old boy from Mexico, smothered after tumbling down a chute into a bin of pea-sized coal.
- Thomas Hermann, thirty-three, burned to death when thrown against an electric wire after being struck by a mule hauling a loaded car of coal. The Austrian died almost instantly.

✦

Did all these men have to die? In a word, no. That was the position of Joseph A. Holmes, the first director of the US Bureau of Mines, who believed the number of deaths far exceeded the inherent hazards of the industry. In 1914, Holmes estimated that one half of the roughly thirty-five hundred deaths and three-quarters of the one hundred thousand injuries that had occurred the previous year could be regarded as "easily preventable."

That sentiment was shared by John Randolph Haynes, special commissioner on mining accidents for the state of California. This leading advocate of social reform delivered a blistering address on that topic before a joint session of the American Economic Association and the Association for Labor Legislation in Washington, DC, in 1911. Haynes, who had grown up among the coalfields of eastern Pennsylvania, didn't pull any punches. "Of all the nations of the earth, America is the most wasteful of the lives of its citizens," he said, acknowledging that a colleague was "not far wrong" in claiming that industry was killing and injuring more people each year "than did bullet and shrapnel in any year of the Civil War." And of all the major industries, he said, coal mining was the worst.

To make his point, Haynes cited a 1908 report compiled by three European mining experts representing Belgium, England, and Germany in response to an invitation from the US government. They found that even though the natural conditions of American mines were safer than their counterparts in Europe, American fatalities in 1907 were five times higher than those in France and Belgium and "in absolute number exceed the total of the whole world outside our Nation." Haynes wasn't shy about dishing out blame: The carelessness of mine superintendents and owners. The ignorance of the miners themselves, many recent immigrants from Europe who had no mining experience but were permitted to handle explosives with minimal training. Lax rules governing the use of safety lamps in gas-filled mines. Flammable coal dust allowed to accumulate to dangerous levels. The use of wooden structures inside mines prone to fires. The reluctance of officials to act on the recommendations of state mine inspectors, who were incompetent in their own right. The improper use of electricity and explosives inside the mines. The failure of some mine operators to create more than a single opening, thereby depriving miners of an escape route in times of emergency.

Haynes called upon Congress to create a permanent commission with full authority over the industry, one with the power to appoint federal inspectors and enact regulations to protect the lives of the miners. "Is it not the least that we can do for these poor fellows," he asked, "to see that the present farce of state regulation should not stand in the way of a strong interstate mining commission that will protect them against the useless, foolish, and unnecessary waste of life which now characterizes our American mining industry?"

✦

The federal government wasn't much help in those early days. On March 3, 1891, Congress had approved an act "for the protection of the lives of miners in the Territories," which by definition only applied to the US territories yet to achieve statehood: Alaska, Arizona, Oklahoma, New Mexico, and Utah. The law created territorial mine inspectors charged with reporting annually on the condition of each mine to the governor and the secretary of the US Department of the Interior. It also set minimum ventilation requirements, required escape shafts, and prohibited children under the age of twelve from working underground.

What the law did not do was give the mine inspector the authority to enforce its provisions. If the mine owner were to ignore calls for corrective action, for example, the inspector had to report that inaction to the governor and the secretary of the interior. If further calls by the secretary were met with similar defiance, the mine inspector had to go to court to seek an injunction to shut down the offending mine until his directives were carried out. In New Mexico, this process proved so cumbersome that it was used only once in the twenty years leading to statehood and the enactment of its own laws.

Nearly two decades would pass before Congress approved the nation's first significant mining law. In 1910, responding to fifty mine disasters that had claimed the lives of nearly 1,800 men in the previous three years, Congress passed the Organic Act, Public Law 61–179, which established the Bureau of Mines under the Department of the Interior. Even then, the bureau's powers were limited to research and investigation; inspection authority was left to the states. The next significant piece of federal legislation—one that would grant federal inspectors the right to enter the mines—wouldn't be signed into law for another thirty-one years.

The New Mexico territory's first mining law was enacted in 1882. While the law set minimum air ventilation standards and called for mine operators to designate an "inside overseer" to ensure the mine was safe prior to worker entry, it was more notable for what it did not do. There were no provisions for enforcement. Nor were there penalties for infractions. It did not call for the creation of a territorial mine inspector. Worse, the law did not apply to new coal mines, only those in existence at the time of its passage.

These two and a half pages of regulations, such as they were, would stand for thirty years. Upon achieving statehood in 1912, the New Mexico Legislature wasted little time in passing a mining law of its own. This regulation, more detailed in scope, established the office of state mine inspector with its qualifications, powers, and duties. It laid out specific responsibilities for mine owners and miners as they related to explosives, haulage ways, timbering, and ventilation. And it eliminated the need for the mine inspector to contact the governor and the secretary of the interior before taking steps to enforce the provisions of the law. Still, mine operators retained the right to appeal in state district courts, and the potential penalties were hardly a deterrent: $50 to $500 in fines, one to three months in jail, or both.

✦

Perhaps the biggest obstacle to mine safety—one that would persist through much of the twentieth century—was the predominant method used to compensate underground men for excavating and loading coal. Rather than setting an hourly rate, coal operators paid these men based on how many tons they produced each day. As a result, every minute not spent digging and loading coal into cars to be weighed was money lost, at least in the minds of many a disgruntled miner. Mine operators countered that this "dead work" was factored into the setting of the tonnage rate.

Of these tasks, "timbering the work place" may have been the most critical of all. Timbering refers to the use of wooden supports to prop up the roofs and sides of tunnels to prevent coal and rock falls, which accounted for nearly half of all coal miner deaths in the US between 1870 and 1914. While some mines employed men specifically for this purpose, it was common practice for underground miners to handle their own timbering before doing what they were paid to do—load coal.

Neither coal operators nor miners disputed the importance of timbering or related dead work. The disagreement was over whether miners should be paid extra for work that, while necessary, couldn't be quantified as easily as the weight of coal.

+

By all measures, 1900–1909 was the deadliest decade for American coal miners. During this period, 157 mine disasters claimed the lives of 3,932 men. The five worst accounted for nearly one-third of all deaths: 362 in Monongah, West Virginia, in 1907; 259 in Cherry, Illinois, in 1909; 239 in Jacobs Creek, Pennsylvania, in 1907; 200 in Scofield, Utah, in 1900; and 184 in Coal Creek, Tennessee, in 1902.

Other records set during this decade:

- 1907: Year with the greatest number of fatalities: 3,242, roughly nine per day.
- 1908: Year with the most rescuers killed in a single incident: 59 in Hanna, Wyoming.
- 1909: Year with the highest number of mine disasters: 19.

Horrific incidents such as these, coupled with individual fatalities, would mar the US mining industry for much of its history. Starting in 1900, no fewer than one thousand men were killed each year until 1946, when fatalities crept downward to 968. In some cases, the deaths resulted from mine owner indifference to safety laws in the pursuit of higher profits, in others, miner inexperience or outright negligence, in still others, just plain bad luck.

Nevertheless, the death toll during this decade would have been considerably higher if not for what became known as "The Miracle of St. Nicholas."

+

In December 1907, between two hundred and fifty and three hundred miners dodged almost certain death in two of the nation's deadliest coal-mine disasters because of the fortuitous timing of the Feast Day of St. Nicholas—and the oddity of the Eastern and Western calendars.

On December 6, 362 workers in Monongah, West Virginia, were killed when an explosion raced through mines No. 6 and 8. On that day, an estimated sixty to one hundred workers who would otherwise have been inside those mines chose to take the day off without pay to commemorate St. Nicholas at morning church services.

"My dad was supposed to be in the mine that day," Leanna Meffe said while attending a centennial memorial service in December 2007. "But it was the Feast of St. Nicholas, and he didn't go. Otherwise, I wouldn't be here."

Two weeks after Monongah, 240 miners were at work in the Darr Mine in Jacobs Creek, Pennsylvania, when an explosion killed all but one of the men inside. The number of dead would have doubled or tripled if several hundred mostly Carpatho-Rusyn immigrants and other Eastern Europeans had reported to the mines on December 19 instead of celebrating the Feast Day of St. Nicholas on that day.

Although the days of these two tragedies were different, the holy day being celebrated was the same. Many members of the Eastern Orthodox faith—Greeks, Russians, Serbians, Slavs, and Ukrainians among them—followed the old Julian calendar, which observed the feast day on December 19, not December 6 in accordance with the modern Gregorian calendar.

"That to-day's disaster does not surpass in loss of life and attendant horrors that in West Virginia is due to the devotion to church duties of a considerable number of the miners," the Pittsburgh *Post* reported of the Darr Mine explosion. "In observance of the church festival many of the 400 or more men regularly employed at the mine did not go to work this morning. . . . Those who escaped through this reason . . . suspended work to celebrate St. Nicholas day."

During a December 2007 service commemorating the one hundredth anniversary of the Jacobs Creek incident, the Miracle of St. Nicholas at Darr Mine icon was presented and blessed at St. Nicholas Orthodox Church, which was founded after the disaster to honor the saint's "life-saving role that day." The icon depicts St. Nicholas, with outstretched arms draped in a priestly vestment, watching over the miners.

Two years later, Congress designated December 6 as National Miners Day, specifically citing the "terrible mining tragedy at Monongah, West Virginia."

OCTOBER 22, 1913

The scenes around the mine and throughout the camp are heartrending. It is terrible. I cannot describe this awful thing that has happened here.
—*Albuquerque Evening Herald*
October 23, 1913

✦

From the moment Dawson General Manager T. H. O'Brien sounded the emergency siren, help was on the way: men from the other mines; men assigned to later shifts; men from the nearby mining camps of Koehler, Sugarite, Van Houten, and Yankee; men from the coalfields of southern Colorado. By 3:00 p.m. the next day, twenty-four hours after the explosion, an estimated two thousand men—"[E]very mine rescue force in the region"—were on the ground, all with one thought in mind: to bring the entombed miners out alive.

If the rescuers needed further inspiration, all they had to do was glance over their shoulders toward the hundreds of distraught women, many with small children in tow, who had made a mad dash to the mine entrance. "The sound of the explosion attracted practically the entire population to the mine and women began to fight frantically to gain vantage points from which they could see the slow progress of the rescuers," said J. C. Roberts, chief of the US rescue station for the district, upon his arrival from Colorado. "Soon they began to interfere with the work and the entries were roped off, while officers were forced to drive back the gaunt, silent, but ever advancing throngs. And at the ropes, straining them forward as they leaned upon them, stood women through the long, chill night, through the bitter, disappointing morning, watching silently and sorrowful, the begrimmed [sic] rescuers as they carried now and then a blanketed form upon a stretcher from the man-way into the improvised emergency hospital at the office building."

Phelps, Dodge & Company was confident that most of the men trapped inside Mine No. 2 would be rescued. In a statement released hours after the explosion, F. C. Searle, division agent for the Dawson Fuel Sales Company, went so far as to say that there was hope for nearly all of them. "There is every reason to believe that practically all of the men entombed can be rescued, as several means of escape are offered from Mine No. 2, which is connected with Mine No. 5 by a tunnel driven through the mountain, and which connects with an air shaft driven from the top of the mountain down into the mine," said Searle, who was based in El Paso, Texas. "This air shaft is equipped with steps and ladders, upon which the entombed men, if they are able to reach the air shaft, can make their way to the top."

Searle's optimism was echoed at New York headquarters by Vice President Cleveland H. Dodge, who declared the mine was "as safe as engineering could make it. . . . Unless the men were killed in the explosion itself it is inconceivable that there has been a heavy death toll."

The rosy views from El Paso and New York differed markedly from the ashen reality on the ground in Dawson.

✦

The first men to arrive, acting under O'Brien's orders, immediately set out to reopen the clogged mine entrance, no small task given the tons of rock and earth that had settled there. Seven hours later, using every tool at their disposal, men working in shifts had cleared only one hundred feet. Nonetheless, the rescuers were rewarded for their persistence. By 10:00 p.m., they had found five trapped miners, all incapacitated by poisonous gases saturating the mine, but able to recover under the care of the small army of physicians now in town.

While the fallen debris would impede the work of rescuers, it was the noxious gases caused by the explosion that posed the biggest threat to the trapped miners. The primary culprit was "black damp," a dangerous buildup of carbon dioxide and nitrogen in the air that displaces oxygen and can result in rapid suffocation. The US Bureau of Mines considered air containing more than 1 percent of carbon dioxide unfit for miners to breathe, warning that levels as low as 3–4 percent could cause shortness of breath, 5–6 percent exhaustion, and 10 percent loss of consciousness or death. The longer the men remained in the mine, then, the less likely it was that they would have enough oxygen to stay alive.

Adding to the urgency was that the huge fan responsible for keeping the mine clear of toxic gases had been disabled by the force of the explosion despite the company's best efforts to guard against it. Three years earlier, Phelps Dodge had invested in an 18' × 6' reversible Jeffrey fan with a capacity of four hundred thousand cubic feet of air per minute. The fan was positioned fifty-three feet from the center of the mine shaft—so it would not take a direct hit in the event of an explosion—and was housed in a fireproof building of masonry and concrete. Explosion doors on the fan house roof were designed to open outward, thereby preventing damage to the fan so that it could resume providing ventilation once the doors were shut.

The fan withstood the explosion. The fan house did not.

"The ventilating fan did not stop running and was not injured by the explosion," said state coal mine inspector Rees H. Beddow, "but the explosion doors and one side of the fan house were blown out, which caused the air to short circuit at the fan, and there was no circulation, except natural ventilation, passing through the mine until this was repaired, which was done in one and one-half hours."

Beddow's estimate of how long it took to get the fan back on line differed from newspaper accounts, which stated the fan didn't begin to circulate fresh air into the mine for four hours. For most of the trapped miners, that would prove to be a distinction without a difference.

✦

For the rescuers, no ventilation in those crucial early moments meant it would take hours, not minutes, to reach their colleagues. They didn't dare enter the mine without donning the cumbersome self-contained oxygen breathing apparatuses of the day, which limited how long they could search for life before risking their own. In the first half of the twentieth century, these were not idle risks. Between 1911 and 1940, twenty-six so-called helmet men lost their lives while wearing these devices in American mines, usually because of defective equipment, inadequate training, a lack of experience, or a combination of the three.

The Dawson-based rescuers needed no reminders of the dangers awaiting them. Many had been training for this day ever since Phelps Dodge opened its state-of-the-art rescue station three years earlier. To their credit, no Dawson rescue men died in the frantic days of the rescue and recovery missions.

The same could not be said for men from other camps.

Day 2: October 23

By 2:00 a.m., nearly twelve hours after the explosion, helmet men working in shifts had rescued seven men from near the entrance, raising hopes that more would be found once they pressed deeper into the tunnel. Sure enough, by midafternoon, that number had risen to twenty-two. Still, the rescuers' euphoria at finding these men alive was tempered by new obstacles observed along the way: a fire in adjacent Mine No. 3 that threatened to reach the trapped miners; connecting tunnels to other mines blocked by fallen rocks and earth; the realization that the source of the explosion lay some three thousand feet from the mine entrance.

While helmeted rescue teams trudged through the mine in search of more survivors, recovery teams began the grim task of removing the dead. By 11:00 a.m., mine officials and teary-eyed loved ones had identified the first six bodies: Arthur English, an American; Felipe Garcia, a Mexican; Walter Johnson, an African American; and Mexicans Ernest Montoya, Juan Trujillo, and Patricio Ulibarri.

At 3:00 p.m., after hours of trying to reach him by long-distance telephone, the *Albuquerque Evening Herald* connected with its correspondent on the ground. Among his observations: The twenty-two men rescued from the mine were badly injured and some could die. Rescuers had discovered many bodies, but these were being left behind while the helmet men sought the living. Dawson mine officials remained dumbfounded by how this catastrophe could have happened here, a place touted by national mining experts as representing the "highest achievement in modern equipment and safety appliances that exists in the world."

"It will be two days at least before we know whether there are any living or not," the *Herald* reporter wrote. "But the most experienced of the rescue men tell me that with the fire belching out of Number 3 shaft and the utter wreck of Number 2, there is not one chance in a hundred that a man of those left under ground will come out alive."

He didn't know about the mule.

✦

Shortly after 5:00 p.m., now twenty-six hours after the explosion, a rescue team was searching for signs of life several thousand feet into the mangled mine. It had been hours since anyone had been found alive, so no one would have blamed the men if they had returned to camp empty handed. Not the mine owners. Not their colleagues. Not the soon-to-be woeful widows. But before returning to base, up ahead in the darkness, the men spotted something that stopped them in their tracks. There, amid the rubble, was a mule—a living, breathing mule. Could a living, breathing miner be nearby?

An hour later, in a room not far from the animal, they found the man who would become the twenty-third survivor. The miner, identified as Jose Fernandez, was unconscious but his rescuers kept him alive using a pulmotor, an artificial respiration device that pumped oxygen into and out of the lungs.

Though he didn't regain consciousness immediately, physicians later announced they expected him to "recover completely." The six men found near him were not as fortunate.

If Fernandez ever spoke to anyone about his experience, there is no record of it. As for the mule, according to one account, "The animal emerged of its own accord and immediately brayed for something to eat."

+

Though they tried, Dawson officials were not able to keep all union "agitators" from entering town in the aftermath of the explosion. Louis Tikas, leader of a large tent colony of striking Colorado Fuel and Iron Company miners seventy miles away in Ludlow, Colorado, was able to reach a Greek boardinghouse to console his fellow countrymen. Nearly three dozen Greeks would die in the explosion, second only to the Italians, including five who lived in that house. That's where Tikas met George Mavroidis, one of the first survivors of the explosion to share his dramatic story with reporters.

"I was working when there came a sudden rush of air, and my light went out," he said. "Gas followed the air. Men dropped all around me. I fell unconscious, and sixteen men died around me. I was stronger than they. I crawled to each of them and made sure they were dead. I was hardly able to breathe. I could not rise. Then everything went black. When I awakened again I was in the mine office and Dr. Brady and a nurse were attending to me."

Six months later, Tikas would be among the casualties in the Ludlow Massacre, considered one of the "bleakest and blackest episodes of American labor history." Shortly after 9:00 a.m. on April 20, 1914, a ferocious gun battle broke out in Ludlow between the Colorado National Guard, armed with machine guns and rifles, and striking miners. When the shooting ended that night, the tent colony was aflame and two dozen people were dead. Among the victims: two women and eleven children who suffocated after seeking shelter in a pit beneath a tent. As for Tikas, he was taken prisoner and shot in the back after a National Guard officer shattered the stock of his rifle over his head.

+

By this time, the Dawson mine disaster had become a national story, worthy of front-page treatment in the *New York Times*, *Washington Post*, and *Los Angeles Times*. Given the large number of European immigrants lost in the explosion, stories began popping up overseas as well. But perhaps the most poignant accounts published in the wake of the calamity came from an unnamed reporter employed at a tiny semi-weekly newspaper thirty-five miles northeast of Dawson, the *Raton Range*:

> Under a smiling October sun our friends came face to face on Wednesday afternoon with a disaster so great, so overwhelming, that as you look from face to face upon the silent groups about the streets, the homes, the mines, you see written but the one word—incomprehension. More than a day has passed and yet the people on whom the dreadful blow has fallen do not understand. They can not as a body grasp the horror in its fullness, and are quiet, stunned. Only now and then is heard the keen wail of a stricken woman as a body at the pit mouth is identified. General and violent mourning, so common under similar circumstances, is entirely absent.

The savvy wordsmith also uncovered a few morsels of good news amid the despair in the shell-shocked town. In one instance, a man had entered the mine on the afternoon of the tragedy only to turn back when he remembered that his wife had asked him to pick up something from the company store. The obedient husband was a safe distance away when the mine erupted. In another, a motor-man left the mine to make a telephone call after several coal cars derailed inside the tunnel. If those cars had not gone off the track, he would have been inside at the moment of impact.

✦

While many newspapers published the names of the first victims to be identified, the *Raton Range* also printed a partial list of the survivors. The newspaper identified them as: Natali Aristidi, B. U. Bartee, Angelo Baski, Eli Cucchi, Andy Donati, Vergins Forni, Joseph Laral, Joe Marcletti, George Mavrides, David Morrison, Lorenzo Natall, Marco Nizzi, Etienne Pages, Passoni Paolo, Charles Short, A. Stringer, O. E. Stringer, R. L. Stringer, Bonocozi Tarilli, C. Ulibarri, and Andre Zanardi.

Like Fernandez, the last of the twenty-three miners to be rescued, little is known about these men, with a few exceptions. Ambrose Stringer found himself fighting for his life inside the gas-filled mine alongside his two teenage sons. "I was working with my two sons, Charles, 15, and Richard, 17, when suddenly our lamps went out," the thirty-nine-year-old miner said a few days after the explosion. "We were half a mile from the entrance, but dragged ourselves to safety. All of us were sick, the gas was so thick. I don't see how the men behind us could have survived."

Less is known about B. U. Bartee, who like Mavroidis and Stringer recounted his story to reporters. "Four other miners and myself ran a mile and a half to safety," he said. "First we heard an awful explosion and then a terrific wind, laden with gas, swept up along the runway. The gas kept getting heavier. All the men behind us must be dead. We barely got out alive."

Marco Nizzi's good fortune was marred by the knowledge that his younger brother, Giovanni, had been killed in the explosion. For Marco, the loss of his thirty-six-year-old brother represented the second time that tragedy had touched his family since his arrival in Dawson; his wife, Mattilde, had died three years earlier.

+

At 8:00 p.m., three hours after the discovery of Fernandez and the mule, ten helmeted rescue men entered the mine in what was quickly morphing from a rescue mission into a recovery operation. They broke into two teams to search for the bodies of William McDermott, the forty-four-year-old mine superintendent, and a hundred others thought to have been in that part of the mine at the time of the explosion.

It was here that James Laird and William Poyser, two young men who had rushed to Dawson from the nearby Koehler camp, ran into trouble. Based on the state mine inspector's report, Laird and Poyser disregarded instructions from the foreman to stop and instead pressed deeper into the mine, overexerting themselves and exhausting their oxygen supply. In a panic, the men removed their helmets and were overcome by the toxic gases.

A government report published years later served up some additional details: The pair's team encountered a rock fall, prompting their leader to order everyone to retreat to the nearest fresh-air base. Instead, Laird and Poyser climbed over the debris, prompting the other three men to follow. Before Laird could turn back and reach the fresh-air base now two thousand feet away, he collapsed. Poyser rushed to the aid of his Koehler colleague before he too lost consciousness and slumped to the mine floor. That was enough to prompt two of the other men to set out for the safety of the fresh-air base, while the crew leader remained behind to administer aid until he was forced to abandon his heroic efforts because of his own dwindling oxygen supply.

Neither of these official reports could compete with the riveting—albeit contradictory—eyewitness tale spun by Roy Simpleman, one of the men to accompany Laird and Poyser into the mine that day. In his version, the two men were walking up ahead when they were suddenly buried under a rock fall. Once pulled from the rubble by their colleagues, Laird and Poyser became disoriented, yanked off their helmets, and ran toward a nearby chamber before collapsing. "The heat and smoke were terrific and I cannot now understand how I lived through it," Simpleman told reporters. After Laird collapsed, Simpleman said he instructed his colleague Walter Kerr to get help while he and Poyser tried to revive their fallen crew member. "Finally, I turned to Poyser and said, 'He's dead, Billy; let's get out of this hell hole,'" Simpleman said. "We started away and just then Poyser's knees gave way beneath him and he sank to the ground. 'I guess I'm gone, too, kid' was all he said. I waited I don't know how long for somebody to come and finally Kerr returned but we could do nothing and after a long time we fought our way out."

News of the accident spread quickly among the rescuers, casting a pall on what up to now had been a smooth operation. For the first time since taking charge that morning, Roberts found it difficult to persuade his rescue teams to reenter the mine. Instead, he had to recruit volunteers. By the time the first group was assembled, Laird and Poyser had been lying in the gas-filled mine for ninety minutes. There they would remain until the following afternoon.

Day 3: October 24

The second government rescue car, dispatched from Kansas, didn't reach Dawson until 8:00 a.m., forty-one hours after the explosion. These rail cars, the brainchild of US Bureau of Mines Director Joseph A. Holmes, functioned as traveling rescue and safety stations to train the nation's miners in first aid, rescue work, and safety practices. In the case of an emergency, they also could be dispatched to the scene of a disaster, providing trained rescue personnel and the latest in equipment.

After being briefed by Roberts, the government team wasted little time before heading out to find Laird and Poyser. Their two-hour oxygen supplies were insufficient for the trip into the mine, so the men—each weighed down by thirty-eight pounds of breathing equipment—had to stop several times at designated fresh-air stations to replenish their tanks. Their task was made all the more difficult by the smoldering fire in adjoining Mine No. 3. Nonetheless, six hours later, under near impossible conditions, the government team safely exited the mine with the bodies of the Koehler miners.

Laird and Poyser's deaths were front-page news across the country, though it was left to a local newspaper to give them their proper due. The *Raton Range* reported:

> Both young men were well known in Raton where they possess scores of friends to whom this additional news has been a severe shock. They were both industrious and good hearted men, whose friendship was prized by

everyone. Their tragic death, met in the performance of their duty, has brought deep sorrow to the camp at Koehler where relatives are living. Their heroic sacrifice will be remembered as one of the pathetic incidents connected with the greatest mine disaster in western mining history.

Laird, a month shy of his twenty-second birthday, was taken to Trinidad, where he was laid to rest at the Masonic Cemetery. Poyser, age twenty-one or twenty-two, was buried at Fairmont Cemetery in Raton, next to his older brother, Thomas, who had been killed in an explosion a decade earlier at the Dutchman mine in nearby Blossburg.

✦

Later that morning, a special relief train carrying Phelps Dodge executives and medical personnel arrived in Dawson. On the night of the explosion, President James Douglas and General Manager Walter Douglas, James's son, had boarded a train in Arizona bound for El Paso. There, they picked up two doctors, five nurses, and an assortment of medical supplies. A Catholic priest from New Mexico who was in El Paso on business requested and was granted permission to accompany the men to Dawson.

By midafternoon on the day of their arrival, Walter Douglas didn't have much new information to share. In a telegram sent at 3:48 p.m. to the New York headquarters, Douglas wrote: "No new developments. Will not know whether any others are alive until later tonight."

Five days would pass before he was able to provide the first detailed company account on record of the mine disaster. In an October 29 letter to New York, he first credited Dawson officials and their wives for establishing a relief corps. He praised O'Brien, the general manager, for quickly taking charge of the rescue work in the absence of McDermott, who was trapped underground. And he singled out several individuals from outside mining companies who had rushed to Dawson in the early hours after the explosion.

Then Douglas updated headquarters on the extent of the catastrophe. As of noon on the day of his letter, seven days after the explosion, 219 bodies had been recovered. Douglas estimated it would take weeks to remove the others, all buried beneath piles of fallen coal and rock. By that time, much to the dismay of their loved ones, religious services no longer were possible.

"The difficulty of bringing out the remains during the past few days has been very great on account of the advanced stage of decomposition; and since last Sunday it has become necessary, as soon as identification is made, to take the bodies immediately to the cemetry [sic] and bury them; it being impossible to embalm or even wash the corpses," Douglas wrote. "We can feel assured, however, that except for those . . . men who were rescued within a few hours of the time of the explosion, every other man in the mine was instantly killed either by the effect of the explosion, falls of roof, or the after damp."

Day 4: October 25

For rescue men still reeling over the deaths of Laird and Poyser, the new day brought little to ease their trepidation. By 4:00 a.m., a team assigned to recover bodies deeper in the mine had to pull back after encountering a heavy presence of carbon dioxide. Then, shortly after noon, several separate fires were discovered, prompting helmet men stationed in other sections of the mine to respond to extinguish the flames. Using the chemical fire extinguishers Phelps Dodge had placed throughout the mine, the men had them under control by 2:00 p.m.

Despite these interruptions, by the end of the day, the intrepid helmet men managed to bring forty-one more bodies to the surface, raising the total to 104. Among the identified dead was William Morgan, a sixty-five-year-old miner who finally ran out of luck after surviving three previous disasters in Colorado and Pennsylvania. "[He] was found leaning against a chamber wall," according to one newspaper report. "His hands were folded across his lap, and a lump of coal was between his teeth."

While recovery teams battled noxious gases and multiple fires in their search for bodies, government crews ran into their own stone wall—literally—in trying to send a motorized trolley car into the mine. The goal? To reach the rescue base established at the air shaft near the thirteenth chamber, which would expedite exploration and the removal of the miners' remains. Aided by the arrival of a second government rescue car from Kansas that morning, the men made progress but had to stop late that night when they discovered mounds of fallen rock blocking the track roughly halfway toward its destination.

Day 5: October 26

By four days after the explosion, all hope of finding another miner alive had been abandoned. Even if someone had survived the impact of the blast, the deadly combination of gases and roof falls in the ensuing days would have made survival impossible. For those families still clinging to hope, that point was driven home by the condition of the bodies awaiting identification in the morgue. Here, frenzied family members cast their eyes on the mutilated remains of men who might—or might not—have been their loved ones, all amid the stink of decomposition. When a definite identification could not be made, company officials wrote "unknown" into the morgue register. "[T]here are those that are identified as 'probably' a certain person," one wire service reported. "To the family whose member he might have been will live always the sorrowful, wondering thought that he who lies buried as their loved one, may have been a man of another name, another nationality."

On this day, a correspondent for the Associated Press accompanied the helmet men inside the mine. His story, published the next day in newspapers around the country, provided the first eyewitness account of the horrid conditions inside the wrecked mine:

> The mental impression of conditions deep into the mine cannot be put, accurately, into words. The tragedy of it all is beyond description. Over wreckage, heaped and strewn throughout every foot of the mine, struggle the men who fearlessly face momentary death to rescue nothing but the dead. Fighting death from black damp, guided only by the flash from their electric torch lights, sometimes walking, often crawling, these helmet-clad heroes defy the law of self preservation in their slow progress to the mine faces in order to establish air currents which will permit unhelmeted men to follow and remove the dead whose loved one are waiting beyond the mouth of the cavern. Yesterday the passage ways were lined with mangled dead . . . The helmet crews in pushing forward into unexplored rooms would come upon other bodies, some yet in a standing posture, some stooping, and others lying prone. And now and then the bright flash of the electric torch would disclose a hand, a foot or a head protruding from under tons of rock, dirt and lumber. No attempt is made by the helmet men to extricate these bodies, a touch upon the protruding member establishing a certainty that no spark of life exists.

Coincidentally, the unnamed AP correspondent was there when rescuers discovered the body of McDermott, the general mine superintendent who had traded places with a foreman about to enter the mine hours before the explosion. Based on where McDermott's body was found, it is believed he and seventeen others were trying to reach the tunnel connected to Mine No. 5 when the party was buried under a pile of earth and rock.

Among those found with him was Henry P. McShane of New York, whose mother was a major stockholder in Phelps Dodge. McShane, age nineteen, had come to Dawson six months earlier to learn the business from the ground up. At first, he had worked in the superintendent's office, but he later moved to a job underground. Despite the raise in pay, the young man was unhappy with the work and was granted permission to return to the office, which may explain why he was with McDermott at the time of the explosion. The superintendent was said to have been "very fond of him."

CHAPTER 8

THE BURIALS

And all through the services, which were mercifully brief, could be heard the chant
of the Austrian widows, the hysterical cry of Mexican women, the moans of Greek
bereaved ones and the sorrowful sobbing of the little group of American women who
so suddenly had been bereft of their loved ones.
—*Albuquerque Morning Journal*
October 25, 1913

✚

"I am very sorry to say that there was very little for the doctors to do."
That was the stark response of the Rev. Harvey M. Shields to an offer from the Santa Fe Chamber of Commerce to rush doctors to the beleaguered coal town two days after the explosion. The Episcopal town chaplain knew that Dawson didn't need help to treat the living. No, it needed help to bury its dead.

The first plea went out nine hours after the blast, asking the coroner of Trinidad for five cases of embalming fluid and all the burial robes and coffins he could spare. Later that day, twenty-five coffins were hoisted onto a Dawson-bound train in Las Vegas, New Mexico, with the promise of more to come. Other communities would join the humanitarian effort, some from as far as 450 miles away. "Coffins are coming from Denver, Las Vegas, El Paso, from Trinidad and other points," the United Press reported. "In box cars, on flat cars and even in baggage cars of the trans-continental flyers, they are coming. The coffin supply for several weeks of Colorado, New Mexico and western Texas is to be used, all at once, in Dawson."

Then there was the matter of embalmers and undertakers. Phelps Dodge didn't have a professional undertaker in town, relying on aid as needed from nearby Raton, so officials recruited a dozen from Colorado, New Mexico, and Texas. Two New Mexico undertakers would spend a week in town supervising this grim work, returning to Raton after preparing 223 bodies for burial. By then, only forty remained entombed inside the mine.

With a steady supply of coffins now on hand, Dawson began the arduous task of praying over and burying its dead. Much of that burden fell upon the shoulders of Shields, the forty-three-year-old pastor of the only church in town. A native of a prominent Pennsylvania family—his father's regiment was the first to enter Richmond after its fall to Union forces in 1865—Shields was no stranger to the American West. He had spent a few years as a boy in Jemez Springs, New Mexico, where his father opened a mission and school under the auspices of the Presbyterian Church. Shields went on to study theology at the San Francisco Theological Seminary in 1889 before becoming ordained in Albuquerque. After assignments in Illinois, Arizona, and elsewhere in New Mexico, he came to Dawson in 1908 accompanied by his wife and two children.

Two days after the explosion, the first funeral service took place inside the old company store, now a temporary morgue. Family and friends crowded around the remains of thirty-six miners, some barely recognizable, in what witnesses described as a short ceremony. Dawson would not have a Catholic church for a few years, so Shields was assisted by the Rev. A. C. Collier, who made the forty-mile trip from Springer to preside over the services for the Catholic miners.

Afterward, the black coffins were carried outside and prepared for the somber, mile-long procession to the town cemetery. Ordinarily, individual caskets would have been lifted into an enclosed horse- or mule-drawn hearse, but the sheer number of victims made that impractical. Instead, for their final journey to the burial site, multiple coffins were crammed onto open-sided carts normally used to haul commercial goods.

✦

George Thomas had a bird's-eye view of it all. The Austrian merchant, who operated a shoe and leather shop in Pueblo, came to Dawson in the days after the explosion to offer support to his fellow countrymen; Austrians made up 4 percent of the workforce at the mines. During his stay, he stood at the mine entrance to observe the recovery work "until it sickened me, and I had to turn away." He explained to the *Raton Range*:

> As each body is recovered, it is placed on a wooden sledge and drawn to the mouth of the mine by a mule. There are nine undertakers working day and night. There is little possibility of recognizing the bodies of many, they are so charred and mutilated. Some had been burned almost to an ash, others had been blown to pieces by the explosion. Decomposition is setting in and this of course handicaps the diggers, so obnoxious is the stench. The unidentified remains are being buried in long trench-like

graves. To give any possible hope of identification, the bodies are numbered and any personal effects, bits of clothing and the like are kept under a similar number, and the graves are kept open temporarily as the weather is sufficiently cold to prevent decomposition, and besides the bodies all are partially embalmed.

Not all of the dead were buried in the Dawson cemetery. Arthur English, among the first recovered miners to be identified, was buried at Fairmont Cemetery in Raton. Mine Superintendent William McDermott was interred at the Masonic Cemetery in Trinidad. His young assistant, Henry P. McShane, was first buried at Dawson Cemetery; a few days later, his well-to-do family arranged for a special train from New York to deliver a steel vault to Dawson for his exhumed body. Upon its return, he was buried at Green Mount Cemetery, a historical burial site in Baltimore that serves as the final resting place for well-known figures such as philanthropist Johns Hopkins and presidential assassin John Wilkes Booth.

✦

Phelps Dodge needed only a few days to estimate the staggering death toll: 263, including the two ill-fated rescue men from Koehler. That work was made easier by Dawson's check-in/check-out system, which required all men entering the mine to deposit metal tokens assigned to them at the check house, where they would remain until retrieved at the end of their shifts. As long as tokens remained on the checkboard, it was presumed men remained in the mine. While this system and variations of it were common in the early 1900s, it wasn't until passage of the Federal Mine Safety & Health Act of 1977 that it became a part of federal law.

By October 27, Phelps Dodge had compiled a preliminary breakdown of the dead by nationality and marital status. The list would be amended slightly over time, but Italians (135), Greeks (37), Americans (36), and Mexicans, (31) made up more than 90 percent of the lost miners. Fifty-nine of the victims were married, fewer than one in four, which would figure prominently in the company's settlement talks with families.

While small in number, one other group was hit hard by the explosion: African Americans. Attracted by higher wages and an opportunity to shed their image as strikebreakers, black miners began arriving in Dawson around 1905. In keeping with the times, they and their families were housed separately from whites about a mile from the mines in "Coon Town"—a practice that would last until the 1930s—though they had access to the entire town and all of its services. Ten African American miners died in the explosion, which, based on the 1910 census, would have represented one-third of the black workforce. Seven years after the explosion, there were only a dozen. When the town closed in 1950, there were no black residents at all.

✦

Phelps Dodge was eager to begin the settlement talks. In an October 29 letter to New York headquarters, General Manager Walter Douglas first broached the company's position on payments to the families of the deceased miners. Under this plan—based on the presumption that the company was not found liable for deaths caused by the explosion—widows would receive $1,000, heirs of unmarried men $500, and each minor child $100. Phelps Dodge would also pay funeral expenses and relocation costs. "In view of the fact that some of the widows and families of the men killed in the explosion of No. 2 mine are anxious to leave Dawson, either for the old country or to go to their relations in other parts of the United States, it has become necessary to make compromise settlements with as many as possible before they leave Camp," he wrote.

While Douglas believed the company's offer to be more than fair, he harbored no illusions that these talks would wrap up quickly, given the number of foreign consuls acting on behalf of the immigrant miners' families. All told, the dead represented roughly a dozen European countries, in addition to Mexico, Russia, and the United States. Making matters worse, Douglas said, foreign government representatives were showing up with what he called "shyster" American lawyers, each hungry for their own slice of the settlement pie.

That was not the only complication. In some cases, widows wanted nothing to do with their consulate, preferring to negotiate either directly or using the representative of their choice. This was the case with the widow of Jakob Subat, a Croatian who had immigrated to the United States at age twenty-nine in 1905. "Mrs. Subat was accompanied by quite an intelligent interpreter and he stated for her that the Austrian Consul had no right or authority in the matter and that she was entitled to handle her own affairs, that this was a right which could not be taken away from her by the Austrian Consul or any other official. . . . So far, every Austrian that I have conversed with say they do not care to have their business handled through any consul's office," General Manager T. H. O'Brien wrote to the company's general counsel. Two months later, Mrs. Subat settled for $1,800. Dr.

John Schwegel, the Austro-Hungarian consul whose earlier efforts to represent her were rebuffed, nonetheless received $200 in what Douglas deemed a "special settlement" given that Mrs. Subat required "more provision" than others.

Not all settlements were created equal, of course. Emmeline P. McShane, Phelps Dodge stockholder and mother of Henry P. McShane, was offered $2,500—the equivalent of a widow with fifteen minor children under the company's original proposal—to compensate her for the loss of her nineteen-year-old son. President James Douglas, in a letter to a company officer, asked him to notify Mrs. McShane of the decision and tell her that a check would be issued upon her acceptance—but only after "we know that she is not going to make any kind of trouble."

Despite the challenge of negotiating with an army of foreign consuls, attorneys, and family representatives, Phelps Dodge made considerable early progress. By November 13, a span of three weeks, the company had entered into agreements with sixty-two families—nearly a quarter—to the tune of $64,091. The settlements ranged from $350 to $1,750 to the family of Giovanni Nizzi, whose older brother, Marco, was among the twenty-three survivors.

While settlement talks would stretch out over several years, Phelps Dodge signed off on roughly 90 percent of the cases in the first fifteen months. As of January 1915, the company had distributed more than $335,000 to the families of 235 deceased miners. Coupled with legal and other fees, the company's expenditure to date of nearly $413,000 was in line with company expectations. The average settlement of $1,427.24 per family was a few hundred dollars more than the annual earnings of a full-time miner operating a coal-cutting machine.

Through it all, Phelps Dodge officials went to extreme lengths to make sure its intercompany communications didn't fall into the wrong hands—or that, if they did, it wouldn't matter. No doubt the company felt it had a lot to lose if, say, the Italian consul knew what the company was offering to settle with the Greeks, or vice versa. In fact, within hours of the explosion in the No. 2 mine, many of the company's telegrams were sent in code, to be followed up by phone or by mail with a handwritten word-by-word translation.

CHAPTER 9

THE SORROW

She would just keep repeating a phrase over and over, like 'Who should I cry for first?
If I cry for George, my Kosti will be sad. If I cry for my Kosti, my George will be sad.'
And she would say this over and over, my mother said, in the Karpathian dialect.
—Fannie Vozos
referring to the Greek woman who lost two sons

✦

The bodies of Carlo, Domenico, and Luigi were among the first
to be recovered and identified. Soon they were joined in the temporary morgue
by Egisto, Geremia, and Pietro. Then Angelo, Beniamino, and Raimondo. Nine in
all. All from the Apennine municipalities of Fiumalbo and Modena in northern
Italy. All Santis.

For Frank Santi, who was not in the mine that day, the loss was inconceivable: three brothers and five cousins.

Angelo was the youngest Santi to die that day. He was a boy of sixteen
when the French passenger ship *La Provence* sailed into New York Harbor on
September 20, 1913, barely a month before the Dawson explosion. Angelo was
accompanied on that voyage by his older brother Raimondo, who was making his
second transatlantic trip to America. Raimondo, now twenty-three, first stepped
foot on US soil in 1905, accompanied by six other Santis, including Beniamino,
Domenico, and Geremia. Nearly eight years later to the day, all five would be dead.

All told, 133 Italians took their last breaths in Dawson Mine No. 2. Of those,
thirty-eight came from the province of Modena, the majority from Fiumalbo
(seventeen) and Monfestino (fifteen). Most were young men from poor farm-
ing communities without enough land to provide for their families. As a result,
they felt it necessary to emigrate to America to "take away a mouth to feed and,
if possible, to earn some money," according to Manlio Badiali, who lives in
Pompeano, about twenty-five miles north of Fiumalbo. He began researching
the 1913 Dawson mine disaster after learning that two cousins of his grandfather—Antonio and Celeste Badiali—died in the explosion, along with Antonio's
brother-in-law, Umberto Giordani, and his cousin, Attilio Garzanillo.

It took only a few days before headlines like "The Dawson Mining Disaster" began showing up in Italian newspapers. But it wasn't until nine days after the explosion that the *Gazzetta dell'Emilia* was able to report with any clarity its devastating impact on its countrymen. Of the Italians known to be dead at that time, twenty-three of the first forty-three victims to be identified were from the province of Modena. Of the eighteen names listed in that day's article, five carried the last name of Santi.

Once news of the mine disaster reached Fiumalbo, town officials sent a telegram to the Italian Ministry of Foreign Affairs, seeking the names of the dead to notify the families. Two days later, after communicating with the consul general in Denver, the commissioner for emigration responded with eleven names, a figure that would soon grow to seventeen.

Villagers rallied around the stricken families. *L'Eco del Panaro*, a local magazine, offered to accept donations. And on November 30, some 5,500 miles from where iron crosses in Dawson Cemetery would soon memorialize the deaths of their countrymen, the Fiumalbo Provincial Council organized a public memorial to pay "due homage of admiration and regret to the valiant workers."

✦

After the explosion, Frank Santi returned to Fiumalbo to console his family. He also became a leading proponent for erecting a monument in the town of 2,500. On May 26, 1914, on behalf of his committee, he sent a letter to Stag Cañon General Manager T. H. O'Brien, notifying him of the committee's intent to "erect an artistic monument in marble and bronze in perpetual remembrance of the seventeen miners" from Fiumalbo.

Citing the extreme poverty in the town, where farmers produced "only one-fourth of their sustenance," Santi asked for a donation from the mining company toward the monument's estimated cost of 5,100 lire, or $1,020 in American currency: "[W]e remembered how generous your people has [sic] been to many matters even outside of your fatherland; and on this occasion we ask you for relief to help us to fulfil our wishes in token of esteem to those who have served you for many years and have died in your land." In return, the committee offered to recognize the company's contribution with engraving at the foot of the monument. The letter was signed by four Santis—Anselmo, Eugenio, Frank, and Giovanni—and Eliveo Brugioni, who was related by marriage to the Santis and also lost relatives in the explosion.

O'Brien forwarded a copy of the letter to Phelps Dodge General Manager Walter Douglas for his consideration. He also included a note expressing his gratitude to the miners from Fiumalbo. "I might state that the class of men received from that section are among the best we get from southern Europe," O'Brien wrote. "Frank Santi was working here at the time of the accident and lost three brothers."

Douglas notified O'Brien that it would be "desirable" for the company to contribute about $250 toward the cost of the monument. Douglas's father did him one better. Based on the recommendation of the company's executive committee, President James Douglas authorized O'Brien to contribute 25 percent "or more if you think it desirable."

The monument, a cenotaph engraved with the names of the lost miners, was erected at the La Piana Cemetery in Rotari, a village in Fiumalbo.

Today, what happened at Dawson those many years ago is a faint memory in the region, according to Manlio Badiali. "The great American mining tragedies such as Dawson, . . . which caused so much pain among the families of the Modena Apennines, are now almost completely forgotten here," he said. "The memory is gone. In the same families affected by the tragedy, the memory is very faint if not absent."

✦

Frank Santi would return to New Mexico, but not before surviving a harrowing experience as an Italian soldier during World War I. Stationed at the Italian–Austrian front, Frank and his company were overrun by Austrian troops. "The one thing that he always remembered about that incident was a fellow soldier being badly wounded," his son Walter recounted years later. "There was no medical attention, and he had to hold him in his arms all night to comfort him, and by morning he was dead."

For Frank, it would get worse. Taken prisoner by Austrian forces, he was sent to Mauthausen, which years later would become home to one of the most infamous Nazi concentration camps. Frank managed to escape, return to Italy, and then set sail for America in 1919. He and his wife settled near Dawson in the mining camp of Swastika, a name derived from the Sanskrit symbol for "well-being" and common to Native American and other cultures. (In 1940, the name was changed to Brilliant after the symbol was corrupted by its association with Nazi Germany.) Shortly after Walter was born in 1923, the family moved to Chicago.

Frank visited Dawson one more time, according to his son, "to look up what friends were left." In 2001, Walter wrote a letter to Jerry Scanlon, an organizer of Dawson's biennial reunions, to request a video of the most recent gathering. In that letter, he mentions that his father lost "3 brothers and 5 cousins" in the 1913 mine disaster, "and it shrunk our family tree fiercely. He came there as a 15 year old boy to help support a large family back in Italy but he paid a dear price by finding them jobs in the Dawson mine. The only redeeming factor of this sordid saga is that God gave him almost 100 years of life after that tragedy."

✦

For Georgios V. Makris and his five fellow Greeks from Volada, the early morning hours of October 22, 1913, were like no other. While differing accounts have taken root over the years, it appears that all six men were warned not to go to work that day because of a roommate's ominous dream.

In one account, the dream is attributed to Emmanuel Meniakis, a brother-in-law of one of the men. Meniakis dreamed of an explosion, of fire, of workers crushed under falling rock, of tunnels clouded with gases and smoke. Unable to return to sleep, Meniakis waited anxiously for his countrymen to wake, recounted his dream, and begged them to stay home, to no avail. They didn't believe in dreams, they told him, and they were not going to give up a day's pay. Meniakis, who did not go to work that day, was inconsolable after learning of the explosion: "Why didn't they listen to me?"

A second version is attributed to Vangelis Choratatzis, who emigrated at sixteen from the Karpathian village of Menetes in 1912. His dream was more symbolic: Foreboding Karpathian skies. A black ship with four smokestacks. Torrential rain. Six men in a small boat. A wave as high as the heavens. Like Meniakis, his pleas to his countrymen to stay home fell on deaf ears. A few hours later, they were out the door on their way to Mine No. 2.

Choratatzis, the dreamer, stayed home.

✦

Cries and wails could be heard throughout the Karpathian village when word of the mine disaster reached Volada. The village priest set off to visit homes touched by the tragedy, but he soon realized there were far too many and that it would be better if everyone gathered in the churchyard.

Fannie Vozos remembers the stories told to her by her mother, who was raised by Maria Makris, the mother of the two boys lost in the explosion. "So that's [the churchyard] where they went and that's when the women would just beat their chests and my mother would point and show me," she said. "They would beat their legs and they would be all bruised up . . . and they would pull their hair out. It was just insane. But that's what they did back in those days. And the church bells would start ringing in the village. It was just . . . a nightmare."

A century later, the Pan-Karpathian Foundation hosted a memorial observance in Volada to honor the memory of the six miners. Speakers recounted the tragic history of that day, shared stories passed down from generation to generation, and watched a documentary about the Karpathian miners compiled by videographer Emmanuel Vozos, a relative of the Makris family.

Maria Makris Caputo was one of the organizers of the event, which was held at the same church, Panagia Plagia, where villagers had gathered to mourn the deaths of the six miners one hundred years earlier.

"Because it was summertime, and a lot of Karpathians go back every summer to Volada . . . we got as many people as we could from the families to be there," said Maria, whose father, Michael, was the younger brother of Georgios and Constantine Makris. "We had a memorial service, and we shared stories of our loved ones."

Maria remembers learning about the mine disaster as a young girl from her mother. "She probably remembers what she heard from other people as the word spread from house to house," she said. "It was pandemonium. The women and wives and mothers were screaming and yelling and tearing at their clothes and their hair like they did back then."

Afterward, Maria's grandmother made her son, Michael, promise her two things. The first was that he would never go to work in the mines like his brothers Georgios and Constantine. The second was that if he ever had a son, he would name him Constantine, after his unmarried brother, so that the name might be passed down to future generations. While Michael broke the first promise to work briefly in a West Virginia mine, he kept the second. In time, his son Constantine Makris would become an Emmy award-winning cinematographer for the long-running *Law & Order* TV series.

✦

Vasilios G. Makris was less than eleven months old when his father and uncle lost their lives in Dawson. In 1936, at the age of twenty-four, he immigrated to the United States and settled in Brooklyn, New York. Four years later, he registered for the draft and served in the US Army, where he was awarded a Purple Heart for injuries sustained in North Africa. After his discharge in 1944, he moved to Manhattan and entered the restaurant business, operating a diner for many years across the border in New Jersey.

George Makris, his son, said his father never spoke much about Dawson. When he did, George said he could tell his father felt "great sorrow" over never getting to know his own father. In his later years, he expressed some regret over never making a trip to New Mexico to visit his father's grave.

George and his wife, Toni, did visit Dawson in the spring of 2007. They walked the cemetery, found his grandfather's grave, and took some photographs. Later that year, George and his wife traveled to New York to tell his father about their trip. "I just remember him tearing up and looking at the pictures and kind of like shaking his head. . . . You know, kind of like in acknowledgment of, 'OK, I now have seen this after all this time,'" George said. "He didn't say too much."

Vasilios passed away the following September, two months shy of his ninety-sixth birthday.

✦

Lloyd Peter Upton, the phosgene gas–stricken doctoral student from New Hampshire, may or may not have had a dream the night before the explosion. But he certainly seemed out of sorts on his way to the mine that morning.

After kissing his pregnant wife goodbye, he walked out the door and headed to work. At some point, Lloyd stopped, did an about-face, and retraced his steps home. Once there, he walked up to his startled wife and gave her a second kiss goodbye. "This was something he'd never done before, and the fact that he was more or less in a daze, or a trance, made it appear that he knew something was about to happen, and he'd never see her again," his nephew, D. Bradley Upton, wrote years later based on an account told to him by his grandmother.

That same day, the story goes, Lloyd's sisters Irene and Marguerite were shopping in Tucumcari. According to Bradley, "All of a sudden Aunt Irene stopped with a funny look on her face, and said, 'Something bad just happened.' Five minutes later the news came down from Dawson, by telegraph, and was all over town in a matter of minutes."

Bradley's final recollection of what happened that day has to do with his uncle's shoes. "Lloyd had just bought a new pair of shoes, and was wearing them for the first time that day," he wrote. "Only one shoe was ever found, more or less in the same area where he was killed, and that was near as he ever came to being identified."

Given his birth into a prominent New Hampshire family—his banker father was revered as "one of the best known citizens of Manchester" upon his sudden death in 1900—Lloyd's own premature death was big news in this industrial city of seventy thousand. "Lloyd Upton is Mine Victim / Manchester Boy Killed in Disaster at Dawson, New Mexico" one headline read; "Manchester Boy Killed in Mine / Dawson Disaster Claims 'Peter' Upton, One Year Married" read another. The original source of the information was a surgeon for the Chicago, Rock Island and Pacific Railroad who had rushed to Dawson to care for the injured miners. Once he learned that Lloyd was among the victims, he wrote a letter to his Manchester-based brother, who brought it to the attention of the city's newspapers.

"Mr. Upton is well remembered here," the *Manchester Union* reported. "He graduated from the high school in the class of 1903 and from Brown University in 1907. He was 28 years old [*sic*] and was married last New Years."

One final clue to Lloyd's job status in Dawson at the time of his death is attributed to a former classmate at Brown, who wrote a letter to his alma mater in 1914 after reading an "incomplete" newspaper account of Lloyd's death. In that two-page handwritten letter, he mentioned that Lloyd had been engaged in some "temporary work" in the Dawson mines. Whether "temporary" meant he had yet to be trained for permanent work or that he and Alice didn't intend to stay in Dawson long is not known.

✦

Dorothy Lloyd Upton was born in Dawson on January 4, 1914, less than three months after her father's death. Alice Upton and her newborn daughter didn't stay there much longer, moving in with family in El Reno, Oklahoma. By the fall of 1917, they were back in New Mexico, sharing a three-room cottage with Alice's mother, Elizabeth, in Solano, where Alice and Lloyd had married but four years earlier. By 1920, all three had settled in California.

Alice remained in California until her death in Fresno in 1996. Unlike her husband, whose life was cut short at age 29, Alice lived to be 103.

She never remarried.

THE CAUSE

The mine itself is wrecked. It was considered a model mine, but then, you know, it is the model mines that explode.

—Peter Hanraty

former state mine inspector for Oklahoma

October 25, 1913

✦

While rescuers raced toward the smoldering mine, while recovery crews carried out the mangled dead, while undertakers prepped the remains for burial, while grieving families struggled to identify their loved ones, while mule-drawn carriages hauled coffins to their final resting places—while all this was taking place, one question remained uppermost in everyone's minds.

What happened?

Simply put, there are two basic causes of coal mine explosions: methane gas or coal dust set off by a sufficient source of heat. In the early days of mining, methane was the primary suspect and with good reason: This byproduct of the formation of coal is released during the extraction process or through cracks above and below the coal seam. Methane is explosive at levels of 5 to 15 percent—9.5 percent is the most dangerous concentration—requiring only a small amount of heat to trigger an explosion.

This is why the role of the fire boss was so important in the nation's mines. Before anyone was permitted to enter, this employee was responsible for inspecting every working section. If he were to find dangerous gases, he would mark off that area—a common method was to place the day's date between two Xs, e.g., "X 27 X"—on a piece of timber or a shovel that he left at a hard-to-miss spot near the entry. Upon exiting the mine, he would record his findings in a ledger for the mine foreman. Then, as a final precaution, the fire boss would stand near the portal and notify each miner of the safety of his assigned work space. Or at least those were his responsibilities on paper.

One of the first recorded mine explosions in the United States attributed to methane—then commonly called "firedamp"—occurred on January 12, 1886, at the Rocky Mountain Coal Company mine in Almy, Wyoming. Based on news reports, "Although the mine had been troubled with gas," that day at 6:00 a.m. the fire boss determined it was safe to enter. Shortly before midnight, a miner's open light ignited methane, sparking an explosion that killed everyone in the mine—eleven men and two boys. The incident prompted the Wyoming Territorial Legislature that year to establish an office of state mine inspector, charged with checking each mine every three months. Lawmakers also banned women (who were considered bad luck inside a mine until at least the early 1970s) and boys under fourteen from working underground.

Like methane, coal dust can be explosive when suspended in air. Eight days before Dawson, coal dust was the source of the worst mining disaster ever in the United Kingdom. On that day, 439 miners were killed when dust ignited at the Universal Colliery in Senghenydd in South Wales. Those fortunate enough to have survived the explosion succumbed to carbon monoxide poisoning.

Methane and coal dust can also work in tandem, with devastating results. In these cases, the methane eruption stirs up dust particles within the mine, generating the necessary heat to ignite the dust and multiply the force of the explosion. That's what happened on April 26, 1942, at the Honkeiko coal mine in the Liaoning province of China. In all, 1,549 people died in what is considered the worst mining disaster in world history.

✦

In Dawson, even before the mine was accessible to investigators, speculation ran rampant over what had caused the explosion. The early favorite: an undetected pocket of methane gas that had seeped into the mine and was ignited by a miner's lamp. An early proponent of this theory was Phelps Dodge General Manager Walter Douglas, who acknowledged that methane had been known to enter the mine from a coal vein above. Two days after the explosion, after spending time underground, he offered his opinion that a small section of the roof had dropped, thereby allowing methane gas to enter several chambers, where it was ignited by a worker's open lamp. J. C. Roberts, chief of the US Bureau of Mines rescue station for the region, didn't dispute Douglas at that time, though he cautioned this was "only a guess."

Not everyone bought into the methane gas theory. Peter Hanraty, a former state mine inspector in Oklahoma, had his own hypothesis after spending a few days in Dawson—and an accidental ignition of methane wasn't it.

Hanraty was no pencil-pushing bureaucrat. He had spent four decades in the industry, starting as a nine-year-old boy in the mines of Scotland. Upon arriving in the United States at eighteen, Hanraty showed an interest in improving the working conditions of American miners—hardly a priority for coal operators of the day—which got him blacklisted in Ohio and Pennsylvania. Undeterred, he traveled to Indian Territory, now southeastern Oklahoma, to work in what were considered the least-regulated coal mines on the continent. There, he joined the Knights of Labor, a once-secret society of Philadelphia garment workers that had grown into a leading labor organization in the late 1800s, and played a key role in a successful strike in 1903 that opened the door for unionization under the United Mine Workers of America. Four years later, Hanraty was elected vice president of the constitutional convention that led to Oklahoma statehood before being named that state's mine inspector.

"There is nothing to this theory about a pocket of gas," he said. "Such things simply don't happen. The explosion was due to some mistake, something left undone or forgotten. They always are. If it had not been for that, there would have been no explosion. This mine had a fine system of ventilation."

Hanraty wasn't the only one who thought the methane explanation was bunk. So did Rees H. Beddow, the state's new coal mine inspector, who was appointed to the post eight months after New Mexico achieved statehood. The West Virginia native had spent two days inspecting Mine No. 2 on October 15 and 16—a week before the explosion—examining the ventilation system and sending air samples to the US Bureau of Mines in Pittsburgh for analysis. Those results showed the air contained 19/100ths of 1 percent of methane, which was considered "very low for a mine of this character." His conviction grew stronger when the post-explosion inspection of the mine found few visible signs of methane.

By the time Beddow released his first official statement on November 4, thirteen days after the explosion, he was sure of it. "Gas played very little part in the explosion of the Dawson mine," he wrote. "The mine was the best ventilated mine in the state. There was from 150,000 to 190,000 cubic feet of air traveling through the mine per minute. This air was divided into many different splits, going into all parts of the mine, thus preventing any accumulation of gas. For the past ten days many of the best gas experts and mining men of the country have been examining the mine and hunting for gas, but not enough has been found anywhere to show up in a safety lamp test."

Three days later, Beddow issued a more definitive statement. He said it had been determined "beyond a doubt" that an "overcharged shot"—where the force of the blasting powder extends outward rather than inward to dislodge the coal—had stirred up and ignited coal dust in the mine, causing the explosion.

An unnamed miner had triggered this deadly chain of events by connecting his copper shooting wire to a live trolley wire while he and 283 of his colleagues were inside the mine, a blatant violation of company rules and state law. "It was caused by an overcharged shot, being fired in room No. 27, off the 9th west entry in mine No. 2," he concluded. "This shot blew the coal out . . . for a distance of 40 feet, creating much wind, stirring up and igniting the coal dust, spreading from this point to all points of the mine."

In essence, the miner had deliberately circumvented the electric shot-firing system that the company had introduced as a safety precaution in all its mines by 1908. Under this system, three entry switches protected by lock boxes controlled the flow of electricity into the shooting wires running throughout the mine, thereby preventing shots from being fired while anyone was inside. At the end of the day, after all the workers had prepared the shots inside their assigned rooms and gone home, the shot firers entered the mine, unlocked the boxes, and cut in the power to the shooting wires. They then retreated to the shot-firing cabin, situated near the mouth of the mine, and signaled to a worker in the substation to turn on the current. Only then was the switch flipped in the cabin, detonating all the shots in the mine simultaneously. Afterward, the current was turned off and kept off until the process was repeated the next day at the same time.

"But all these precautions amounted to nothing because a man wanted to load a few more cars of coal that day," Beddow said. "He fired his shot from the trolley wire, thus starting an explosion that killed 263 men and destroyed much valuable property. The lesson taught by this disaster has been a dear one, and should be sufficient to enable the operators to realize fully the danger lurking in the coal dust of the mines."

Beddow's conclusion was cause for relief at Phelps Dodge headquarters in New York. By placing the blame squarely on the back of a reckless miner, the mine inspector had absolved the company of liability, potentially strengthening its hand to negotiate more reasonable settlements with families of the deceased miners.

✦

Not everyone thought that Phelps Dodge deserved a free pass. This became crystal clear courtesy of some on-the-ground reporting by William G. Shepherd, a journalist who had made a national name for himself for his chilling eyewitness account of the Triangle Waist Company fire in New York City's Garment District. The March 25, 1911, fire—the deadliest workplace disaster in the city's history prior to 9/11—claimed the lives of 146 workers, mostly girls and young women of

Jewish and Italian descent who faced the ghastly choice between burning alive or being overcome by smoke above or jumping ten stories to certain death. Dozens chose the latter.

When Shepherd arrived in Dawson two years later, he once again found himself amid the stench of charred corpses. This time he was reporting for E. W. Scripps's *The Day Book*, a Chicago-based tabloid newspaper dedicated to championing America's workers with "extensive coverage of working conditions, wages, union organizing, and labor unrest." In other words, this was exactly the type of publication that would never see the light of day inside the Phelps Dodge company store.

Writing under the eye-catching headline "Was Stag Canon Mine Horror Just Out-and-Out Murder?" Shepherd surmised that the explosion was no mere accident. First, he reported that a mine guard had notified Superintendent William McDermott at 6:00 a.m. that day that "dust-gas was filling the mine!" Thirty minutes after the explosion, the guard rushed to the mine entrance and told anyone within earshot: "My shoulders are clear. I told the officials this morning that the mine wasn't safe to work in!"

Second, since McDermott was among the men killed, Shepherd speculated that the superintendent "undoubtedly" had entered the mine to check out the guard's report of coal dust and gas. "McDermott did not want to risk the loss of one day's output of coal," Shepherd claimed. "So he risked his own live [*sic*] and the lives of nearly 300 men."

Based on his conversations with Dawson miners, Shepherd reported that mine officials had installed "eight or ten" more coal-cutting machines to boost production in response to a major labor strike in neighboring Colorado. "These machines made additional dust, which should have been removed by additional fans, but the mine's equipment of fans could not handle the increase of deadly dust," he wrote.

✦

A labor-friendly journalist was not the only one to point a finger at the company. John C. Schwegel, the Austro-Hungarian consul in Denver, shared some of his concerns with Walter Douglas in a letter dated November 22, exactly one month to the day after the explosion. Citing a "thorough investigation" by his vice consul, Schwegel accused the company of allowing working conditions to deteriorate under the leadership of McDermott, who had replaced the respected Joe Smith as superintendent in January.

Schwegel wrote that McDermott had cut back on the extent and frequency of sprinkling within the mines to wet down the coal dust; in fact, he claimed that Mine No. 2 had been sprinkled only once in June and then only in anticipation of a visit by the state mine inspector. He also claimed that McDermott had ordered the removal of ventilation doors, thereby eliminating the need for four trappers—boys stationed underground to open and close the doors as needed to direct fresh air into the mine—saving the company five dollars a day. And he claimed that McDermott had ceased Smith's practice of keeping special records on every room in the mines: "If a rock was loose, special timberman [sic] were sent in, also if there was gas, nobody was allowed to work. These rules have not been observed under Mr. McDermott, the successor of Mr. Smith."

For his part, General Manager T. H. O'Brien dismissed Schwegel's allegations as "bar-room gossip." In a letter to Walter Douglas, O'Brien wrote that Schwegel was "far from being correct" about sprinkling and ventilation, saying the latter was "practically four times more than was required by law." As for the removal of the doors, O'Brien said the company had invested a "considerable sum" on airway improvements, thereby making the doors unnecessary. "The changes were in line with the best mining practice," he wrote. "Possibly the company should have been censured for not having the doors changed previous to March, certainly not after the improvements had been made."

✦

Some theories were a bit more fanciful, if not downright preposterous, a reflection of simmering tensions between coal mine operators and labor union organizers around the nation. Prime among them was that small quantities of explosives had been smuggled into the mine over several weeks and concealed until they were detonated with a time clock around 3:00 p.m. Why then? Because "one of the main objectives" was to do so when McDermott was in the mine. This tip was attributed to an unidentified Secret Service agent once employed by the Southwestern Interstate Coal Operators' Association, who identified the ringleader as "Salivator Dicolly," a onetime resident of Dawson. The Secret Service agent's source: an Italian with the nickname "Big Garibaldy."

This sensational scheme was described in a November 3 letter from the head of coal mining operations for the Chicago, Rock Island & Pacific Railway Company to the railroad's president. A copy was forwarded through an intermediary to Phelps Dodge President James Douglas, who acknowledged that he had heard "vague rumors" of rogue Dawson miners working in cahoots with the

Western Federation of Miners, a labor union with a reputation for militancy. Douglas relayed the information to O'Brien, saying that it was "within the range of possibilities that there may have been this malicious intention to blow up the mines," though by this point the state mine inspector had already issued his definitive report on the cause of the explosion.

✦

That coal dust was suspected as a major factor in the Dawson explosion should have come as a surprise to no one. The inherent dangers of the dust had been raised more than a century earlier after the 1803 explosion of a colliery in Wallsend, England, which claimed the lives of thirteen men and boys. "The workings were very dry and dusty, and the survivors who were most distant from the points of explosion were burnt by the shower of red-hot sparks of ignited dust which were driven along by the force of explosion," according to the chief of the Newcastle coal miners.

Still, it would be another eighty years before the explosive properties of coal dust were accepted as a matter of science, thanks largely to a study published by two British mine inspectors in 1886. After investigating six mine explosions between 1880 and 1885, coupled with a review of other mine disasters in the country's long history, they concluded that "coal dust was the effective agent in most of the great mine explosions."

The road toward enlightenment was bumpier in the United States. One of the earliest coal mine explosions where dust was considered a factor took place on March 13, 1884, at the Pocahontas mine in West Virginia, where all 114 men in the mine were killed. A committee established by the American Institute of Mining Engineers found "unusual dryness of the mine" and a "very large quantity of dust in an extremely fine state of division." The committee's conclusion: "We believe that the explosion was due mainly to dust."

In New Mexico, the first official reference linking coal dust to a mine explosion occurred nearly two decades later. On March 29, 1901, three men were killed around midnight at the Colorado Fuel and Iron Company's Weaver mine in Gallup. Newspaper reports detailed the extreme force of the blast. "The iron doors weighing 1,000 pounds and several pit cars were blown out onto the tipple," the *Albuquerque Weekly Citizen* reported. "The shaft was ruined. The 40-foot frame chimney above it was reduced to kindling wood."

Jo E. Sheridan, US mine inspector for the territory of New Mexico, arrived in Gallup four days later to begin his examination into the cause of the deadly explosion. His conclusion? That blown-out shots had "agitated the coal dust . . . to reach the point of ignition and explosion."

Sheridan did not stop there. Seizing on his opportunity for a teaching moment, he fired off a letter to the roughly two dozen mining companies in the New Mexico territory, making sure they were aware of his findings in Gallup and reiterating the importance of keeping coal dust under control. In that letter, Sheridan acknowledged that not all mine owners were sold on the connection between mine explosions and dust. He wrote: "Heretofore the officials in charge of the several coal mines of this Territory have been careless in guarding against this great danger of coal-dust explosion. Many of them even now dissent from the opinion that very violent explosions may be caused by coal dust and lack appreciation of this great danger."

Sheridan was an early believer in the danger posed by the excessive accumulation of coal dust. His letter to mine owners was written nearly a decade before the creation of the US Bureau of Mines and the subsequent opening of the government's Experimental Mine in Pennsylvania. To drive home his point, he peppered his annual inspection report that year with thirty-four references to "dust" or "dusty."

In Dawson, mine owners should have been well aware of the need to control the buildup of coal dust inside their mines even without Sheridan's reminders. In a cautionary letter to O'Brien, Beddow had warned that he found "the haulage ways much dryer [sic] and a greater accumulation of slack coal and dust" during his most recent inspection than he had a few months earlier.

The date of that letter? December 23, 1912.

Nearly ten months to the day before the deadly explosion.

CHAPTER 11

THE INQUEST

Only rarely did coroners' juries find a coal operator or mine official responsible for fatal accidents in the mines. Instead, they almost always found that accidents either were unavoidable or were due to the carelessness of the deceased or his co-workers.
—James Whiteside

✦

The coroner's inquest into the deaths of the Dawson miners commenced at 11:00 a.m. on November 15, 1913, a Saturday, before Justice of the Peace T. L. Kinney—the same T. L. Kinney who served as the company-appointed town supervisor. Kinney's presence in Dawson predated Phelps Dodge: he had arrived in 1903 to accept a chief clerk position for the Dawson Fuel Company after holding similar jobs in New Mexico and Colorado. Phelps Dodge named him town supervisor in 1908.

Kinney would become one of Dawson's most dedicated citizens, adding to his official duties the secretary to the school board, precinct chairman for the New Mexico Republican Party, and delegate to his party's state convention. The colorful Indiana native was also a fixture in the town's civic life, assuming leadership roles in many of its fraternal organizations. Case in point: Kinney's selection as "best looking man in the Dawson Club" in 1923—credited in part to "a special haircut"—after beating out 109 contenders for the club's "highest honor" and one dollar in prize money. (The contest was so successful that the club's secretary contemplated offering a two-dollar prize at the next meeting to the "homeliest man in the club.") The judge was also known at times to inject some levity when meting out justice to miscreants brought before the bench. Kinney would pick up a Sears, Roebuck & Company catalogue, open to a random page, point his finger at an item, and set the fine accordingly.

✦

R. H. Worcester was the first witness to be questioned by George E. Remley, the thirty-two-year-old county attorney who, years later, would serve briefly as acting governor while president pro tem of the New Mexico Senate. Worcester, a construction engineer, had been outside the mine when recovery teams brought out many of the bodies, including that of Superintendent William McDermott.

Q: Did you see the body of Mr. McDermott?

A: I did.

Q: And will you describe to the jury the condition of the body when you saw it?

A: Why the face was burnt, and somewhat mangled around the mouth—the lips were burned and broken, although considerable of his mustache was there. His hands were badly torn, and his legs, or his feet at any rate, were uninjured.

Q: When did you see this body?

A: I saw it after it came out of the Mine, in the Blacksmith Shop.

Q: Did you see any other bodies about the same time?

A: Yes, sir.

Q: Approximately in what numbers did you see the bodies?

A: I must have seen close to one hundred bodies, all told, as they came out of the Mine.

✦

Rees H. Beddow, the state mine inspector, testified next. If Worcester was called to confirm that McDermott and the others had died in the explosion, Beddow was there to talk about his investigation. When Remley reminded him that the jury was examining whether the deaths were caused by the commission of a crime, Beddow didn't mince words.

"Well," he replied, "it is my opinion that there was a crime committed."

Beddow, who was in the wrecked mine between 6:30 and 7:00 on the morning after the explosion, testified that he spent his first few days ensuring the ventilation system was working properly, trying to remove bodies, and checking on reports of fire. He then turned his full attention—roughly fourteen days in all—to investigating the cause of the explosion. It didn't take him long to pinpoint the precise location. "[I] concluded in the first day after I started to investigate that the explosion had been started in the 9th West, or the South Entry off the 9th West in that Mine," he said.

"What caused you to conclude so?" Remley asked.

"Well, on account of the direction of the explosion, of the force of the explosion," Beddow replied.

Accompanied by Tim Tinsley, the mine foreman who had swapped places with McDermott, and five helmet men, Beddow reached the south entry off the 9th West about the fourth day of his arrival. While poor ventilation forced them to turn back after forty feet, they were able to see enough to conclude that the blast had originated somewhere in that area. Everything was blown out into the 9th West entry, he said, including the timbers used to support the roofs while men worked inside the rooms. Empty coal cars were scattered about, and some loaded cars—weighing about two tons—had been blown off the track. As a reminder of the human toll, they found the bodies of two men "that had blown up the 10th West from the parting about a distance of fifty feet."

At first, Beddow suspected what he called "a local explosion of gas," but neither he nor his fellow investigators could find a measurable amount capable of triggering such an explosion. During the next eight to ten days, similar tests for gas conducted in other parts of the mine also came up empty. So Beddow, joined by J. C. Roberts of the mine rescue station and James W. Paul of the US Bureau of Mines, returned to the 9th West entry to conduct additional tests. Again, they found no gas in the rooms along this entry, but something else caught Beddow's eye when he reached Room 27: signs that a shot, an explosive charge, had been set off there.

"[I] called the attention of Mr. Roberts and Mr. Paul to this, and they came down and looked at it, and they agreed with me that there had been a shot fired there," Beddow said. This was not just any shot, but an overcharged one with "entirely too much powder in the hole. The coal had been blown a distance of probably thirty or forty feet, and it appeared to me that was the cause of the explosion." Next to where the shot was fired was a car filled two-thirds with coal, a miner's identifying check token hanging on the side.

Remley, eager to pursue any clues that might lead to who fired the deadly shot, pressed Beddow for more details:

Q: Do you remember the check number at this time?
A: Why, I have a note of it, but I haven't it with me, as I didn't bring my note book along, and I couldn't testify as to the correct number.
Q: I will ask you to look at your notes during the intermission, so that you may refresh your memory as to this check number.

Why Beddow didn't think this detail important enough to bring to the inquest—particularly given his earlier statement that he believed a crime had been committed—is a head-scratcher, especially after he explained the relevance of finding that check token to the jury: "Well my object in getting the check number was to see who worked in the room, so that I could find out whether the man had been working the day of the explosion, and when I got out I inquired who worked in that room, and whether they had been sending out any coal on that day, and the check man gave me the man's number and name and told me that he had gotten out five and a half or six tons of coal that day."

If Beddow ever examined his notes for the check number during intermission as Remley specifically requested, there is no evidence of it. After he returned to the stand that afternoon, he never mentioned the check number nor the identity of its owner.

✦

While the inspector had nothing else to say about the "who" part of his investigation, he had plenty to say about the "how" and "why." Beddow said it was clear the overcharged shot had blown coal "about thirty or fourty [sic] feet," stirring up coal dust along the way.

Q: There was dust in the room when you got there?

A: Yes sir, there was a heavy deposit of dust and soot on everything, which showed that there had been a great commotion in there, and more or less flame.

Beddow proceeded to go into great detail on how the mystery miner connected his shot to a detonator and trolley wire 150 feet away, violating company rules and state law. After having no success learning the check number found on the coal car near the shot, Remley turned his attention to bodies found near the point of impact with the trolley wire:

Q: With respect to the place where a man could bring these wires in contact, where were the bodies found?

A: One of them was found, I should say, about fifteen feet up the Entry, and the other was about fifteen feet below where these switches were located.

Q: Did you learn the name of either of these bodies?

A: No sir, I did not.

After some further questioning, Remley tried one last time to elicit any information that would help determine who fired the fatal shot.

> **Q:** What I am trying to get at is this—from your examination of the mine at that particular point, and your finding the bodies there, were you able to advance any opinion as to who fired the shot, formed this electric connection, and how it was done?
> **A:** No sir, I could form no opinion as to who done it, but I have an opinion as to how it was done.

Undeterred, Remley tried one more time:

> **Q:** Do I understand that, from your examination of the conditions, you are of the opinion that either one of these two men did make that connection?
> **A:** No sir, I don't say that. That connection could have been made by these men, or by anybody else, and the shot wouldn't have been fired until the motor [car] came down there and the current came on the trolley line, then it would have immediately gone off.
> **Q:** Then you believe that somebody did make that connection?
> **A:** Yes sir.
> **Q:** And that connection was the cause of the explosion?
> **A:** Yes sir.
> **Q:** But you don't say who made the connection?
> **A:** No sir.

Under further questioning by Remley, Beddow addressed the motivation for a miner to set off an explosion while he and others were inside the mine.

> **Q:** In what way would he be benefited by firing this shot?
> **A:** He could load more coal that day than if he hadn't fired the shot, otherwise he would have to quit work.
> **Q:** And I presume the miners are paid by the amount of coal they get out?
> **A:** Yes sir, they work on a tonnage basis.

Jo E. Sheridan was Beddow's predecessor as the US mine inspector for the territory of New Mexico. Unlike Beddow, who arrived the morning after the explosion, Sheridan didn't get to Dawson until November 5 after being asked to come by General Manager T. H. O'Brien. But, like Beddow, based on his forty-five years of mining experience, Sheridan began his investigation suspecting that the ignition of gas caused the explosion, a common finding during his thirteen-year tenure as territorial mine inspector. He soon learned that this wasn't the case here.

After his weeklong investigation, while there were some minor discrepancies with Beddow's findings, Sheridan concurred that the explosion had originated between Rooms 26 and 27 when a miner connected his shot to the live trolley wire. "My opinion is that a shot had been left properly connected," he said, "and that when the motor came in it threw the automatic switch in, putting the electric power on to the trolley wire."

✦

O'Brien was the fourth and final witness to testify. Initially, the Stag Cañon general manager was asked by Remley to explain the company's policy for firing shots—always by trained shot firers stationed outside the mine after all the men had checked out for the day—and then to elaborate on the check-in/check-out system employed to ensure that was the case. O'Brien explained that the underground workers deposited numbered check tokens assigned to them in a cabin near the mouth of the mine before entering and picked them up on their way home. In that way, O'Brien said, the shot firers would know whether anyone was in the mine before they fired off the shots electronically that evening.

Remley then turned his attention to a different check used by miners, the one they attached to their coal cars so they could be credited for the amount of coal they loaded on a given day. Specifically, he wanted to know the owner of the check found on the car next to the source of the explosion that Beddow could not—or would not—identify during his testimony earlier that day.

> **Q:** I would like to have some evidence as to who the miner was who fixed this shot that Mr. Beddow and Mr. Sheridan have testified to. Have you any knowledge with regard to that man?
> **A:** Check No. 667 was working in that place.
> **Q:** You have been in the mine at that point?
> **A:** O yes, several times.

Q: What was the check number on the car that Mr. Beddow testified to?

A: No. 667.

Q: It was the same check number?

A: Yes sir.

Q: Do you know the name of the man who owned that number?

A: That check number was owned by Thomas Pattison.

Q: I take it he was a negro?

A: No sir, he was not.

Q: Is Mr. Pattison living or dead?

A: He is dead.

Q: Do you know where the body was found?

A: No.

Q: Has it been identified?

A: It has been identified and shipped, but as to where the body was found I couldn't say, as I didn't see the body at that place.

Dr. F. B. Evans, a member of the jury, asked the final question of O'Brien:

Q: I would like to ask Mr. O'Brien if Pattison, No. 667, was the only man checked in to that room on that day?

A: Yes, he was the only man, working on the pillar.

With that, Remley brought the testimony to a close and reminded the jury of the criminal nature of the proceeding: "You understand, while this is not a criminal prosecution, yet it is a criminal investigation, and you and I are here to ascertain if not only one crime has been committed, but other crimes, and if any of you have reason to believe that other crimes have been committed, and know of witnesses and can give any light on the subject, let us hear from you."

At 3:00 p.m., after four hours of testimony, the jury was escorted into the mine for a firsthand examination of the evidence brought before them. Of particular interest was the room off the 9th West entry where they were told the explosion originated. Afterward, they were instructed to appear in Kinney's office at 8:00 p.m.

❖

That same night, the six jurors returned the following verdict:

"We the undersigned Justice of the Peace and Jury, who sat upon the inquest held this 15th day of November, 1913, on the body of William McDermott and others, found in Precinct No. 13 of the County of Colfax, find that the said William McDermott and others came to their deaths by reason of an explosion in Coal Mine No. 2, operated by the Stag Canon Fuel Company, at Dawson, New Mexico, on October 22nd, 1913 caused by a shot having been unlawfully fired by an unknown employee of such company at the time working on pillar No. 27, 9th West Entry, No. 2 mine, which employe [sic] met his own death in such explosion."

The statement was signed by Kinney and the six jurors. The verdict was released at 8:00 p.m., the exact time the jury was instructed to meet in Kinney's office.

There was no mention of Thomas Pattison.

✦

While the jury's verdict appeared to reflect the evidence presented, a ruling against the company would have been highly unusual. That is because coroners' juries, often through wanton corruption, sheer incompetence, or political pressure, invariably came down on the side of the coal operators. Between 1904 and 1914, for example, coroners' juries in Colorado's Huerfano County reviewed ninety-five coal-mine fatalities. Of these, eighty-five were blamed on the deceased's own negligence; only one found major fault with mine management. On occasion, even state mine inspectors, whose reputation for being chummy with coal operators was an open secret, spoke out. In 1914, James Dalrymple, coal mine inspector for the state of Colorado, took the Las Animas County coroner to task for ruling "in case after case where a miner has been killed—'no inquest necessary.'" And the *United Mine Workers Journal*, admittedly no friend of coal operators, griped only partly in jest that coroners' inquests were "not as rigid as the inquiry the coal company would make if a dead mule was brought out of the mine." That was in keeping with a common lament among miners that their bosses considered mules more valuable than men because the animals cost more to replace.

In Dawson, the collegial relationship among the parties did not go unnoticed. Among the complaints: the jury consisted entirely of company employees; County Attorney Remley regularly conferred with Phelps Dodge attorneys before, during, and after the inquest; Remley "took his meals" with the company's lawyers, an accusation O'Brien would deny; and the official stenographer, another company employee, initially refused to provide copies of the transcript upon request to an interested party.

Similarly, coziness between mine owner and mine inspector was evident in when—and how—Phelps Dodge first learned of Beddow's finding that a miner's overcharged shot caused the explosion. On November 4, Beddow released a public statement saying that coal dust, not gas, was responsible but noted that what "stirred up and ignited the coal dust has not been determined up to the present." It wasn't until three days later, on November 7, that he released a second statement attributing the cause to the overcharged shot.

Yet, on November 5 at 2:27 p.m., O'Brien sent a telegram containing that very information to Walter Douglas, who was stationed at the company's copper mines in Bisbee, Arizona. The timing suggests that O'Brien was in possession of this knowledge one day after Beddow's first pronouncement that he didn't know what set off the coal dust and two days before he blamed it on the overcharged shot.

Like many of the telegrams exchanged among Phelps Dodge officials during this period, this one was sent in code. "The Mine Inspector has conclusively located cause of explosion and will so report and testify and in which I concur, the same being a dust explosion caused by a secretly and criminally exploded shot by an employee working under contractor by connecting a wire to the trolley wire," O'Brien wrote in a handwritten translation of the telegram. "This conclusion fully sustained by physical evidence existing and still practically in place."

Beddow's "special report" to Governor William C. McDonald, detailing his findings on the Dawson explosion, was dated November 10, five days after O'Brien's telegram.

+

A century later, the identity of the miner who set in motion the catastrophic chain of events that claimed the lives of 263 miners, including his own, remains a mystery, though what evidence exists points to Thomas H. Pattison. He was the only miner working in the room where the blast originated. His identifying check number was found attached to the coal car in that same location. He was the only miner identified by name—and more than once—during the four-hour inquest hearing. And, perhaps more noteworthy than conclusive, in his letter to O'Brien complaining about the fairness of the inquest, Austro-Hungarian Consul John C. Schwegel mentioned the miner by name: "I understand that the explosion was caused by a shot fired by Tom Patterson [sic], Check No. 667." While O'Brien contested some of Schwegel's allegations in a letter of his own, the consul's reference to Pattison was not among them.

So who was Thomas Pattison?

Born to John Henry Pattison, a coal miner, and Mary Ann Williams, a Welsh immigrant, in Pennsylvania in 1884, he was working in a coal mine by the age of fifteen. In 1904, he enlisted in the US Army's Coast Artillery Corps, serving as a private in the 44th Company until his honorable discharge three years later. In 1910, he married Mary Donley and within a few years moved 1,500 miles west to work in the coal mines of Dawson.

Pattison's body wasn't found until five days after the explosion. Upon identification, the thirty-year-old's remains were sent home his to parents in Punxsutawney, Pennsylvania, where he was buried in Clayville Cemetery.

To be fair, it should be noted that while New Mexico law forbade firing shots while men were in the mine, the practice was fairly common in American coal mines. In fact, a US Bureau of Mines circular published in 1916 gave its blessing to the practice—with the proper precautions: "If shots are prepared, loaded, and fired under the supervision of a competent shot firer, where no gas is present and the coal dust is well watered, there is no great danger in firing the shots while the miners are in the mine."

That was not what happened inside Dawson Mine No. 2 on October 22, 1913.

CHAPTER 12

BACK TO NORMAL

Dawson and the industry that makes it its headquarters are two of the things that are bringing New Mexico to the forefront of the country's industrial progress. Dawson is not a coal camp. It is a city. Over 6,000 people reside there; it is a city in government, in civic pride, in progressiveness.

—Ralph Emerson Twitchell

✦

If Rees H. Beddow had spent any more time in Dawson in 1914, he would have needed his own office. The New Mexico mine inspector made five trips to the mining town that year, on top of the first four days of November 1913 investigating the cause of October's explosion. All told, his trips in January, February, May, July, and September covered thirteen days, six inspecting the wrecked Mine No. 2. There wasn't much to report on his first visit—"found quite a number of men cleaning up"—but when he returned four months later, he observed two hundred and twenty-five miners, fifty-two company men, four boys, and twenty mules working underground. While he noticed some dryness in spots, he found the mine in "good condition"—an assessment he repeated in his later inspections.

Beddow also took note of safety improvements implemented by Phelps Dodge in the aftermath of the disaster. The company placed air humidifiers and steam radiators in all mines to dampen coal dust, installed new sprinklers to wet the top of coal cars for their trips out of the tunnels, and purchased new steel cars designed to prevent loose coal from spilling and being crushed into dust.

But those weren't the only things to grab Beddow's attention. During one of his visits, he was invited to attend the company's monthly safety meeting inside the rescue station, as well as, in his words, to "fill up on good eats." Here, officials from the general superintendent down to mine foremen met each month to discuss a particular topic related to safety inside and outside the mines. Beddow came away from that session with more than a full belly. "I was very favorably impressed with the results of the meeting, as all present were deeply interested in what was said and done," he said. "It was plain to be seen that they all were

thinking of means of improvements, and when you can get men thinking seri-
ously, much good is going to be accomplished. I was very much pleased to see
this co-operation among the mine officials of this company, and trust that these
meetings will be profitable to all concerned."

Beddow was back the following January for that month's safety meeting
and "banquet."

✦

Phelps Dodge made several strategic decisions that year to mitigate the impact
of any future dust explosions. In order to confine them to the smallest possible
area, the company limited the average daily production in each mine to 750 tons.
For Mine No. 2, this was done by installing barriers and effectively splitting it
into Mines No. 2 and 3. Similar divisions were under consideration for Mines
No. 1 and 5.

The company also ended its practice of allowing underground miners to
load their holes with explosives and connect them to the shooting wires at the
end of their shifts. Instead, specially trained men took over that job after the
miners had left for the day. Mine officials ramped up safety measures, too, making first-aid lessons mandatory for designated workers in each of the mines.

✦

In the spring of 1914, two *Denver Post* staffers toured New Mexico coalfields to
report on the state's mining industry for the paper's readers back home. By pure
happenstance, they were in Dawson in late May for the company-sponsored
memorial service for the men killed in the previous year's mine disaster. The
story began:

> Dawson, the biggest coal mining camp in this state, paused for half a
> day yesterday to do honor to the memory of 263 miners whose lives were
> lost in an accident on October 22, last. Everything in the town and its
> environs closed down except the post-office and the railroad, while every
> man, woman and child in the camp moved over the hills to the cemetery
> which one mishap has nearly filled. To those who are familiar with the
> management of the properties centered about Dawson there was prob-
> ably nothing unwonted in this dolorous gathering, but to an outsider it
> appeared to be one of those demonstrations which reveal a breathing soul

in an occasional corporation, and this belief was reinforced by the tales the miners themselves tell of the generous and practical sympathy shown to the bereaved families by the Phelps-Dodge interests, which own the various mines.

Phelps Dodge spent months planning for this observance, from ordering special iron crosses and wreaths to drawing up blueprints to erect fences around the graves of the deceased miners and the cemetery. Perhaps no one was more active in this endeavor than Dr. James Douglas, the firm's president, stationed at the company's New York headquarters. No detail was too small for Douglas, whether it was the cement blocks to be sunk underground to hold the iron crosses ("Cement blocks for crosses should be about 8" square") or the crosses themselves ("The crosses are a fancy of my oen [sic]. I will pay that bill.")

As conveyed in the *Denver Post* article, the company's extensive planning and attention to detail was not lost on the thousands who gathered for the spring service. "It was estimated that from 2500 to 3000 people were in attendance at the ceremonies," Stag Cañon General Manager T. H. O'Brien wrote to Douglas days later. "The crosses and decorations made a very beautiful effect and the relatives and friends of the deceased were greatly pleased with the arrangements."

No less impressed with the ceremony—as well as the "splendid conditions in the coal camps at Dawson"—were the visitors from Denver: R. G. Dill Jr., the reporter who wrote the story, and Josiah Maloney, a twenty-year veteran of the paper. "It was one of the most solemn and impressive sights I ever saw," Maloney said. "The band—one of the best bands I ever heard—played softly all through the exercises, 'Nearer My God to Thee,' and the whole ceremony was one of the most beautiful things I ever witnessed. No part of it was more impressive than the solicitous care the management took to see that no hitch occurred in the proceedings and that every woman and child were [sic] taken care of while the crowd gathered."

✦

While the explosion prompted changes in *how* coal would be mined in Dawson, it had little to no impact on *how much*. Dawson retained its position during this period as one of the top two coal producers in the state. In 1914, for example, the St. Louis, Rocky Mountain & Pacific Company (1.57 million tons), with its twelve mines, and Dawson (1.34 million tons), with five, accounted for 96 percent of all the bituminous coal produced from New Mexico's forty-four working mines.

They were also responsible for all 826,417 million tons of coke in the state, though here Dawson held a nearly two-to-one advantage over its rival.

For Dawson, it only would get better. By 1916, three years after the explosion, production reached an all-time high of 1.44 million tons. During that year, railroads accounted for 80 percent of its total sales, a dependency that would come back to haunt Dawson years later. Now, however, business was so good that the company began work on a new mine, driving two parallel entries roughly 1,200 feet for what would become Mine No. 7. (Mine No. 6 had been formed by the splitting of No. 1 in 1916.) This period also marked Dawson's largest mine employment, peaking at an average of 1,640 workers in 1915.

Dawson's coming of age was not lost on observers of New Mexico history. "Dawson is the banner coal producer, the mammoth mineral deposit, the almost sole fuel source for an area equal in size to one-sixth of the United States," wrote historian Ralph Emerson Twitchell. "All of which will be admitted as evidence that it is a place of considerable importance."

✦

Phelps Dodge would never achieve these levels of production and employment again, but that doesn't mean the company sat on its hands through the early 1920s. On the mining side, it opened a new state-of-the-art washery and a new boiler plant and dug three new mines: Nos. 8, 9, and 10. Mine officials also increased the use of coal-cutting machines to compensate for a shortage of labor brought on by World War I. In 1915 and 1916, thousands of American miners left for better-paying jobs in the nation's munition factories and related industries, where wages averaged about 20 percent higher. "The decrease in production [in 1917] was due to the shortage of all classes of mine laborers during the latter part of the year," according to the company's 1917 annual report. "It has become practically impossible to procure skilled diggers, and in order to maintain the production, mining machines have been introduced, and their installation will be continued throughout the coming year."

Phelps Dodge was also active in the community at large during this period. Among other structures, the company built a schoolhouse, a dispensary, nurses' quarters, and a Catholic church in 1916; ninety-one homes to meet the rise in married workers in 1917; a grade school and high school to accommodate between four hundred and five hundred students in 1920; a dairy to supply milk to the town in 1921; and a three-room school and conversion of the company store warehouse into a basketball gym in 1922.

But the company had much more in mind at this time than tending to the physical needs of the community. Driven by labor unrest in neighboring states and its undisguised contempt for unions, the company established a Welfare Department in 1920 to—in the words of New Mexico historian Richard Melzer—"kill union activity with a type of corporate kindness," or what he called "welfare capitalism." The basic goal was to transform their largely immigrant workforce into obedient American citizens while rooting out suspected radicals during the postwar Red Scare hysteria that gripped the nation.

The Welfare Department, not uncommon in company towns in the early 1900s, became deeply rooted in promoting the educational, health, and social benefits of life in Dawson. And there were many of these, to wit: a visiting nurse to provide home health care, night classes for foreign-born workers to help them become American citizens, dozens of fraternal organizations and social clubs, all manner of athletic pursuits (including a semiprofessional baseball team), and large social events on the Fourth of July and Community Day in the fall to foster community spirit. Demonstrating that no task was too small, the department even coordinated the distribution of free shade trees for residents.

A key component of this movement was the formation of a Welfare Committee, an elected body that met twice each month to identify issues in need of attention and recommend solutions to the bosses. Representatives were elected by nationality or race and by mine district; craftsmen and the machine shop also shared a seat. To be eligible, candidates had to have been employed for at least one year and be able to speak English. Presumably to foster open discussion, supervisors were prohibited from serving, which meant that the Welfare Department director was the lone conduit to management. While this body gave workers a seat at the table, it had no real authority to institute significant change. As it turned out, it was more successful at organizing garden contests and reminding residents to keep the streets clear of wandering livestock than bringing any meaningful improvements to the lives of the miners.

Perhaps the most visible change introduced by the Welfare Department was the *Dawson News*, a weekly newspaper that debuted on February 3, 1921. Predictably, this was more of a company house organ than an independent news source, but it did serve its purpose as described in the maiden issue by Jay T. Conway, the newspaper's director and editor: "Unlike most weekly publications of its kind, the chief motive for its existence is not commercial in character. Its fields of usefulness, therefore, will be restricted solely to the particular purpose for which it is published—the advancement of Dawson's community interests and of the Welfare Department."

Conway's front-page news stories that day were in keeping with that promise: coverage of the dedication ceremonies for the new Dawson High School, which the newspaper described as "probably one of the best equipped and most conveniently arranged school structures in this part of the State," and the opening of a new sanitary dairy that represented "One of the most import-ant contributions made in recent months to the health, convenience and general well-being of the people of this community." Briefs inside the paper touched on the reopening of a boardinghouse that had been severely damaged by fire, the sentencing of a miner to sixty days in the county jail after pleading guilty to drunk and disorderly conduct, and the placement of "no loafing" signs in the lobby and halls of the opera house and other public places to "save a certain class of small boys in Dawson some serious trouble." The newspaper would enjoy an eight-year run, its final issue published on October 31, 1929, two days after "Black Tuesday" and the nation's calamitous stock market crash.

✦

Not all was within Phelps Dodge's control during this period. Like every other community in the country, Dawson was subjected to the ebb and flow of events playing out nationally and around the world.

In 1917, New Mexico passed a prohibition amendment to the state consti-tution effective as of October 1 the following year. "The consequent abolishment of the saloons will remove a certain amount of diversion which hitherto has been enjoyed by the employees," the company acknowledged, "and we should devise some method of providing a satisfactory substitute." In the fall of 1918, the global influenza dubbed the Spanish flu spread through town, claiming the lives of seventy-nine residents and placing an enormous strain on the hospital and its medical staff.

President Woodrow Wilson's decision to enter World War I in April 1917 also upended life in Dawson, particularly for the European immigrants now put in the position of fighting for their adopted country. More than fifty men and boys—some with last names like Cincornella, Haprtsilakos, and Sinkovich—joined the war effort, along with dozens more from the nearby coal camps of Brilliant, Gardiner, Koehler, Sugarite, Van Houten, and Yankee.

Five Dawson soldiers were wounded in action, some severely. Two never made it home alive: Alonzo Aragon, a twenty-five-year-old New Mexico native killed during France's Meuse–Argonne offensive, the deadliest campaign in US history; and John Karantzias, a twenty-eight-year-old Greek immigrant who was one of the twelve thousand American casualties during the Battle of Soissons in July 1918.

Roughly 150 Dawson men answered the call when the United States entered World War II in December 1941. Barbers. Coal loaders. Dairymen. Janitors. Machine operators. Nurses. Pick miners. Twelve never returned, their names recorded for posterity on a monument near the entrance to Dawson Cemetery. Two died in captivity in prisoner-of-war camps.

Robert Lucero nearly joined them. But he survived the infamous Bataan Death March and, in his words, "three years, six months, one day and three hours" in captivity in a Japanese POW camp in the Philippines. "My biggest hope was that I'd be able to see my family again in Dawson," Lucero wrote later. "I hung on to that . . . Just before Thanksgiving, I got a train from Lamy [New Mexico], to Raton, where my brother Dave picked me up. I came into Dawson at night, and I guess it was a surprise. Dad and mother knew I was alive, but they weren't expecting me. There was a lot of crying and hugging, and it was good to be home. I'd been away from Dawson for four years, and that was much too long."

During the 1996 Dawson reunion, Lucero told an *Albuquerque Journal* reporter that thoughts of Dawson had helped him to survive the Bataan Death March. "All I wanted to do," he said, "was to come home, see these hills, smell the food, be with the people here."

OH, NO, NOT AGAIN!

Nearly everyone in town went over to Dawson to see if they could help, and I will never forget the scene. Families were gathered at the entrance of the mine crying, screaming and milling around. Children were asking "Is my daddy alive?" and wives and mothers could only hope and pray that their loved ones would be safe.
—Enes Federici Caraglio Covert

✦

May Dee Lunsford was teaching her class of fifth-graders when a loud boom echoed through the canyon on the chilly afternoon of February 8, 1923. Immediately, the children's shouts of "Mine explosion!" filled the room, but Lunsford tried to calm her excited charges.

"Oh, no," she said. "They are just blasting for the new houses."

If only.

"Miss Lunsford," a young student cried out as he burst through the doorway. "There has been an explosion and Pearl Dupont's father is caught in it!"

Lunsford rushed out into the hall, where she found the school's teary-eyed principal.

"Is it true?" she asked.

"Yes," he replied. "There has been an explosion in Number One."

✦

Pearl Dupont's father was not in the mine when it erupted around 2:30 p.m. that day. Scott Dupont, the underground mine superintendent, was standing just outside the portal, getting ready to go inside, when he was thrown back several feet by the force of the blast. He suffered burns and cuts to his face but, like General Manager T. H. O'Brien ten years earlier, he worked until he collapsed from exhaustion.

This wasn't the only similarity to October 22, 1913. The reinforced-concrete entryway was severely damaged by the explosion—one chunk broke through the wall of the wooden motor house two hundred feet away—making it difficult for rescuers to gain quick access to the mine. Fresh air stopped circulating for a time, not because the fan was damaged, but because the fan house doors had blown off. Inside the mine, fallen rocks and timber blocked the most direct paths to the entombed miners. Outside, a first-aid station was set up and staffed by physicians, nurses, and volunteers. Others provided relief to the rescue teams, now working in four-hour shifts, to ensure that hot coffee and sandwiches were served as the men came off duty.

"The bakery made the bread and roasted the beef," May Dee Lunsford said. "Part of the teaching force worked there because there was no school. I was with the group that served the food at the mine entrance—a beef sandwich and black coffee."

Later, her brother would face a far grimmer task.

"My brother also worked in the cemetery," she said. "It was his job to open each casket and record the number of the metal tag in a plat book."

✦

As soon as they heard the explosion, women and children hurried toward the mine entrance, hoping and praying that their loved ones would come out alive. A reporter with a keen eye for detail captured the scene: "The women, some hatless despite the wintry breezes, others tightly wrapped in shawls, some tight lipped and dry-eyed, while others were sobbing and hysterical, waited for some sign to indicate whether their 'men folks' would be brought from the mine."

Enes Covert was there, too. Born in a "tiny little house behind the tailor shop" on September 7, 1907, Covert was in her Dawson High School classroom when what sounded like a clap of thunder prompted her and her classmates to rush outside. Seeing nothing out of the ordinary, they returned to class.

"It wasn't until I arrived home after school that mother told me the bad news," she wrote years later. "Dawson's No. 1 mine had exploded and 122 men had been in the tunnels."

Covert watched as rescue crews entered the mine to search for survivors—or worse. That was when she recognized one of the volunteers: John Caraglio, a photographer who, hours earlier, had been at the high school taking pictures of seniors for the class yearbook. The same John Caraglio would later befriend, court, marry, and raise four daughters with her.

✦

Superintendent Daniel Harrington, stationed at the US Bureau of Mines' Denver office, learned of the explosion ninety minutes later when notified by an Associated Press reporter. He immediately wired Stag Cañon General Manager William "W. D." Brennan to offer a bureau rescue car and other assistance. Brennan, having already secured the aid of a Colorado Fuel and Iron Company rescue car from nearby Trinidad, told Harrington that this wouldn't be necessary. Nevertheless, Harrington ordered bureau rescue cars to Dawson from Hanna, Wyoming, and Ajo, Arizona. He set out for Dawson on the Wyoming car and "P. G." Beckett, general manager of all Phelps Dodge coal properties, on the Arizona car. By the time they arrived two days later, Worthington "W. W." Risdon, the state mine inspector, was already there.

While Dawson officials welcomed the arrival of the federal government's trained rescue teams with their life-saving equipment, they were better prepared for this kind of work than they had been a decade earlier. The company owned ten two-hour breathing apparatuses—newer equipment designed by James W. Paul of the Bureau of Mines and approved for use in 1920—and five of the older half-hour Draeger devices. Some forty Dawson miners had completed training on the equipment and another twenty-eight were in the process of earning their certificates. Still, for the most part, the breathing devices proved not to be needed. By the next morning, ventilation had been restored enough to clear the mine of dangerous gases.

✦

Technically, this was not the first mine disaster at No. 1. Three years earlier, on April 14, 1920, five men had been killed during the nightly setting off of explosives inside what were supposed to be empty Mines No. 1 and 6. The mines, whose entrances were a few hundred feet apart, connected underground.

That night, in accordance with company rules, six trained shot firers entered the tunnels to plant their explosives for detonation by an electric system once they had exited. Then they made their way to the shot-firing cabin, where they signed their names and logged the time in a register to affirm the mines were empty. After the shots were fired, the men were supposed to reenter the mines to inspect their work before heading home for the night.

Everything was in order until the company electrician flipped the switch inside the substation at 8:25 p.m., setting off the charges to dislodge the coal for loading the next morning. Instead, possibly due to an improperly set shot, he triggered a huge explosion inside Mine No. 6, demolishing its fan building and damaging the fan for No. 1.

Worse, the mines weren't empty after all. Unbeknownst to the electrician, during his five-minute walk to the substation, four shot firers had reentered the mine. A fifth man—a laborer—was in the mine as well. None survived the blast.

In his report to Governor Octaviano Larrazolo, submitted five weeks after the incident, New Mexico mine inspector Jo E. Sheridan had yet to determine the cause of the explosion, but he left no doubt what led to the deaths of the shot firers:

> In flagrant violation of the mine rules, these men returned to the mine and were killed in the explosion, within eight hundred feet from the portal of the mine. The sole incentive which these men had in entering the mine was that they might make their final inspection of the various places where the shots were fired as quickly as possible and get through their work for the night. By going into the mine as far as possible, before that last switch was thrown, and the shots fired, they would be that much nearer to their working faces to make the examinations and would get out of the mine a few minutes earlier.

The five men left three widows and eleven fatherless children.

Not much is known about these victims with the exception of one, thanks to research conducted in recent years by his great-grandson, Stephen Reed. Albert James Reed, age fifty and married with four children, got a job as a coal miner in April 1917 in Walsenburg, Colorado. He remained there until at least February 1919, after which he made the trip across the state line to work in the Dawson mines. Reed's death certificate lists his cause of death as "explosion in mine," stating that he suffered severe burns over his entire body. There was no autopsy; his death was confirmed by physical examination two days later in Raton. While the death certificate records his place of burial as Dawson, his name is not listed in Dawson Cemetery records as one of the men buried there.

+

On the morning of February 8, 1923, 140 men had checked into Mine No. 1, one of the original three opened by the Dawson Fuel Company in 1902. Eighteen men had left the mine because of illness or other reasons prior to the explosion, leaving 122 trapped inside. By 4:00 p.m., the portal had been cleared enough for the first rescue teams to enter. Brennan, the general manager, accompanied them and remained on the job until 3:00 a.m., when "exhaustion forced him to seek rest."

"The work of entering the mine and excavating, through the caved in tunnels, is a task which presents no little risk to the rescue party," the Associated Press reported. "The fumes in the mine still are dense, despite the use of the large mine fan." Indeed, four rescue men were overcome by fumes and had to be carried out by their colleagues to be resuscitated. Falling debris from the roofs and walls posed a constant danger and made it necessary for workers to retrace their steps to clear the tunnel for the crews behind them.

By the next morning, rescue teams had recovered the bodies of seven miners, including Albert English, age fifty-six, whose brother, Arthur, had been killed in the 1913 explosion. Later, rescuers would find the body of his twenty-nine-year-old son, mine foreman Albert English Jr., now the third in the family to die in the Dawson mines. They were buried side by side—"FATHER" and "SON" carved into their respective headstones—at Fairmont Cemetery in Raton. Seventeen-year-old Fred English, one of Albert and Elizabeth's ten children, was among the volunteers to join the search for the bodies of his father and older brother.

A temporary morgue was soon opened in a nearby office building to house the first bodies. By the next morning, when a howling snowstorm cleared the portal of the few remaining vigil-keepers, the remains of only forty miners had been recovered.

Unlike ten years earlier, Phelps Dodge's first public assessment offered no reason for optimism. In a statement released to the Associated Press, the company stated: "Owing to the fumes which permeated the mine following the explosion, very little hope is entertained that any of the men who were in the mine will be found alive."

That statement would turn out to be true—in a way.

✦

Guerino "Shorty" Scarafiotti didn't hear the explosion but knew something was amiss. The vibrations under his work boots in adjacent Mine No. 6 told him all he needed to know. When his foreman asked for men trained in the use of rescue gear, Guerino volunteered. So did his brother, Guido. When they got outside, they could see smoke pouring out of No. 1. They headed to the No. 6 lamp house to get fresh lamps before hurrying back to the wrecked mine. Superintendent Scott Dupont lay on the ground near the portal. The brothers thought he was dead.

The volunteers gathered at the No. 1 lamp house, where they were instructed on the dangerous task before them. They were reminded to walk slowly to conserve their limited supply of oxygen and to keep track of their distance from the mine entrance to ensure they had enough to get back. With that, they checked out their equipment, suited up, and broke into teams of four before entering the smoky mine.

Maneuvering through the fallen debris, the Scarafiottis came upon what at first looked to be an abandoned motor car—until they saw an unrecognizable motorman "burned black where he sat." The next bodies to be discovered, roughly one and a half miles into the tunnel, looked much different. Neither scorched nor mutilated, the men appeared to have been running toward the entrance when they were overcome by carbon monoxide and collapsed to the floor. Crew members were equipped with a pulmotor to revive the living, but they quickly saw that it wouldn't be needed; these blue-lipped men were dead.

In Guerino's words: "At this point we returned to the surface because we were using way too much air since we were working too hard and using more than we normally did in training. When we got back outside it was after dark, and they had brought big lights up and many families were present. Me and Guido made sure that our families were told that we were OK. We also checked to be sure that we didn't have any family working in #1 that day and thank goodness we did not."

After grabbing sandwiches sent down by the company store, the Scarafiotti boys changed equipment and reentered the mine with their team. They headed to where they had left off, passing other crews removing bodies along the way, when they spied what looked to be a group of miners. They were sitting with their backs to the wall, lunch pails open before them. But they, too, were dead.

"As I shined my light on them, I recognized among them both a father and son that lived near us, and I felt really bad and had to sit down," Guerino recalled, referring to the English family. "I will always remember how they looked like they were just asleep. At this point we marked the location and started back for air. When we got back outside there were plenty more volunteers to help, and we didn't go back in, nor did we ever help remove bodies. . . . You didn't want to go back inside again after seeing something like that, and Guido and I never told the families what we saw, and we were asked plenty. I prayed that they went fast and didn't suffer."

✦

W. W. Risdon was no stranger to Dawson or to the state mine inspector's post, for that matter. Originally appointed by Governor William C. McDonald to replace Rees H. Beddow in 1916, Risdon held the position for three years before he was replaced by Jo E. Sheridan, the former territorial mine inspector, in 1919. When Sheridan died suddenly during his first year, Risdon returned and served through 1925. His third and final term would run from 1927 to 1931—roughly a dozen years in all.

Risdon had visited the Stag Cañon mines numerous times, his most recent inspection having taken place the previous July. He also happened to be there on February 22, 1918, when he got word of a mine fire in Carthage, which would add yet another sad footnote to Dawson's snakebitten history.

Upon his arrival in Carthage, Risdon suggested to Carthage Fuel Company President Powell Stackhouse Jr. that he contact Stag Cañon General Manager T. H. O'Brien and ask for two experienced mine safety men. O'Brien obliged by sending Thomas Brown, superintendent of Mine No. 2, and David Murphy, a Dawson mine inspector. Both had trained in rescue work and fighting underground fires.

On February 26, four days after the fire, Brown and Murphy arrived at 3:30 p.m. By 6:21, they were inside the mine, part of a five-man crew whose goal was to inspect the first seven hundred feet. The men made their mark without incident—but the same could not be said for the caged mouse they brought with them to detect the level of toxins in the air around them. After walking a bit farther toward the source of the fire, the crew pivoted and headed back toward the entrance.

The men had retraced about one-third of their steps when someone noticed that Murphy was struggling to breathe. James Cunningham, the team leader, promptly adjusted Murphy's breathing apparatus, which brought immediate relief. Murphy assured his crewmates he was fine and would need no further assistance. It wasn't long, however, before he again showed signs of distress. While Cunningham tended to Murphy, he noticed that Brown looked wobbly, too. Within minutes, both men were down.

Unable to carry them out, the rescue team exited the mine, refreshed their oxygen tanks, and returned in a mine car to retrieve them. They found Brown exactly as they had left him, but Murphy had turned onto his back and disconnected his breathing apparatus. Brown recovered. Murphy did not. "Work to resuscitate Murphy began 7:54 and continued until about 12:01," Risdon wrote in his report. "Two doctors were in attendance and at no time were either of them positive that they could detect any sign of life."

One possible explanation for this unnecessary death was that Murphy was unfamiliar with the older Fleuss breathing apparatus used in Carthage, having been trained on the more advanced Draeger equipment. A later report specu-lated that Brown and Murphy, by talking to each other "incessantly," might have inhaled carbon monoxide during their exploratory mission.

Risdon had great respect for Murphy's knowledge and experience, perhaps greater than that of "any of the other men in the party," he said. And, contrary to some reports, Murphy had assured him he was comfortable using the Fleuss breathing apparatus. Still, Risdon advised him to be careful before entering the mine, emphasizing that there were no lives at stake because all of the men had escaped safely. According to Risdon, "He said to me, 'I am not going to take any chances, and you don't need to be uneasy about me.'"

Murphy, the son of an Irish miner, was forty-four years old. He became the third trained rescue man associated with Dawson to die in this manner, joining James Laird and William Poyser, who perished in the 1913 rescue mission.

✦

Just minutes after the 1923 explosion, Risdon, stationed in Albuquerque, received a terse telegram from Stag Cañon General Manager Brennan stating that "mine number one had blown up." Risdon didn't waste any time. The state mine inspec-tor boarded a train that evening for Raton and arrived at 5:10 the following morn-ing. Five hours later, he was on his way to Dawson and arrived by noon.

Risdon's first stop was at Brennan's office to find out what steps had been taken to restore ventilation and assemble rescue crews to enter the damaged mine. Both jobs had been under way well before his arrival, though rescuers would have to stand down Friday morning for about an hour while the over-loaded fan motor was replaced with a larger unit.

That was when two men walked out of the mine.

✦

Charles George Skandale was a long way from home. Born on the Greek island of Crete, he was twenty-three years old when he came to America in 1909. He left home for much the same reason as thousands of his countrymen during the early 1900s: to make his fortune in this promised land, then return in a few years to share his newfound riches with his family.

Skandale brought some skills to his new home. He had learned to make leather belts, saddles, and shoes under the tutelage of his craftsman father, but these weren't the skills he would pursue. Upon his arrival at Ellis Island, he hitchhiked his way across the country to Utah, where he met up with some cousins who had already found jobs at a coal camp. When that coal supply began to run low, Skandale moved south and was working in the Dawson mines by 1918.

Skandale found something else in Dawson besides a good-paying job: Elizabeth, a young Greek girl from Lakos, a small town on the southern tip of the Peloponnese peninsula in southern Greece, who had emigrated a year after he had. Soon, they married.

Like many miners' wives, Elizabeth never got used to the danger of his work. Years later, her granddaughter, also Elizabeth Skandale, wrote that her grandmother "worried about her husband going into the mine everyday. It just didn't seem right to her, for men to go deep into the earth to dig coal. It was the mine explosions she feared most. She wondered when he would get a job above ground, when she could go and see him at lunch. This kind of life where she always wondered if he would make it home in the evenings had to change. But she kept all this to herself."

+

Filomeno diMartino was already digging coal by the time Skandale arrived in Dawson. Born in San Pietro Avellana, a small town roughly ninety miles north of Naples in south central Italy, diMartino was twelve years old when he immigrated to the United States with his brother and sister in 1904, according to a family history compiled by distant cousin Mark DiVecchio. They settled in Denver, but by 1910 diMartino was living in Dawson with a couple from his home town. The US census that year listed the nineteen-year-old's occupation as "miner."

DiMartino returned to Italy but was back in the United States by May 1915, accompanied by Oliveta Iannacchione, his new bride. Together, they traveled to Dawson, where diMartino resumed work as a coal miner. By 1920, they had a four-year-old son and a home of their own.

That's where they were living on the morning of February 8, 1923.

+

On that day, Charles Skandale was up bright and early at 4:00 a.m. He grabbed his jacket, laced up his black work boots, and stepped out into the frosty February air to wash up. After a breakfast of hot cereal and coffee prepared by his wife, he packed his lunch pail—the bottom half filled with drinking water to last the day, the top part with a jelly sandwich—grabbed some warm clothing, and began his daily walk to the mines. When he arrived, the foreman assigned him and diMartino to the deepest part of Mine No. 1. They grabbed their picks and shovels and rode a motor car to their assigned spot.

They had finished eating lunch when they heard a low rumbling sound that grew louder and louder until the impact of the explosion knocked them off their feet and onto the mine floor. Breathing became difficult, leading them to believe—correctly—that the fan had stopped circulating fresh air into the mine. The force of the explosion knocked out the mine lights, and the two men turned off their headlamps to conserve the batteries for their hoped-for escape. Rather than make a mad dash to the entrance, a certain death sentence amid the deadly gases, they decided to stay put. That's when, somewhat miraculously in the total blackness, they found diMartino's undisturbed lunch bucket a few feet away.

"The mine lights were out. Feline [sic] had a water bucket that some how hadn't been turned over. We tore the bottoms off our sweaters, soaked them in water and tied them around our nose and mouth," Skandale told reporters later. "Then we just sat there by the water bucket and waited. We knew we were dead men if we moved and got into the current of gas. It was as though years went by."

They waited not years, but hours—roughly sixteen in all—during which Skandale and diMartino lay stretched out on their bellies, their damp sweaters wrapped around their faces as crude breathing devices. The men spoke little during the night, trying to conserve their precious oxygen, even when they heard voices nearby. Neither dared to call out.

✦

The next morning, Skandale felt "a breath of fresh air" on his face. He gave diMartino a nudge and both lowered the damp sweaters from their faces. The air, in the words of Skandale, was "sweet," a sign that the overnight ventilation had driven out the dangerous gases. They scrambled to their feet and began to walk toward the mine entrance. That was no easy feat considering the darkness—the batteries to their headlamps had died during the night—and the debris scattered before them. Within minutes, they came upon several men, presumably the miners they had overheard talking earlier. They were dead.

"They continued stumbling their way along the ragged edges of the tunnel walls while their hands were cut and bleeding, tripping over huge boulders and broken timbers," Skandale's granddaughter recounted. "As they neared the mouth of the mine they were met by the rescue party who escorted them out. My grandfather walked out of the mine unassisted as a cheer rang out from the crowd." That's when his wife, her cheeks now glistening with tears of joy, reached out and wrapped her arms around him, saying over and over: "You're the only ones, you're the only ones to live."

For his part, diMartino did his best to put everyone at ease.

"We ain't hurt," he said. "How about some coffee?"

✦

Reporters on the scene were eager to share with readers this stranger-than-truth tale of survival. An account by Frank H. Bartholomew, a United Press staff correspondent, was splashed on newspaper front pages across the country. He wrote:

> Dawson today heard from the lips of Charles Kantal [sic] and Feline Martini [sic], miners who walked miraculously as though guided by a divine hand from their tomb a 'mile below sunshine,' the story of the mine disaster in which 122 men were trapped. Kantal and Martini for 16 hours kept a grim vigil in . . . Number 1 Mine near where 120 of their comrades also imprisoned, lay dead, dying or waiting for the air to be pumped in. It seemed that all the pathos of the Dawson tragedy centered about the little box-like Kantal home today. Weeping women and wide eyed children gathered around Kantal and Martini to hear about the fate of the others entombed.

At the end of the interview, Skandale agreed to pose for a photograph with his wife and two young sons, George and Nick. Before the photo was taken, a third young boy tried to join them. "Juan, come here," a young Mexican woman called to him. "They don't want your picture. You—you're just an orphan kid now."

Despite his death-defying escape that day, Skandale suffered more than cuts and bruises. His older brother, Antonio, was among the 120 men who didn't make it out alive.

✦

Charles Skandale did not hesitate to go back into the mines after the explosion, though he later took a job working above ground. He left Dawson before the town closed and moved to Los Angeles. His granddaughter, who was nineteen when he died, said he never spoke much about Dawson, though one time he did share his story with her that she recounted for a college paper in 1981.

"He was a quiet man," Elizabeth said. "When we used to go to his house when he lived in LA, he used to sit in the corner in his special chair. He was a man of few words, to be quite honest with you."

Elizabeth recalls her father, George, an outstanding Dawson athlete who played for the University of New Mexico in the 1939 Sun Bowl, telling her how her grandfather used to complain about working all day in the mines for nothing because "all he'd hit was slate." She also remembers her grandfather becoming "very quiet" each year on February 8. "Until his death in 1979, at the age of 93, my grandfather held the anniversary of the day of the explosion as a day of bad luck," Elizabeth said. "He would stay close to home and do very little. But as if to test his superstition, the one time he did leave the house to go to another town by car, he was involved in a serious car accident. He again escaped with little injury; that was the last time he would ever test fate."

✦

Less is known about Filomeno diMartino's life after the explosion. Two years later, while still in Dawson, he and his wife were blessed with the birth of a daughter. But eight days before Christmas—on the same day as her baptism before family and friends at St. John the Baptist Church—she died. The family remained in Dawson for another year before moving to Pittsburgh in 1927. By 1930, diMartino had landed a job at the city's salt works plant, and he and Oliveta were the proud parents of six children: four boys and two girls. In 1942, when he registered for the draft at age fifty, he was working for the Federated Metals Division of the American Smelting & Refining Company. He died sixteen years later in 1958.

✦

Unlike the 1913 mine disaster, where three-quarters of the victims were European immigrants, native-born Americans (37 percent) and Mexicans (23 percent) bore the brunt of the 1923 explosion; Italians (15 percent), Greeks (13 percent), Austrians (7 percent), Montenegrins (5 percent), and one Russian made up the remainder. This was reflective of changes to the Dawson workforce during this period. By 1920, Mexicans (46 percent) had surpassed Italians (20 percent) as the dominant group inside the mines, followed by Americans (16 percent), Slavs (12 percent), and Greeks (6 percent).

WHAT HAPPENED THIS TIME?

*[T]he mine was very dry, plenty of dust in that place; I don't see no sprinkling for a
long time.*
—Filomeno diMartino

✦

After the euphoria over the miraculous escape by two trapped
miners had dissipated, mine officials and rescue teams resumed the grim task
of recovering the dead. As of 8:00 the night after the explosion, workers had
removed thirty-four bodies, fewer than one-third of the 120 believed to be inside.
Four found near the center of the mine were badly burned ("their forms were
seared almost beyond recognition" according to a news report), suggesting that
the blast occurred nearby.

Getting to the other remains was no easy task. "In the mine, some buried
beneath huge mounds of debris, others lying behind mammoth obstructions that
blocked rescue workers and others far back, somewhere in the dark depths of the
many passage ways not yet cleared, are 86 men," the Associated Press reported.
"Dawson has not abandoned hope that they will be brought forth alive."

Before the day had ended, most of the folks who had braved the winter cold
to keep a steadfast vigil near the portal had returned to their homes. For those
who had lived through the disaster of 1913, the mood was all too familiar.

"Huddled in little groups about some of the homes were work-worn women
who gave consolation to those whose homes had felt the hand of death," observed
one correspondent. "On the streets of Dawson tonight, toil-begrimed men trod
the streets in small groups. There were no cheery handclasps, no hearty laughter—only the stolid demeanor of men who had lost a comrade or a brother."

Waking the next morning to newspaper reports listing the dead by name
did little to alter the mood of resignation.

✦

While rescue crews pressed into the deepest crevices of the wrecked mine and

Dawson began the somber task of burying its dead, mine officials faced a new challenge: sightseers. They arrived by the carload from nearby towns, hoping to catch a glimpse of the calamity that had unfolded days earlier. By and large, officials blocked the "tourists" from reaching the mine entrance, but they had less success keeping them from the opera house, now a temporary morgue. On this day, the bodies of sixteen Greeks and three Italians rested in open coffins, awaiting the arrival of a Greek priest from Pueblo, Colorado, to preside over their funeral services the next day.

Meanwhile, the first set of religious observances got under way at private homes, churches, and gravesites. The Rev. Joseph A. Couturier, pastor of Dawson's St. John the Baptist Church, and a visiting priest tended to the Catholics, while the Rev. J. S. Russell comforted the Protestants. Russell could have used some consoling of his own: The pastor would leave Dawson with the gratitude of the grieving families and the body of his son-in-law.

✦

On February 12, while recovery teams searched for the remaining fourteen bodies, mine officials were no closer to pinning down the exact cause of the explosion. Not that there hadn't been early rumors and speculation. Most pointed to the ignition of a methane gas pocket by a worker striking a match to have a smoke, the sparking of an electric coal-cutting machine, or an electric trolley car rolling through a gaseous part of the mine. None would turn out to be true.

That afternoon, an Associated Press correspondent got a firsthand look at the "utter devastation" inside the mine: "Ripped from the roof, as if clawed away by a brobdingnagian's hand, gigantic blocks of slate, coal and rock litter the passageways, piled in helter skelter confusion in the dark and windy tunnel through which the rescue crews for four days have been laboring with the bodies of their unfortunate comrades. That members of the working crews have not been injured or killed by falling debris during that period is little short of miraculous."

In the meantime, as had been the case ten years earlier, company officials extended a helping hand to families reeling from the loss of their loved ones. P. G. Beckett, general manager at Phelps Dodge, released a statement to the press assuring that "every provision possible" was being made to assist these families—the process of compensating them was already underway—while deploring the loss of life inside one of its mines. He also pledged to do everything humanly possible to find out what had caused the explosion.

The answer to that question would come soon enough.

✦

Justice of the Peace T. L. Kinney, as he had done a decade earlier in his role as coroner, swore in the six individuals who would serve on the jury on February 14. They would question nine witnesses ranging from company officials to coal diggers in their official charge to "determine the cause of the death of Albert English, Jr. and others found dead on February 8th, 1923."

W. D. Brennan, who had replaced T. H. O'Brien as Dawson general manager in 1920, was the first witness. Brennan, age forty-five, testified that he learned there had been an explosion inside one of the mines after receiving a telephone call at 2:30 p.m. When he reached Mine No. 1, he found that what remained of the entrance was clogged with debris and that the fan, while still working, had become ineffective because of damage to the surrounding fan house door. "Taking charge at once of the men who were there, I arranged to have the return air course blocked, so that the fan would again commence to remove air from the mine," he said. "After about twenty minutes of work on this, I felt that it was safe to start to proceed into the mine."

After rounding up some volunteers, Brennan testified, he entered the mine and headed down the main haulage road, one of three parallel entries that extended 5,800 feet into the mountain. A quarter of the way from the entrance, the men saw several dozen motor cars used to haul coal out of the mine. Making a note of their location, Brennan then divided his crew into two teams and instructed them to commence work to improve ventilation in this part of the mine.

In later trips, Brennan sought out the precise location of the explosion by examining what he called the "direction of forces": that is, the point where the initial impact of the blast was evident both inward and outward. His first clue was a sliver of wood—roughly a foot long and "a little larger than my thumb"— driven into a piece of timber in the direction of the portal.

Brennan found similar signs of force heading in the opposite direction. He also noticed that the lead motor car had been pushed back toward the mine interior and that the bodies of the now-deceased motorman and miner's helper had been blown back in the same direction. For Brennan, all of this led to one conclusion: that the blast had originated near that lead trolley car, some 1,500 feet into the mine.

By the time Brennan had finished testifying, he had identified the cause: Several of the lead motor cars had derailed on their way out of the mine, striking some timbers that supported live trolley wires. When the wires came in contact with an iron car, they arced and ignited the stirred-up coal dust.

Brennan said he had ruled out any other causes, in part because he and his team were able to determine that none of the electric coal-cutting machines found in the mine were turned on at the time of the blast. He was pressed by a juror on that very point:

Q: You mean by that that all the machines weren't running in the mine?
A: The other motors we found with the controllers off. The motor-man was undoubtedly instantly killed, and the mining machines were all found in various conditions, but in no case in such a condition as to lead anyone to believe they were in operation.

✦

Henry "Scott" Dupont, the underground superintendent who almost died that day, was the next witness. Dupont, age forty-six, had worked in Dawson for nineteen years, assuming his leadership position, like Brennan, in 1920. He began by describing what he saw just before the mine exploded: "Why, about two thirty I walked up to the mouth of the mine and started to walk in, and I looked down and seen what looked like the flash of a head light of the motor coming out, and I stopped and turned around and I was looking at the trolley switch and at that time the blast came and threw me out and it injured my leg, and I didn't get in until the next morning at about eight o'clock."

When Dupont entered the mine the next morning, he said, he found three of the motor cars off the track, burns and scorch marks on the trolley line, and fallen timbers all around. The brake in the lead car was engaged. This evidence led him to believe, as did his boss, that the derailment had set in motion the series of events that led to the death of the 120 miners.

✦

Edmond Thomas brought a different perspective to the proceedings, though he reached the same conclusion. Thomas, the foreman for Mine No. 1, was downtown when it exploded. He had forty years of experience working underground, all but one since 1908 in Dawson. The fifty-three-year-old miner was familiar with the driver of the motor car that day and testified that there was no way he would have applied the brakes in that spot unless something was wrong. "I have been in the mine hundreds of times and ridden out on that motor and he never brakes at that point; he would have gone farther than that without setting the brake. . . . That man knew there was something wrong or he wouldn't have set a brake at that place," he said.

✦

The final two witnesses introduced elements that would play a significant role in the formal investigative report: coal dust and sprinkling. The first man, interestingly enough, was Filomeno diMartino, one of the two survivors, who described himself as a thirty-two-year-old "coal digger." Kinney posed the questions:

Q: Can you tell us anything about the explosion; what happened or what you did at the time?
A: I can't tell, but the mine was very dry, plenty of dust in that place; I don't see no sprinkling for a long time.
Q: Did you see anything in the mine or on the way out that might have caused the explosion?
A: I never take a look at the time I come out.
Q: You didn't see anything that you think might have caused the explosion?
A: No, I was in a hurry to come outside and save myself.

Domenick Palumbo, the final witness, was a veteran of the Dawson mines, having begun work there in February 1905. The thirty-nine-year-old identified himself as a coal digger and shot firer, though on the day of the explosion he was filling in for a fire boss who had quit. He had checked the mine for gas that morning but was home at the time of the explosion.

Q: You didn't find anything in the mine that you think would cause an explosion, did you?
A: No, only the way there was dust for two or three days, the pipe must have been frozen up. And when I come up I try have them fix the pipe . . .
Q: Did you go in the mine after the explosion?
A: I was the eleventh man in.

✦

Before the day was out, the jury had issued its verdict. As Brennan had first testified, the jurors concluded that the explosion was caused when derailed motor cars took down a live trolley wire attached to the felled timbers, creating an arc that ignited coal dust.

The official finding read: "We, the undersigned justice of the peace and the jury who sat upon the inquest held this 14th day of February, on the bodies of Albert English, Jr., [mine foreman], and others, found in precinct No. 13 of the county of Colfax, State of New Mexico, find that the deceased came to their deaths by reason of a dust explosion in Mine No. 1 of the Phelps Dodge Corporation, at Dawson, New Mexico, on or about the 8th day of February, 1923; that said explosion was caused by the derailment of an outcoming trip, which knocked down the timbers to which the trolley feed line was attached, raising a quantity of dust, which was ignited by an electric arc, resulting from the feed wire coming in contact with one of the iron pit cars."

✦

While the jury succeeded in addressing the *how*, it did little to answer the *why*. For starters: Why was the mine so dry? Why was coal dust permitted to accumulate at such dangerous levels a decade after this contributed to the second-worst mine disaster in American history? What about witness Domenick Palumbo's reference to the "frozen up" pipe? Was the mine not sprinkled regularly to wet down the coal dust in the days leading up to the explosion? And, if so, why not?

State Mine Inspector W. W. Risdon provided the answer less than two weeks later in his February 20 special report to Governor James F. Hinkle. He wrote:

I have been told by the men in charge of the mine that on Saturday the 3rd of February, five days before the explosion occurred, some one closed a valve in the pipe line thus shutting pipes. The extreme cold weather of Saturday night, Sunday and Sunday night froze the water in the pipe line and, therefore, the mine had not had any water on the roads for five days preceding the explosion.

Risdon concluded that what had occurred on February 8 in Mine No. 1 was a dust explosion: "The accumulation of fine dust on the top of the cross bars and in the crevices of the roof together with the accumulation of dust on the roadways for lack of sprinkling furnished sufficient fuel to propagate the explosion throughout the mine."

Left unanswered in Risdon's report were the questions of who had closed the valve and why.

✦

Two months later, sprinkling was among the issues addressed in a comprehensive eighty-one-page report compiled by Daniel Harrington, supervising engineer for the US Bureau of Mines' Denver office. While hardly a scathing report—Harrington went out of his way to note there was "no intent at making offensive criticism"—it did point out some weaknesses in the company's approach to coal dust, electricity, rock dusting, shot-firing, sprinkling, and ventilation, concluding with thirty-one suggestions or recommendations.

Harrington acknowledged the many safety measures put into place by Phelps Dodge at considerable expense over the years before broaching the elephant in the room: the two mine disasters in a ten-year span that together had claimed the lives of nearly four hundred men. "[It] is evident," he wrote, "that something is lacking otherwise there would not occur at least three [probably more] serious widespread explosions in Dawson mines within a 10-year period. . . . While comparisons are odious and frequently unfair, it does not seem out of place here to refer to the fact that no explosions are known to have been experienced in the neighboring Van Houten and Koehler Mines, said to be operating in the same seam and under essentially similar conditions."

Like Risdon, Harrington called attention to the frozen pipes and the absence of sprinkling in the days leading up to the explosion. But he took this one step farther based on his own examination of the interior of the mine during his stay in Dawson. In short, he found the sprinkling system insufficient. He wrote: "An inspection of some room necks of abandoned places, as well as a few trips into entries on which no hauling was being done, indicate that seldom, if ever, is sprinkling done in such places and much fine dust was seen on the floor as well as on timbers and ribs. It would appear that sprinkling when done is confined chiefly to interior haulage entries and to working rooms, entries and pillars."

Harrington conceded that he had seen "comparatively little" of the mine—and then, under less than ideal conditions—yet it was enough for him to conclude that sprinkling was being done only "spasmodically rather than continuously and systematically."

Not surprisingly, then, four of Harrington's recommendations mentioned sprinkling in some form, including designating two men to do "nothing but sprinkle" unless ordered to do otherwise by the company. These men also should file regular written reports not only with the mine foreman, but with higher-ups such as the safety engineer and general manager.

✦

Two weeks later, several New Mexico lawmakers, aghast at the state mine inspector's findings, called for a state investigation to determine if any laws had been broken. "A sweeping investigation of the Dawson disaster, which cost the lives of 120 men in the Phelps Dodge Corporation's No. 1 mine, February 8, will be proposed in the house this afternoon, according to announcement made by Democratic Leader [Coe] Howard and Rep. Edgar F. Puryear," the *Santa Fe New Mexican* reported on February 24.

Lawmakers introduced a joint resolution calling for the establishment of an investigative committee consisting of four members, two each from the state House of Representatives and the state Senate. Further, they asked the governor and attorney general to appoint a special counsel to work with the committee and, more troubling for the company, to "take steps to prosecute in case any violations of the law are brought to light."

Phelps Dodge wasted little time trying to sidetrack this inquiry, releasing a statement the next day putting its actions in the best possible light. In the run-up to the explosion, the company said, it was adhering to its own safety rules by using the motor cars to haul out the fine coal particles and dust created by the use of electric coal-cutting machines deep inside the mine. It was that dust that was primarily responsible for the explosion after the cars ran off the track. The company acknowledged that the sprinklers had not been working inside the mine that day but blamed that solely on the system freezing the previous Sunday during "a severe cold snap" that had left it "not . . . fully thawed out." The company also used the opportunity to cite its rapid response to the humanitarian needs of the affected families: it had issued compensation checks four days after the explosion even though it had up to four weeks to do so under state law. What was more, rather than basing payments on the average wages of the deceased, "the company in every case had paid the maximum compensation provided by the law."

Did the statement help? Well, it certainly didn't hurt. Hours before the legislature was scheduled to take up House Bill 289, there were signs of trouble.

"Company Makes Explanation of Mine Explosion / Sentiment at Santa Fe is Changing Against the Investigation Proposed by the Legislature," read a front-page headline in that day's *Albuquerque Morning Journal*. The story attributed the reported change in attitude to the realization that federal and state officials had already investigated the explosion and that Phelps Dodge "took immediate charge of all dependents and continues ministering to them."

Meanwhile, the *Santa Fe New Mexican* reported that while passage of the bill was "virtually certain" that night in the House, the same couldn't be said for the Senate. Several senators said they would support the bill only if convinced something good would come out of it. Others called the $5,000 appropriation attached to the bill insufficient, given that the probe was also expected to examine safety conditions at coal mines statewide.

The House passed the bill, 19–16, but it failed to achieve the two-thirds vote required by an attached "emergency clause." Two later attempts fell short, the second one by a single vote. When the legislature adjourned for the year on March 9, the push for an investigation into the 1923 Dawson mine disaster died with it.

✦

The legislature's failure to establish an investigative committee ended any chance of answering some key lingering questions: Why did the coal cars run off the track that day? If coroner's jury witness Edmond Thomas was to believed, the motor driver had made the trip countless times without incident, so what was different on February 8? Who was the "some one" who closed the pipe valve five days before the explosion? Assuming that it wasn't a wildcat act, who ordered that it be done? Was it General Manager Brennan? Mine Superintendent Dupont? Someone else?

Neither Brennan nor Dupont was asked that question during the coroner's inquest, but it's difficult to believe that Dupont, as the underground superintendent, would not have been aware of the danger posed by the frozen water lines in a dusty mine. He was no novice, having worked his way up over two decades in the Dawson mines from driver to superintendent. And as a witness to the devastating mine explosion a decade earlier, he would have known as well as anyone the risk posed by coal dust. Yet, whether acting on his own or under orders from his boss, he kept the mine running for days without a functioning sprinkler system to wet down the dust, which ignited and caused the deaths of 120 miners. Either way, he became a popular target of blame within the community for what transpired on that day.

Dupont remained as superintendent for another twenty-two years. While it is impossible to know how the explosion affected his disposition, letters from disgruntled miners to Phelps Dodge headquarters suggest that it changed for the worse. On September 30, 1926, Richard Stanley mailed a handwritten letter to the company president to complain about Dupont's "unhumane" treatment of miners, claiming he was abusing them without cause. On that very day, Stanley wrote, Dupont had told him that if he didn't like it, he should "take my tools out."

He noted that he was not alone in his complaints. "I want to work for this Comp but under Scott manage is impossible," he wrote in rudimentary English. "So I am truesting [sic] you to take some action up on it."

Perhaps to his surprise, Stanley received a letter from Phelps Dodge President Walter Douglas less than two weeks later. Douglas acknowledged receipt of his letter "criticizing the Superintendent's treatment of men underground" before coming to Dupont's defense, writing that he had known "Mr. Dupon [sic] for some years and he has never struck me as one who is unsympathetic and rough." Still, Douglas said he would look into the complaint on his next trip out West.

Several years later, a typewritten letter signed by "All miners in Dawson Camp" made similar complaints, accusing Dupont of laying off miners in retaliation for taking a day off due to sickness and being "so grouchy that if a miner goes to him to explain something he just flies at them like a bull-dog."

"All the miners have become so disgusted with him that if they could lay hands on him they sure would finish him up," they wrote. "This has been going on for years but just now lately he has become so fierce that if they don't change Supers and put some one else in his place something severe will happen to him, because all the miners are too disgusted and they want a new Superintendent."

In this instance, Phelps Dodge Vice President Cleveland E. Dodge forwarded the letter along with a dismissive note to General Manager Beckett. "Enclosed is a letter from Dawson, which is evidently written by a man with a grievance," he wrote. "We are not worried about it, but I am sending it on to you in case you wish to forward it to Mr. Brennan."

Whether or not the complaints were warranted, Phelps Dodge never acted on them, assuring Dupont of a long run as superintendent in Dawson. All told, the Oklahoma native served twenty-five years in that post before leaving in 1945. Seven years later, at the age of 75, he died in Tucumcari, for many years the end of the line for the Dawson Railway.

Figure 1. (*above*) John Barkley Dawson, shown here with third wife Lavinia, acquired the land
that would later become his namesake town to operate a ranch, not to mine the millions
of tons of coal that sat under his property. (Dawson Family Papers, Special Collections &
Archives, University of California–San Diego)

Figure 2. (*below*) Dawson native Fred Becchetti created this illustration from an aerial photograph depicting the town as it appeared in the early 1900s. (Courtesy of Fred Becchetti)

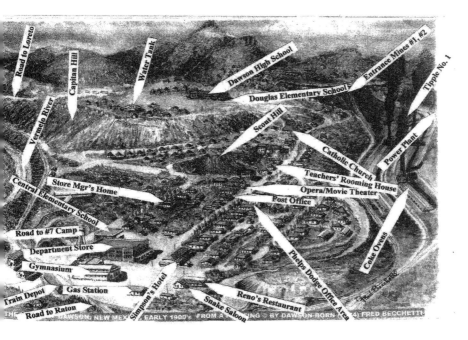

Figure 3. (*above*) A loaded coal train leaves one of the Dawson mines circa 1925. (Courtesy of Florence Swopes in memory of George Wallace Gulley, New Mexico Bureau of Geology and Mineral Resources, Historic Photograph Archives, Socorro, NM 87801)

Figure 4. (*below*) Miners load coal into a shuttle car with the help of a Joy loader in this undated photo. The white material on the wall is rock dust, which was applied as a safety measure in Dawson after the 1913 mine disaster. (Courtesy of Phelps Dodge Corporation, New Mexico Bureau of Geology and Mineral Resources, Historic Photograph Archives, Socorro, NM 87801)

Figure 5. (*above*) A bird's eye view of Dawson one late afternoon circa 1920. (Courtesy of Collier Collection, New Mexico State Records Center, New Mexico Bureau of Geology and Mineral Resources, Historic Photograph Archives, Socorro, NM 87801)

Figure 6. (*below*) Coal cars were used as mobile scoreboards to keep underground workers up to date on Game 7 of the 1924 World Series. The Washington Senators, leading 1–0 after five innings, went on to defeat the New York Giants 4–3, in 12 innings. Hall of Famer Walter Johnson was the winning pitcher. (New Mexico State University Library, Archives and Special Collections)

Figure 7. Frank Santi, shown here with his 1922 Ford Model T, lost three brothers and five cousins in the 1913 Dawson mine disaster. He returned to Italy after the explosion, served in World War I, then returned to the United States in 1919. (Courtesy of Walter Santi)

Figure 8. Brothers Constantine and Georgios Makris were among the six Greeks from the island of Karpathos to lose their lives in the 1913 mine explosion. (Courtesy of Fannie Vozos)

Figure 9. Georgios Makris wrote this letter to his wife, Stamatina, four days after arriving in Dawson on March 7, 1913. Seven months later, both he and his brother Constantine would be dead, victims of that year's mine explosion. (Courtesy of Tina Leslie)

Figure 10. Lloyd Peter Upton, a New Hampshire native, graduated from Brown University in 1906 with plans to return in the fall as a postgraduate medical student. Instead, he moved to New Mexico, built a ranch, married—and took a job in the Dawson mines weeks before the 1913 explosion. (Courtesy of Brown University Archives, *Liber Brunensis*, 1906)

Figure 11. (*above*) This cenotaph, located in the village of La Piana in the province of Modena, memorializes eleven Italian miners who were killed in the 1913 mine disaster. Frank Santi, who lost eight relatives in the explosion, was instrumental in securing a financial contribution from the Dawson mine operators to help pay for its construction. (Courtesy of Manlio Badiali)

Figure 12. (*below*) This commemorative plaque contains the names of the 17 Italian miners from the village of Fiumalbo who lost their lives in the 1913 mine explosion. Eight carried the last name of Santi. (Courtesy of Manlio Badiali)

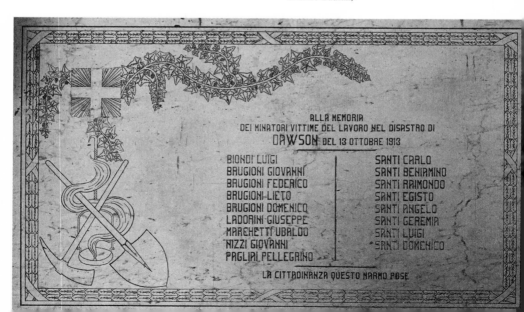

ALLA MEMORIA
DEI MINATORI VITTIME DEL LAVORO NEL DISASTRO DI
DAWSON DEL 13 OTTOBRE 1913

BIONDI LUIGI
BRUGIONI GIOVANNI
BRUGIONI FEDERICO
BRUGIONI LIETO
BRUGIONI DOMENICO
LADORINI GIUSEPPE
MARCHETTI UBALDO
NIZZI GIOVANNI
PAGLIAI PELLEGRINO

SANTI CARLO
SANTI BENIAMINO
SANTI ARIMONDO
SANTI EGISTO
SANTI ANGELO
SANTI GEREMIA
SANTI LUIGI
SANTI DOMENICO

LA CITTADINANZA QUESTO MARMO POSE

Figure 13. (*above*) The Dawson mine disaster of 1923 resulted in the deaths of 120 miners. The explosion was triggered when an outgoing motor car derailed, stirring up coal dust that was ignited by an electric arc in the downed trolley feed line. (New Mexico State University Library, Archives and Special Collections)

Figure 14. (*right*) The reinforced-concrete entryway to Mine No. 1 sustained heavy damage from the 1923 explosion. The force of the blast sent a chunk of concrete through the wall of a wooden motor house two hundred feet away. (New Mexico State University Library, Archives and Special Collections)

Survivor of Mine Disaster

George Kandal, one of the two survivors of the Dawson (N. M.) mine explosion where 122 miners were entombed, is shown here greeting his wife and two sons after his rescue. Kandal was entombed for 16 hours. This photo was taken a few minutes after he reached the open air.

Figure 15. Charles Skandale was photographed with his wife, Elizabeth, and sons George and Nick after walking out of the mine sixteen hours after the 1923 mine explosion. He and Filomeno diMartino were the only survivors. This uncredited photograph, which refers to Skandale as "George Kandal," appeared in newspapers across the country.

Figure 16. Amalia Trujillo, a nurse at Dawson
Hospital, walks along the railroad tracks in this
circa 1918 photo. Her husband, Alfredo, was
killed in the 1923 mine explosion. (Courtesy of
the Trujillo family)

Figure 17. Dawson Cemetery, "rediscovered"
in 1990 by two brothers out for a day of metal
detecting, was accepted onto the National Register of
Historic Places on April 9, 1992. (Photo by Roberto
Rosales)

Figure 18. Dolores Huerta, a celebrated American labor leader, was born in Dawson in 1930. She took some time during the 2022 reunion to visit the grave of her uncle, Marcial Chavez, who was killed in the 1913 mine disaster. (Photo by Roberto Rosales)

Figure 19. Joe Bacca points to the survey map at the entrance to Dawson Cemetery. This longtime chairman of the Dawson New Mexico Association and his family have played a key role in organizing the biennial reunions and maintaining the historic cemetery. (Photo by Nick Pappas)

Figure 20. Edward Zavala replaces artificial flowers at the grave of his father at Dawson Cemetery in 2019. Jesus V. Zavala is believed to have been the last miner buried at the cemetery before the town closed in 1950. (Photo by Nick Pappas)

Figure 21. Pam Thompson and her husband, Dick, traveled from their Illinois home to visit the grave of her great-uncle, Chester N. C. Davis, at Dawson Cemetery in 2021. Davis was among the 263 men killed in the 1913 mine disaster. (Photo by Nick Pappas)

Figure 22. Pietro "Pete" Scarafiotti displays some of the Dawson mementos he has collected over the years during the author's visit to his Arizona home in 2022. He is the founder and administrator of the Dawson Facebook page. Pete's great-grandfather and great-uncle were among the first Dawson miners to enter Mine No. 1 as part of a rescue team after the 1923 mine disaster. (Photo by Nick Pappas)

Figure 23. (*above*) Vivien Pick has devoted years to researching Dawson Cemetery, culminating in the creation of a large survey map near the entrance that helps visitors find the gravesites of their loved ones. (Photo by Roberto Rosales)

Figure 24. (*below*) Carlos Tenorio has attended five Dawson reunions with his family, his first as an infant in 2004 and his most recent in 2022. His generation holds the key to the long-term future of the reunions. (Photo by Roberto Rosales)

WRITING ON THE WALL

[S]igns of Dawson's dying were apparent to even the most casual observer. Deserted
buildings were conspicuous in every section of town. The town pool was abandoned,
and the number of organized social activities were drastically reduced after 1945.
—Richard Melzer

✦

Dawson recovered from its second major mine disaster, though annual coal production (997,637 tons) and the average number of employees (1,548) never again reached 1923 levels. Both remained stable until the stock market crash of 1929 ushered in the Great Depression of the 1930s, decimating the coal industry from coast to coast. Over the next three years, US coal production tumbled 40 percent—from 608 million tons in 1929 to 359 million in 1932—and it would take another ten years before the nation's annual production reached even 1929 levels.

The Great Depression's impact on Dawson was just as devastating. In 1928, a year before the crash, an average of 1,004 men produced 842,166 tons of coal from the town's nine mines. By 1932, those numbers had plunged to 293 men, 258,159 tons, and three working mines. In fact, by the end of that year, only Mine No. 6 remained in operation.

Dawson's quality of life suffered, too. "Single workers were the first to be laid off, but not even married men could expect to work more than two or three days a week in these hard times," according to historian Richard Melzer. "Many husbands relied on credit from the company store to get by while others enlarged their yard gardens, shot game in the wilderness, or sought temporary work on nearby farms. Some men wandered as far away as California and Wyoming to find employment during the worst periods of the depression."

The economic downturn didn't spare the next generation of young men, who had become accustomed to securing mining jobs immediately after high-school graduation. Some found temporary work while waiting for an opening, a process that could take up to two years. Others opted for relief work with the Civilian Conservation Corps established by President Franklin D. Roosevelt under the New Deal in 1933. Still others bid farewell to Dawson for good.

✦

To its credit, as had been true a decade earlier after the 1923 explosion, Phelps Dodge moved quickly to introduce new safety measures to guard against yet another catastrophe. Key among them: rock-dusting the main entries and installing rock dust barriers, wetting down coal at the work spaces and on its way out of the mine, and experimenting with storage batteries to power its motor cars and cutting machines to determine whether it was feasible to do away entirely with dangerous wiring inside the mines.

The use of rock dust—pulverized limestone or other inert material—to prevent or mitigate coal dust explosions was a relatively new phenomenon. In 1913, based on research conducted at its Experimental Mine outside of Pittsburgh, the US Bureau of Mines concluded that the application of rock dust was a "positive means of limiting or preventing explosions of coal-dust in mines." In essence, in the event of an explosion, it absorbs the heat that otherwise would ignite the coal particles. Still, the use of rock dust in the nation's bituminous mines did not occur overnight. By 1930, it was being applied to fewer than 10 percent of American mines, making Dawson one of the early pioneers.

State Mine Inspector W. W. Risdon gave his blessing to this work when he returned to Dawson four months after the 1923 disaster. At Mine No. 1, he found the roadways being covered with adobe dust—another form of rock dust—and that dust barriers were under construction in accordance with US Bureau of Mines standards. While he found fault with the company's policy of wetting down the roofs and walls every day—a practice he said had proven "disastrous" and caused "many heavy falls of roof"—Risdon concluded the mine was in "good condition."

Phelps Dodge's renewed commitment to mine safety only intensified the next year, particularly in rock dusting and sprinkling. Before the year was out, President Walter Douglas sent a letter to the US Bureau of Mines office in Washington, asking if Edward H. Denny, district engineer for the bureau's safety division in Denver, could visit Dawson that winter with an eye toward safety improvements.

Denny's report, submitted in February of 1925, heaped praise on the company, offering but five safety recommendations that he acknowledged were "limited and in part a matter of opinion." These addressed fire protection, mining machines, roof falls, the distance between trolley tracks and walls, and the placement of electrical wiring. The report commended the company on its blasting practices, timbering, and "very complete and effective safety organization."

"The writer considers that the Dawson mines, if maintained in the condition obtaining at time of his visit, are safe from danger of general coal dust explosion," the report stated. "Measures taken toward dust explosion prevention are numerous and adequate and effectively carried out."

The 1923 mine disaster would be Dawson's last.

✦

This is not to say that Dawson stopped making news altogether. Four years after the explosion, the mining town was rocked by scandal. On December 12, 1927, Angelo Frazzini, the Dawson postmaster, was shot and killed in his home during a scuffle with his young wife. The accused? Pearl Dupont, the daughter of the underground mine superintendent.

This was a tragic end to what had begun two years earlier as a storybook romance. In October of 1925, Frazzini, then a twenty-two-year-old postal clerk, and Dupont, a sixteen-year-old student at Dawson High School, ran off to Raton to get married, apparently without the blessing of the girl's father. After several weeks on a honeymoon trip that took them to Denver, Kansas City, and Chicago, the newlyweds returned to Dawson. Frazzini was named the town's postmaster two years later.

On the night of the shooting, according to news reports, Frazzini and his wife were wrestling over a handgun when it discharged. A single bullet tore through Pearl's right hand before lodging in her husband's abdomen. He was rushed to Dawson Hospital, where he died thirty minutes later, never regaining consciousness. As for his wife, she was said to be "suffering severely from the shock and the gunshot wound in her hand."

A coroner's jury, impaneled the next morning by Justice of the Peace T. M. Utley, confirmed the cause of death as a gunshot wound from a Colt .45 fired during a scuffle but found that the "discharge . . . was accidental." Afterward, Assistant District Attorney Fred Voorhees told jurors that he didn't believe there was enough evidence to bring the case before a grand jury, but that he would refer it to the district attorney for his consideration. A grand jury indicted Pearl for the murder of her husband a few days later.

Justice of the Peace Ray C. Haner convened a preliminary hearing in Raton to consider the murder charge against Pearl Frazzini on February 28, 1928. Pearl took the stand in her own defense, testifying that the gun that fired the fatal bullet was in her husband's hand when it discharged. That key point was underscored by her attorney, Archie H. Darden, a member of a prominent Raton law firm that listed the Phelps Dodge Corporation among its clients. Voorhees, acting as the prosecutor, conceded that the evidence didn't support the murder charge but might be sufficient to warrant a verdict of involuntary manslaughter. Haner felt otherwise. Ruling that the evidence showed "no crime had been committed," the justice of the peace dismissed the charge.

Besides newspaper accounts, not much is known about the circumstances that led to the shooting that December night. Some insight is contained in two letters written by Stag Cañon General Manager W. D. Brennan to Phelps Dodge General Manager P. G. Beckett later that month. In the first, written on the day the coroner's jury issued its verdict of an accidental shooting, Brennan explained that the couple had married two years earlier despite the objections of Pearl's father, who wanted her to finish high school first. "From all general appearances they were a very happily married couple and seemed to be very congenial," he wrote. "From information I have been able to derive, I think that she got the revolver in a moment of temper and threatened to use it on herself," prompting the struggle that culminated in her husband's death. "He was never conscious and made no statements. She is still in quite a hysterical condition."

In the second letter, penned eight days later, Brennan expressed surprise that the prosecuting attorney had sworn out a warrant for the girl's arrest to be served later that day: "This was rather of a surprise to me as I thought the matter would die down. There is some little feeling among the boy's parents, who are Italian, against the girl, but to date have done nothing to reflect back on Scott [Dupont, Pearl's father]. He has kept himself pretty well in the back ground."

Given Dupont's position, of course, there was rampant suspicion in town that he had used his considerable influence to tip the scales of justice in favor of his daughter. That certainly was the sentiment of Angelo's family, who later accused him of taking steps to run them out of town. Angelo's stepfather, a miner, was demoted to the "most horrific job," according to the family; he refused the position and, as a result, was let go. In time, the family packed up and moved to Cañon City, Colorado. Before doing so, on the one-year anniversary of Angelo's death, the family placed an "in memoriam" notice in the town newspaper:

In memory of our dear beloved son and brother, Angelo Frazzini, who passed away a year ago today, the 12th of December, 1927.
A smiling face from us is gone,
A voice we loved is still,
A vacant chair within our home,
Which never can be filled.

Even before the Great Depression undercut Dawson's coal production by nearly half in 1930, Phelps Dodge and the nation's coal operators were facing a new obstacle: the growing popularity of oil and natural gas as cheaper sources of fuel. The company acknowledged this transition as early as 1925, when it cited the impact of oil on its declining coal production over a three-year period. By the following November, recognizing that the smelters of the Southwest had "practically discontinued the use of coke for smelting ores" in favor of oil-burning furnaces, Phelps Dodge shut down its 446 beehive ovens used to make coke, once a significant part of its business. In 1927, the company conceded that fuel oil, at current prices, was a "strong competitor of coal in our territory and it seems likely that natural gas may also affect our sales adversely."

Phelps Dodge did not sit idly by in the face of this nationwide transition. In a concerted bid to cut costs, the company introduced five mechanical loading machines in 1928, replacing the more labor-intensive hand-loading process. It also kept up its reliance on coal-cutting machines to supplement men wielding pickaxes. By the end of the year, the forty-six machines in operation were responsible for more than one-third of all the coal produced.

Nevertheless, despite its best efforts to compete in this new energy arena, Phelps Dodge began scaling back its coal-mining operation and, with it, the size of its labor force. Production fell to 389,345 tons in 1930, barely a quarter of its peak year of 1.44 million tons in 1916. Likewise, the number of employees, now averaging 474, was down from its all-time high of 1,640 in 1915. By the time 1932 came to a close, only one of the ten mines in operation during the company's heyday—No. 6—was being mined for coal, a job requiring roughly three hundred workers.

Even that mine nearly shut down—along with the entire town—three years later.

✦

Phelps Dodge had little tolerance for labor unions, strikers, or troublemakers. That was true in Dawson in 1913 when it blocked "agitators" from outside camps from helping in the aftermath of the first mine disaster. And it was true in Bisbee, Arizona, in 1917 when Phelps Dodge ordered more than one thousand striking mine workers to be rounded up and shipped by rail in cattle cars 150 miles to Hermanas, New Mexico, in what became known at the Bisbee Deportation.

While criticized for its role in this incident, Phelps Dodge avoided any legal penalties when a US District Court judge dismissed a grand jury indictment on the grounds that no federal laws had been broken. Likewise, a kidnapping charge brought in an Arizona state court ended in acquittal.

This intolerance resurfaced in 1935 after the United Mine Workers of America and the nation's coal operators reached agreement on a new eighteen-month wage contract, ending an eight-day nationwide coal strike. The agreement came on the heels of Congress's approval two months earlier of the National Labor Relations Act, which guaranteed mine workers and others the right to organize, form, or join unions and engage in collective bargaining on behalf of their members.

The new contract called for pay hikes of nine cents a ton for men who dug and loaded coal, fifty cents a day for those compensated at a daily rate, and 10 percent for "deadwork." John L. Lewis, the legendary president of the UMWA, was "jubilant" over the agreement, telling reporters: "We got everything we asked for."

For its part, Phelps Dodge agreed to abide by the terms of the settlement, even though it was not obligated contractually to do so. The company posted a notice that read "effective Oct. 1, the increased miners' scale will be paid." But when the mine whistle sounded that morning, to the company's surprise, no workers were to be found. "The men are not working and I do not know when they will work," Superintendent Gilbert Davis told reporters. "We are ready to operate when the men are willing to work."

Unbeknownst to Davis, that would not be for quite some time. Later that day, the striking miners made it known they would return under two conditions: a recognition of their UMWA Local 6419, which had been chartered in 1933, and a union contract with Phelps Dodge. Up to that point, the company had refused to entertain either. When told of the union's demands, Davis acknowledged that "we have not signed with the union and never have had a contract." He also described the current impasse as a "waiting game."

Phelps Dodge waited until October 10—when the strike had entered its tenth day—before making a move. On that day, it posted formal notice that unless the miners returned by October 14, the company would shut down the mine for good.

This was not the first time the company had threatened to shut down the mine and, by extension, the town of Dawson. Two years earlier, shortly after forming its UMWA local, between two hundred and fifty and three hundred Dawson miners refused without notice to show up for work on October 2, later notifying the company that they would not return without union recognition and a signed contract. Phelps Dodge waited nearly a month before issuing an ultimatum: return to work by November 2 or face closure of the mine. On October 30, after a late-night meeting, the men agreed to return to work on November 1, even though the company had not agreed to recognize the union. Mine officials did sign off on a higher pay scale and to allow miners to select a checkweighman of their own to guard against miners being cheated during the weighing of the coal.

✦

This time, when the striking miners did not return by the October 14, 1935, deadline, Phelps Dodge followed through on its threat. On that day, a Monday, the company began to board up the mine entrance and posted notice that all occupants had to vacate their company-owned houses. "Everything is quiet here and it's going to be more quiet," Davis said in a statement. "We cannot let a little coal mine dictate to the policies of a large corporation like Phelps-Dodge."

The company's threat also caught the attention of Frank Hefferly, president of the UMWA's Denver-based District 15. On October 15, he sent a telegram to Lewis, the union's national president, alerting him to the company's decision to board up the mine and initiate eviction proceedings, "giving men and families three days [sic] notice to vacate company houses. Have taken this matter up with Governor [Clyde] Tingley of New Mexico. It would be helpful if your office could contact office Phelps Dodge Corporation New York protesting eviction procedure and urging settlement."

State Labor Commissioner Charles Davis met with Gilbert Davis, the mine superintendent, in Dawson the next day to hammer out a settlement between the two parties. Three UMWA representatives also attended: Ed Munden, representing the Denver district office; Robert Montgomery, head of the Dawson-Raton UMWA; and Sylvester Lorenzo, president of the Dawson local. After the meeting, Munden said the miners had authorized Lewis to act on their behalf and that he, Munden, would negotiate with Phelps Dodge officials toward a settlement. Davis, the state labor commissioner, emerged from the meeting hopeful, reporting that "a little headway" was made and that he would update the governor and the state's two US senators on the status of the talks. Davis, the mine superintendent, was less enthused, saying only: "There is no change in the picture."

If Phelps Dodge officials were willing to give negotiations time to work, they had a funny way of showing it. On October 19, three days after this meeting, Dawson's Davis posted a notice urging the striking miners to act. "You are advised that the position of the Phelps-Dodge corporation remains unchanged, and there is no room for a discussion or conference between the two sides of the subject of a contract. It is for the employes [*sic*] of Dawson to decide whether they desire to work at Dawson and a decision must be made quickly."

That decision came four days later, following a meeting in Dawson between Charles Davis and UMWA representatives. Following that session, District 15 President Hefferly announced: "After a complete investigation of the Dawson situation and a conference with Davis and then with the men, I recommended that the men resume work and report to their individual and respective positions without discrimination." In return, Phelps Dodge agreed to refer the dispute to the Bituminous Coal Labor Board, a federal dispute-resolution panel that had been created with the passage of the Bituminous Coal Conservation Act of 1935. The Dawson miners returned to work the next day, ending their three-week strike.

✦

The next fifteen years would be no less contentious, some of the difficulty brought on by World War II. On May 1, 1943, President Franklin D. Roosevelt ordered the federal government to seize the nation's coal mines after the UMWA refused to back down on its call for a nationwide coal strike effective that day. The Dawson mines remained under government control—with the exception of two weeks in October—until June 26, 1944. Coal production jumped 25 percent during the war years to nearly 375,000 tons, with a short-lived bump in the labor force to 377. By the time the war ended in 1945, the number of workers had fallen back to around 300.

For Dawson, 1943 was memorable for something besides the federal government's takeover. On November 3, two days after Dawson miners joined with five hundred thousand others in another UMWA-led nationwide strike, the men returned after Phelps Dodge agreed to recognize the union. In early 1945, a dozen years after the union's first call for such recognition fell on deaf ears, Dawson Local 6419 entered into its first contract with the company.

On May 8, 1945, Hefferly wrote to Lewis, notifying him of the agreement while trumpeting the union's leadership to bring it about:

> Enclosed you will find copy of the National Bituminous Coal Wage Agreement, which has been executed by and between the Phelps Dodge Corporation, Stag Canon Branch, Dawson, New Mexico, covering approximately 350 men employed in and around the coal mine operated by the said company. I think it will do no harm to repeat that after a period of

more than eleven years, since we organized a local union in Dawson, New Mexico, and a continuous struggle with this company, we were finally able to wield sufficient influence to cause the corporation to execute the standard union shop wage agreement.

✦

The labor peace that followed Phelps Dodge's recognition of the UMWA local was short-lived. On April 1, 1946, Dawson miners walked off the job in support of a nationwide strike by four hundred thousand mine workers, which prompted another government seizure of the mines. When the strike ended fifty-nine days later, the union had secured an hourly wage hike of 18½ cents, the establishment of an industry-financed welfare and retirement fund, and a medical and hospital fund paid for by deductions already made from the miners' pay. Six months later, the Dawson miners went out on strike for another seventeen days, again as part of a nationwide coal strike called by Lewis.

The two shutdowns, while no doubt an annoyance to Phelps Dodge, had little impact on coal production, which only declined 6 percent that year. The company credited the introduction of new mechanical equipment for boosting its coal output rate per shift. Production rebounded nearly 13 percent the following year to just shy of four hundred thousand tons, the most since the pre-Depression year of 1929.

Dawson miners joined another nationwide coal strike on March 15, 1948, this one driven by the UMWA's call for pensions. It lasted four weeks and ended with a compromise agreement between the union and the nation's coal operators to provide pensions of $100 a month for miners sixty-two years of age or older with twenty years of service if they retired after May 28, 1946. The strike ended four weeks later and was marked by a one-day moratorium in Dawson so miners could load about five hundred tons of coal for delivery to the state hospital in Las Vegas to keep "inmates of the hospital warm."

For the year, coal production fell nearly 10 percent, to 357,114 tons, but that wasn't the only ominous news for Phelps Dodge. The company had embarked on a drilling program that year to seek out fresh coal reserves but found the results to be disappointing.

"Indications are," the company wrote in its 1948 annual report, "that operations will be short-lived at this branch. Branch earnings have been insignificant for many years."

CHAPTER 16

CLOSING TIME

They have a Marshall plan for Europe. They are putting a coal mine in France back into operation. New processes and all that. But nothing for Dawson.
—F. W. Koelling
Dawson mine superintendent
May 21, 1950

✦

Phelps Dodge's downbeat assessment of its future in Dawson turned bleaker in 1949, thanks in part to persistent labor demands by the United Mine Workers of America and its charismatic president. John L. Lewis initiated a series of strikes—some nationwide, some regional—along with periodic calls for shorter workweeks. Dawson miners supported a half-dozen full and partial strikes that year, including a nationwide walkout by four hundred thousand workers in September over the suspension of benefit payments to their pension and welfare fund. On November 10, with the strike approaching the eight-week mark, Lewis called a three-week truce. When that deadline arrived, however, Lewis instead instructed members to cut back to a three-day workweek.

The new arrangement, which pleased neither owners nor workers, was short-lived. Within two months, about one hundred thousand UMWA members were back on strike. Participation more than tripled before the union and the industry reached its March 6, 1950, agreement on a new twenty-eight-month contract that was hailed by both sides. For the nation's mine operators, the agreement gave the industry its "first real opportunity for stability in the last decade." For Lewis, his UMWA had "again accomplished the impossible," put additional "bread and butter" on the table of miners' families, and allowed the industry to focus on "producing coal in quantity for the benefit of the American economy at the lowest cost permitted by modern techniques."

He made no mention of the Phelps Dodge letter he had received a week earlier.

✦

Gerald O. Arnold was the author of that letter. As Dawson's general manager, he had signed the first contract with the UMWA local in 1945. He had presided over the laying off of ninety miners in 1948. And on February 25, 1950, a Saturday, he had the job of posting the official notice that Phelps Dodge would shut down its last mine by April 30. The notice was a copy of the letter he sent to Lewis.

> Dear Sir:
>
> We herewith give you notice of our plan to close down the Dawson mine on or before April 30, 1950. Effective April 30, 1950, we hereby cancel all obligations and agreements, either expressed or implied, which may be a part of any wage agreement with your union; this applies especially to the wage agreement made effective July 1, 1948, and presumably extended to cover present operations, and to any subsequent wage agreement which may become effective between now and April 30, 1950.
>
> It is the intent to operate the Dawson mine until April 30, 1950, provided the action of your union makes such operation possible and economically advisable.
>
> Yours very truly
> G.O. Arnold,
> Manager

The announcement received tepid treatment in the next day's newspapers. The *Santa Fe New Mexican* and *Albuquerque Journal* published short dispatches from the Associated Press, both relegated to one-column placement under small headlines. While the *New Mexican* played the story at the bottom of its front page ("Phelps Dodge to Shut Mine at Dawson"), the *Journal* story was buried on page four ("Raton Coal Mine Closes April 30; 300 Workers Hit."). Neither article offered much insight in their half-dozen paragraphs. In fact, other than a *Journal* editorial two days later addressing rumors that the Southern Pacific might now abandon its Dawson–Tucumcari rail line, daily newspaper coverage was silent until the weeks leading up to the mine's April 30 closing.

✦

While the shutdown may not have come as a shock to everyone—Phelps Dodge had signaled its intent to "shut the Dawson property down permanently at some time in 1950" in its 1949 annual report to stockholders—the news dealt a devastating blow to the miners and the community at large. It also foreshadowed worse news to come, given that there wasn't much future in a company-owned mining town with no working mines. Sure enough, the other shoe dropped a month later with the posting of a new notice in the window of the company store on March 31: Dawsonites had ninety days to get out of town.

To All Residents of Dawson:

As disclosed by other information posted recently, we wish to verify the fact that the Dawson Mine will cease operation Friday night, April 28, 1950.

Except for Power House employees, and such few other persons as may be specifically excepted, because of Corporation or related duties, all residents of Dawson will be expected to vacate their premises on or before June 30, 1950.

Persons desiring to continue residence in Dawson through May, and possibly all or part of June, will please make arrangements to cover their rental and service charges with Mr. J.T. Shelton, Town Supervisor; unless arrangements are made to take care of these charges, electric and water service will be discontinued after May 15, and eviction notices will be served immediately.

House coal will be sold only on such days as the mine may work between now and April 30, 1950. No coal will be sold during May and June.

Medical service will be discontinued after Saturday, April 29, 1950.

G.O. Arnold, Manager

✦

The timing couldn't have been worse. For miners and their families, money set aside as rainy-day funds had already dried up over the previous nine months while the men were on strike or working three-day weeks in solidarity with the national union.

Meanwhile, jobs at other coal camps in the region—at least those still in business—were in short supply. In Colfax County alone, Gardiner (1939), Sugarite (1941), and Brilliant (1949) had shut down in the previous decade. Housing was also scarce, though Raton officials made it known they would try to accommodate former Dawson residents. To make matters worse, money the company had contributed over the years into the union's welfare fund could be used only for pensions or hospitalizations. In order to qualify for pension money, according to the bylaws, an applicant had to be at least sixty years of age *and* have worked in a mine during the previous year. For miners under age sixty, there was no special relief money other than a few weeks of unemployment benefits available from the state.

"It will be hardest on the old fellows," said Nick Gonzalez, secretary of Dawson's UMWA local, "too old to get another mine job and not old enough to qualify for a miner's pension."

Karl F. Guthmann, editor of the nearby *Roy Record*, observed that sentiment firsthand when he visited the town in early May. "Sad is the plight of many of the miners and others who have been residents of the camp for as long as 40 years," wrote Guthmann, a former railroad worker who once lived in Dawson. "One of the old timers told with tearful eye of the large number who are without funds even to move their household effects to another town. Most of the number are inexperienced at means of livelihood other than the jobs found about the mines and many are too old to make application for other employment."

Faced with these obstacles, some Dawsonites embarked on a longshot plan to satisfy both their short-term housing and long-term employment needs. Two weeks after Phelps Dodge announced the town would close, they filed petitions with US Senators Clinton P. Anderson and Dennis Chávez of New Mexico, seeking permission to remain in their Dawson homes for a few more years until construction began on a Vermejo River irrigation project. With a new dam to be built a few miles outside of Dawson, they reasoned, jobs would become available for the displaced workers. President Harry S. Truman had vetoed the project the previous year, but there was a move afoot to revise it more to his liking.

US Representative Antonio M. Fernández, who had grown up in nearby Springer, joined with Rep. John E. Miles to introduce a scaled-down version of the Vermejo irrigation project bill in the House, similar to the one initiated in the Senate. In making the case for the legislation on May 1, 1950, on the House floor, Fernández argued that it was important to move quickly to provide employment to those men left jobless by the closing of the Dawson mine. He told his colleagues: "These miners and their families who have depended on coal production at this mine for half a century will find themselves in a serious predicament. This project will have to be reconstructed sooner or later and prompt action on the part of the Congress at this time will relieve the hardships attended upon the losing of their jobs by these miners."

Truman signed off on the legislation in September. Two years later, the US Bureau of Reclamation and the Vermejo Conservancy District approved a $2.92 million contract to begin construction. On April 7, 1953, the project got underway with a ceremonial ground-breaking attended by 1,200 people.

All played out as Dawson residents had envisioned three years earlier—albeit more slowly—when they put forward the plan to remain in their Dawson homes until these new jobs became available.

Phelps Dodge had a different idea. Six days after closing the town, the company sold all its above-ground possessions to an Arizona salvage firm for $500,000.

✦

Miner Fred Bergamo had the honor of dumping the last carload of coal at the tipple on April 28 at 3:00 p.m. Bergamo, a Dawson native who had celebrated his thirty-seventh birthday days earlier, was the tipple foreman. To mark the historic occasion, fifteen men gathered around the empty coal car—"Last Car Coal Dumped, Dawson, April-28-50" handwritten in white on the front—for a ceremonial photograph. Afterward, the men joined their colleagues for a round of food and drink paid for, appropriately enough, with the remains of the tipple crew's funeral wreath fund.

Later that night, residents packed the opera house for a musical perfor-mance by one of their own, Augustine Hernandez, a guitar-playing coal miner who had come with his parents to Dawson from Mexico as a young boy. On this night, Hernandez did more than entertain with his usual favorites. He performed "¡Adiós a Dawson!," a special song he had composed after learning that the town would soon be no more. (See front of book for lyrics in English and Spanish.)

"It was the last concert that they had there at the opera house," said Roberta Hernandez Perez, his daughter. "And from what I understand from my sister and my mom, there wasn't a dry eye in the house."

Two weeks later, Dawson High School hosted its thirty-first and final grad-uation ceremony for twenty seniors. While handing out diplomas, the school board president referred to the graduates as members of the "last but not least class." Fred Cericola, in his valedictory address, acknowledged that in any other year many of his fellow male graduates would be preparing to work in the mines. "Now we have an opportunity to do something else," said Cericola, whose father, Jay, had earned the unwanted distinction nine months earlier as the last man to die in the Dawson mines when he was buried under a pile of fallen rock.

By this point, seven weeks before the Phelps Dodge–imposed June 30 dead-line, signs of the town's demise were impossible to miss: Empty coal cars outside the mine portal. Mining machines above ground. Boarded-up buildings. Cars and trailers crammed with personal possessions. A poorly stocked company store.

✦

Samuel Shapiro headed to Dawson on June 6, the same day his National Iron and Metal Company had agreed to purchase all of Phelps Dodge's above-ground holdings. That Phelps Dodge had turned to the Phoenix-based salvage firm was no accident. Shapiro had already done similar work for the company, dismantling industrial plants in its Arizona copper-mining towns of Clarkdale, Clifton, Douglas, and Morenci.

But those jobs paled in comparison to his new assignment: clearing out an entire community that once was home to about six thousand people. There were four hundred houses, three schools, two churches, a three-story company store, a gymnasium, a hospital and dispensary, a hotel, an opera house, a post office, the town train depot, and more. National Iron and Metal now owned not only the buildings but the furnishings inside, from pencil sharpeners and desks to bowling balls and pool tables. And then there was all the mining equipment Phelps Dodge had accumulated and relied upon during its forty-five years of operation in Dawson. It was said, somewhat in jest, that the only things the company didn't sell to Shapiro were the hospital's medications, which were destined for "a qualified buyer under government permits."

Shapiro was no small-town operator. A year earlier, working with two other firms, he had spent five months in Tokyo securing five thousand tons of brass and one thousand tons of lead for shipment to Houston. The company then turned around and sold the metals to customers in Asia and Western Europe and around the United States. Apparently, he had similar expectations for Dawson. "In his mind's eye," an Arizona reporter wrote at that time, "Shapiro envisions some of the scrap he will have salvaged in the year-long job of demolishing Dawson as a skyscraper in Gotham, pagodas in the Orient, or even in the battery of your next year's automobile."

Shapiro didn't waste much time. Within days of closing the deal, he sold the estimated four hundred houses to Dugan Guest of Albuquerque. In turn, Guest made the homes available to potential buyers to either knock down for the building materials or to move to other locations.

A prime beneficiary of this new cottage industry was Homer Bennett, who ran a house-moving business based some 250 miles south in Clovis near the New Mexico–Texas line. By mid-July, Bennett, his six employees, and their families had set up camp in Dawson with six trucks. Dawson homes were soon on their way to Clayton, Des Moines, Raton, and other New Mexico communities, as well as to neighboring states. The Dawson contract did wonders for Bennett's business. ("Clovis Man Moves Ghost Mining Town" read one headline in a Texas newspaper.) He became so busy that he found it necessary to take out an advertisement in the *Clovis News-Journal* to dispel rumors that the home office in Clovis was closed. Before he was finished, he had purchased five brand-new trucks that would come in handy for his next big job—moving two hundred homes from the old mining town of Lowell, Arizona, to nearby communities to make way for what was heralded at the time as "one of the largest open pit copper mines in the world."

The developer? Phelps Dodge.

+

The doleful dismantling of this once-grand mining town took a little over a year. By the fall of 1951, pieces of Dawson were scattered around the country like autumn leaves on a blustery day. The coal washer was taken apart, moved, and put back together in the coalfields of West Virginia. The Dawson Hotel, which had once provided a comfortable place to stay and "quality food at reasonable prices" to visitors from around the country, was knocked to the ground, its wood and nails used to build a private home in Tulia, Texas. One of Dawson's landmarks, the three-story company store, was taken apart brick by brick by a Trinidad contractor, who planned to use them to build houses in his hometown. The ornate Catholic church was demolished, although its religious items were made available to other churches.

"It's a little sad," said Sidney O'Neil, who had overseen the project for National Iron and Metal since Day 1. "But I guess there was nothing else they could do."

O'Neill spoke those words on October 5, one day before he and the remaining National Iron crew headed home after fifteen months of working out of the old Phelps Dodge office building in Dawson.

"It's all gone," he said. "There's nothing more to sell."

+

Marlene Hancock Kotchou, who was ten years old when the town closed, got to stick around a little longer. Her father, William Hancock, a Dawson native who for years ran the movie projector at the opera house, was one of the few men to keep his job as an employee of the Dawson-based Frontier Power Company, which provided power to Trinidad, Walsenburg, and other communities in southern Colorado and northern New Mexico. They lived in one of the dozen or so homes that Phelps Dodge retained for those working at the power plant and the cattle ranch.

Kotchou's maternal grandparents, Robert and Nellie Wilson, both emigrated from Scotland and arrived in Dawson separately between 1910 and 1912. Robert worked at the mines with his brother, John, who was killed in the 1923 explosion. Robert and Nellie took in his five children even though they had seven of their own.

While it has been more than seventy years since Kotchou called Dawson home, not all of her childhood memories have faded with the passage of time, especially the town's reaction to news of the end of World War II. "I remember sitting on the porch outside, and everybody was outside when the war ended," she said. "Firecrackers were going off, and people were yelling and screaming in the streets, and there was just one big celebration."

The Hancocks lived across the street from the elementary school, where Kotchou remembers one of the big treats for sixth-graders was ringing the outside bell. "When you were in sixth grade you got to go upstairs in the school and you got to hang out the window and ring the bell," she said. Kotchou never got the chance. She was in fourth grade when the town shut down.

Kotchou also remembers one of the treats of living in an abandoned town, though she ended up getting in trouble with her good friends David and Fritzi DiLorenzo at the old company store: "We used to go up in the store to the third floor. They used to have a bakery up there, and they had a bread chute down. And we used to get wax paper and slide on that down to the first floor. We got caught. They told my parents."

In October of 1950, the Springer Electric Cooperative of New Mexico received a $1.17 million loan from the US Rural Electrification Administration to purchase Dawson's four-thousand-kilowatt power plant for $390,000. The loan also covered the construction of new distribution lines in four counties. The acquisition became official on December 7, leaving William Hancock without a job.

Kotchou and her family soon moved to Tucumcari, where her father managed two downtown movie theaters and a drive-in. Later, they all relocated to Bisbee, Arizona, where Phelps Dodge hired him for a job in its copper plant.

✦

The editorial writer at the *Albuquerque Journal* wasn't off base when commenting on rumors about the potential impact of the town's closing on the Southern

Pacific's rail service to and from Dawson. On August 29, 1950, the Dawson
Railway Company, owner of the Dawson-to-Tucumcari line, and the Southern
Pacific, which leased the 132 miles of track, asked the federal Interstate
Commerce Commission for permission to discontinue service on the sixty-
three-mile stretch between Dawson and Roy because of the downturn in traffic.
The application drew protests from farmers, ranchers, and town and county
officials along that portion of the line, who argued that it would have a negative
impact on their livelihoods. Of particular concern was abandoning the town of
French, situated eighteen miles from Dawson, where the line connected with the
Atchison, Topeka & Santa Fe Railway and, with it, markets as far east as Chicago
and as far west as San Francisco.

Ultimately, the State Corporation Commission of New Mexico sided with
the opponents and argued on their behalf before the ICC in Washington—with
some success. On March 18, 1952, the commission handed down a partial victory for the Southern Pacific, granting it permission to abandon only the eigh-
teen-mile stretch between Dawson and French, but not the forty-five miles
between French and Roy. In reaching its decision, the commission set aside the
recommendation of its own examiner, who had recommended full approval of
the railroad's request.

The opponents' victory appeared to be short-lived when the ICC granted the
Dawson Railway and Southern Pacific approval to abandon the French-to-Roy
leg on February 14, 1956. But the commission revoked its decision five months
later after organizations such as the American National Cattlemen's Association,
National Wool Growers Association, and New Mexico Cattle Growers Association
argued that the railroads had failed to prove they were losing money on the line.

The Southern Pacific waited another seven years before approaching the
ICC again, this time seeking to abandon not just the forty-five miles from French
to Roy, but the entire 114 miles to the end of the line in Tucumcari. The railroad
argued that it had lost $118,000 in 1959 and another $83,000 in 1960 on this
branch, prompting the ICC to conclude there wasn't enough traffic to justify its
further operation. On August 23, 1961, the commission authorized the request,
effectively bringing to an end the storied history of the old Dawson Railway.

The news came as a shock to New Mexico officials and other interested parties.
The State Corporation Commission, which had fought the two previous attempts,
immediately cried foul, claiming that the state hadn't received proper notice of a
hearing. The dispute came to an end the following spring when a court sided with
the Southern Pacific and set October 31 as the date for the train's final run.

✦

On that day, William G. Boswell boarded the Southern Pacific train in Tucumcari, just as he had countless times before. The sixty-six-year-old engineer had spent more than two-thirds of his life working on the original Dawson-to-Tucumcari run, first for the El Paso & Southwestern Railroad and later for the Southern Pacific after it acquired the EP&SW in 1924. He was there in February of 1917 as a new twenty-one-year-old crew member. He was there as part of the wrecking crew on October 25, 1922, after an out-of-control train derailed two and a half miles west of Cabeza, killing an engineer and a brakeman. And, now, here he was as the engineer of a one-car ceremonial train, leading the passenger car "Polly" on her final journey.

During those years, Boswell witnessed the rise and fall of many communities along the route: Dawson, Colfax, Lloyd, French, Taylor, Abbott, Mills, Roy, Solano, Mosquero, Cabeza, Medio, Campana, Atarque, Canadian, Bascom, and Tucumcari. Fewer than a handful of these towns exist today.

Boswell was accompanied for part of the run by fifty first-graders from the Forrester Elementary School in Springer, ten miles south of French. The students and their teachers were treated to an up-close look at the diesel engine before boarding the Polly on its final run—an image recorded for posterity by an *Albuquerque Journal* photographer.

Joining them on this historic ride was Karl Guthmann, now retired from the editorship of the *Roy Record*, who had visited Dawson in its closing days to report the news for his readers. Half a century had passed since Guthmann had first ridden the train, five years after the Dawson Railway made its debut in 1903. For this trip, he was fortunate to claim the last available ticket in Tucumcari and an opportunity to reminisce.

At one time, he recalled, each of the stations along the route was manned by a telegrapher-agent and a section crew consisting of five or more workers. On this final run, the only working station was in Roy—and that was to close by day's end.

For Boswell, that final ride still held a special place in his heart two decades later. "I was the engineer on the last run back from Dawson," he reminisced to an *Albuquerque Journal* correspondent as a retired eighty-three-year-old in 1979. "And the section gangs were coming behind me disconnecting the signals."

DAWSON CEMETERY

We had expected to find the remnants of a ghost town there. There was nothing, save for the skeleton of a huge set of coke ovens, a metal shed, and, most importantly, a cemetery.

—Dale Christian

✢

Dale Christian wasn't sure what to expect when he and his brother, Lloyd, left Albuquerque one summer day in 1990 for the three-hour trip to Dawson. He knew the old mining town had been closed for decades. He knew its history had been marred by tragedy. And he knew that his older brother, a metal-detecting enthusiast visiting from Minnesota, would be champing at the bit to scour the grounds for some hidden hints of history.

Neither foresaw this.

"We were both shocked at the cemetery. It looked like a miniature Arlington," Dale told New Mexico newspaper columnist Morrow Hall after their visit. "It contained row upon row of white iron crosses. It appeared to be abandoned and uncared for."

That didn't sit well with the Christian brothers, Dale in particular. He contacted the New Mexico Historic Preservation Division, a branch of the state Department of Cultural Affairs, to inquire about the cemetery. The people he spoke to didn't even know it existed, according to Dale, but he did manage to pique their curiosity, so much so that they asked him to revisit the old graveyard and return with specific measurements.

Several weeks later, Dale presented his findings.

"When I gave them the outside boundary measurements, I saw expressions of total amazement," he said. "They said they expected a site with two or three graves. What I provided was a football field. I counted the graves, and provided pictures. There were over 383 graves at the site, apparently abandoned and forgotten, even by the State of New Mexico."

✢

The Christian brothers were close during their boyhood in Minnesota but went their separate ways after high school. Lloyd, the older of the two, spent most of his life within a two-hundred-mile radius of Pipestone, graduating from the local high school in 1960. He entered the US Navy and served four years aboard the *USS Oriskany*, a San Diego–based aircraft carrier named after one of the fiercest battles of the Revolutionary War. Upon his return, he found work at a Pipestone bakery and later as a photo developer for the EROS Data Center in nearby Garretson, South Dakota. The job at the US Geological Survey's science center was a good fit for the happy-go-lucky Lloyd, who was well-liked by his coworkers and known for his colorful tie-dyed T-shirts.

If Lloyd was the carefree jokester, Dale was the humorless genius. Blessed with an IQ north of 150, he bade goodbye to Pipestone to pursue a chemical engineering degree at the University of New Mexico and married Martha Martinez, a Hewlett-Packard Company secretary, in 1969 prior to graduation. Dale's first job was for the Shell Oil Company in Washington state—their only child, Laura, was born there—before he circled back to take a public utility job with Public Service Company of New Mexico. In the late 1970s, he helped to engineer the design of Solar One, a $140 million project in Daggett, California, touted at the time as the world's largest solar power plant.

To each of his activities, Dale Christian brought intelligence, passion, and a healthy dose of skepticism. In college, he delighted in discovering errors in engineering textbooks. A history buff, he found amusement in what he considered military design blunders, such as the Allied tanks that sank into the mud during World War I. And he distrusted the federal government once he became convinced an invention he had developed for military use had been copied and credited to someone else. "He was brilliant, meticulous, very detailed, very orderly, very 100 percent German," Laura Christian recalled in an interview nearly two decades after her father's death at the age of fifty-nine in 2002.

Laura remembers her father's excitement once he began to research the cemetery. "He was very passionate about this. He was upset at the atrocity, that it had been lost. . . . He tried to revive it, so to speak, in a historical sense, because he loved history. He was trying to find the beauty in that."

Dale had an additional motivation: anger. The brothers' discovery of used hypodermic needles spread across the old burial ground upset him.

"He was pretty angry about that," his daughter said. "He had no tolerance for things like that."

✦

New Mexico Historic Preservation Division officials got far more than they bargained for in 1990 when they asked Dale, now retired, to calculate the dimensions of the miners' section of the cemetery. He drafted a five-page document dated October 11 that detailed the history of the cemetery—roughly the size of a professional football field—culminating in a recommendation for the state to pursue its placement on the National Register of Historic Places.

For the next eighteen months, Dale worked hand in hand with state officials and others to make this a reality. He helped Corinne Sze of Research Services of Santa Fe complete the formal application form for the National Park Service, the agency that maintains the list. He compiled US Geological Survey maps showing the precise location of the cemetery. He took dozens of photographs and slides, paying particular attention to the style of the individual grave markers and the languages of their inscriptions. He conducted research into Dawson's history by reviewing microfiche files of the *Raton Range*, a local newspaper that had reported extensively on the twin disasters. He created a topographical map of the site based on a 30" × 30" aerial photograph. He tracked down a US Bureau of Mines document listing all major mine disasters between 1900 and 1984. He counted and recorded 596 graves spread among the three sections of the cemetery, including about 360 in the portion dedicated to victims of the two mine explosions. He even took the time to caution Dr. Mary Ann Anders, the state's architectural historian, should she decide to visit the cemetery, writing: "[I]f you do go to the site be careful as it is remote. I've been there twice: both times I've found large rattlesnakes in the high grass areas."

On February 18, 1992, state officials submitted the nomination form to the National Park Service for its consideration, checking the box to indicate that in their opinion the property met the criteria for placement on the National Register.

✦

Acceptance was no slam dunk. Despite their best efforts, the nomination faced a considerable hurdle: the National Park Services' strict criteria for cemeteries. "Ordinarily cemeteries, birthplaces, or graves of historical figures . . . shall not be considered eligible for the National Register," the agency's regulations state. But the criteria used to evaluate properties contained one key exception: when a cemetery "derives its primary significance from graves of persons of transcendent importance, from age, from distinctive design features, or from association with historic events." This language opened the door for state officials to argue that Dawson Cemetery met the criteria for inclusion. They also cited two other sections of the regulations they believed were on point, dealing with properties "associated with events that have made a significant contribution to the broad patterns of our history" and those "that have yielded, or may be likely to yield, information important in prehistory or history."

The completed nomination form cited three specific areas of significance: coal mining, ethnic heritage, and social history. It identified the period of significance as between 1906 and 1941. And it listed under significant dates 1913 and 1923, the years coinciding with the town's two major disasters.

On April 9, 1992—roughly eighteen months after Dale and Lloyd first laid eyes on their "miniature Arlington"—Dawson Cemetery was entered onto the National Register of Historical Places. The notification came eight weeks after the cemetery was formally placed on the state version, the New Mexico Register of Cultural Properties.

✦

If Dale Christian helped to put Dawson Cemetery on the map, Vivien Pick made sure that people knew how to navigate it. In 1998, six years after the National Register acceptance, Pick (then Vivien Andrews) published *Dawson Coal Mine Cemetery Inscriptions: Dawson, Colfax County, NM*. The thirty-seven-page booklet consisted of 695 names, most pulled directly from the information inscribed on their tombstones. The list included all 383 miners killed in the 1913 and 1923 explosions, even if they had been buried elsewhere or their markers could not be found. Each name was accompanied by a date of birth and/or death and the nationality of the deceased, if known.

Four years later, Pick did that one better. After acquiring the original cemetery survey map dating back to the 1940s, she created another document that linked each name to plot, block, and grave numbers. In 2005, when a giant board displaying the map and accompanying information was erected near the entrance to the cemetery, visitors for the first time were able to quickly determine the precise location of a particular gravesite.

That Pick had a hand in this was no surprise. The granddaughter of a Dawson miner, her fascination with cemeteries took hold at an early age and only intensified after being introduced to genealogy in her late teens. "As a child, I used to walk the cemetery that was near our house and read the names," she recalled in an interview for this book. "It was just something that always attracted me. . . . I would wonder about people's lives, or if it was a short life, or if it was a long life, or something like that. It was just whimsical, I guess. Morbidly whimsical, maybe."

It was around this time that Pick learned she had a personal connection to Dawson Cemetery. She remembers her mother telling her that her own mother used to take her there as a child to look for the tiny graves of her brother and sister: Donald died at two; Sarah was an hour old. "My mother had no details on where the children were buried other than near a big rock that fell off the mountain toward the back of the cemetery. . . . She used to call it the 'baby cemetery.' That's where her mother would take her when she was little so she actually could see where Donald and Sarah were buried," she said.

In 1983, Pick and her family moved to Cimarron, a village twenty miles southwest of Dawson. By then, she had attended the 1980 and 1982 Dawson reunions and was becoming familiar with the history of the region. Her familiarity grew exponentially a few years later when the owners of the Old Aztec Mill Museum in Cimarron asked her if she would create a database of everyone buried in Dawson Cemetery. "One of them brought me the list and basically said, 'OK, we've done all we can do, and do you want to do anything with this?'" she said. "They knew I was associated with Dawson. And I go, 'Sure.' And that's how I got started in it. I decided I would finish their list."

So in late 1995 or early 1996, she and her husband, Bob, took their two Australian shepherd dogs, Daisy and Willow, and began walking the cemetery to record the names and nationalities of the hundreds of people buried there, a project that would take several years to complete. At first, the obstacles appeared insurmountable. Some of the engraved headstones were barely decipherable, particularly those made of sandstone, weathered by years of New Mexico rain, sun, and wind. Other inscriptions were in multiple languages and needed translation. A few of the couple's cemetery walks were cut short by intense heat or torrential rains.

What was it like walking through the cemetery, day after day, pencil and paper in hand, jotting down the names, dates of birth and death, and other accompanying information of people she never knew?

"I remember feeling a sense of peace walking through there, a connection with the families," Pick said. "These are names that I have known all my life, even though I didn't know the people, because of the stories I had heard . . . It wasn't eerie. It wasn't scary. It was basically a place of reverence that I really [had] a lot of desire to save the history of."

While Pick is not related to any of the miners killed in the 1913 and 1923 explosions, her grandfather, Alvin Davis, played a role in the latter. Davis, a miner who worked thirty miles to the north in Van Houten, was familiar with Dawson, having walked there once a week to take classes in first aid. When word of the explosion reached his camp, he was among the men who responded to work on the search and rescue teams. He would remain in Dawson, one of many miners hired to replace the 120 men who perished in the explosion.

The decision to stay wasn't a difficult one. Compared to other coal camps in the region, Dawson had many advantages. The men were paid in actual wages, not scrip that could be redeemed only at the company store. They lived in comfortable housing, which in time included indoor plumbing. Social activities abounded.

"When they had to leave in '38," Pick said, "my grandmother cried all the way back to Oklahoma."

✦

On October 20, 2013, the Dawson New Mexico Association hosted a centennial commemoration ceremony at the Raton Museum, which included the donation of a plaque by the Office of the Italian Consul General of Los Angeles in memory of "all those who perished and suffered in the explosion at Stag Cañon #2 mine." Later that morning, following the Divine Liturgy at St. George Greek Orthodox Church in Albuquerque, the local chapter of the American Hellenic Education and Progressive Association (AHEPA) sponsored a program in recognition of the Greek immigrants and others who died in the explosion. On the following Sunday, St. Elias the Prophet Greek Orthodox Church of Santa Fe led a multidenominational memorial service at the cemetery, during which the names of all miners killed in the two explosions were read aloud.

Georgia Maryol, who helped organize the two events, never lived in Dawson but remembers her father speaking in Greek to his friends about the mine disasters when she was a child growing up in Albuquerque. Many years later, she researched the history of Dawson and visited the cemetery. "It's like something I've needed to do for a long time," she said at the time about playing a role in the two remembrances. "It has something to do with being that my father was from Greece and he came over here with the clothes on his back. . . . Just like all these people came over with the clothes on their back. . . . I know he knew the coal miners. It's something in the soul."

✦

Pam Thompson did not attend that graveside memorial service. While she had known since the 1970s that an ancestor had been killed many years before in a coal mine accident, she didn't know where until she came across an online article in the August 2019 issue of a New Mexico magazine. There, under the headline "Abandoned Coal Town Still Has a Story to Tell," was a photograph depicting a large tombstone of a miner killed in the 1913 disaster.

Engraved on the headstone?

"Chester NC Davis."

Her great-uncle.

The photo prompted her to open a box left to her by her grandmother, Pearl Davis, which contained a letter Chester Davis had written to her several months before his death. That led to a new discovery, something Thompson couldn't believe she had missed when she first looked at the yellowed envelope years earlier: a "bold, black postmark" that read Dawson, New Mexico.

Davis was living with his parents and five sisters in Toluca, Illinois—a coal town in its own right—when he left home in the spring of 1913 at the age of seventeen for a job in the Dawson mines. In that letter to his older sister dated July 7, he said he was writing to "let you know that I am alive" and that he planned to send some money home soon. He also mentioned he had won $6.75 playing pool, then the equivalent of three months' rent on a two-room house. Davis closed his letter by saying he would be home for Christmas, "and then what a time I will have."

Davis never made it home for Christmas. Neither did Ben Loger, a fellow Toluca native who joined him in Dawson a few days before the explosion. They were rooming together in the days leading up to their deaths.

Upon learning of the explosion, John Henry and Emily Davis traveled to Dawson to identify the remains of their son and make arrangements to have them shipped home to Toluca. Upon their arrival, however, the couple learned that their son's body had been buried the previous day. When the grave was opened, they were unable to make a positive identification because of injuries to the man's face. They decided to leave his remains buried in Dawson.

One hundred and eight years later, in August of 2021, Pamela and her husband, Dick, visited Dawson Cemetery for the first time to pay their respects to her great-uncle. They were struck by the five-foot-tall stone monument at his burial site, a rarity among the many graves marked only by white iron crosses. Pam believes his parents made arrangements for the marker either during or after their trip to Dawson.

"It's just real now," she said before leaving the Dawson burial grounds that Sunday afternoon. "The cemetery is a very nice cemetery, but it's sad to see so many miners' crosses here in one place and all the loss that has happened."

✦

Joe Bacca approaches the wrought-iron gate that leads into the nine-acre ceme-tery and removes the padlock and chain that keep it secured to an adjacent post. Clad in a blue-and-green striped shirt and a pair of blue jeans on an overcast morning in August of 2019, Bacca is there to show off the recently completed preservation work to a journalist and a Raton couple, who visit the cemetery sev-eral times a year to replace the sun-faded plastic flowers that adorn their fami-ly's graves. The renovations—the installation of an eight-foot-high game fence, drainage work, and a general sprucing up of the grounds—were funded by the charitable arm of Freeport-McMoRan, the Phoenix-based international mining company that acquired Phelps Dodge in 2007. The work represented the most extensive upgrade of the cemetery in at least thirty years.

A year earlier, Bacca and Bruno Ridolfi, a professional engineer, had walked the graveyard to assess what could be done to improve its deteriorating condi-tion. In February 2019, Ridolfi hand-delivered their proposal and request for funding to Harry "Red" Conger, at that time president and chief operating officer of Freeport-McMoRan Americas, whom he had met years earlier while both were studying toward mining engineering degrees at the Colorado School of Mines in Golden. He didn't have to wait long for an answer.

"The historic Dawson Cemetery represents a part of mining history, and we wanted to honor the memories of those laid to rest there," Tracy Bame, pres-ident of the Freeport-McMoRan Foundation, announced a month later. "We are pleased the grant-funded restoration work will improve the cemetery, which hosts the Dawson Reunion every two years where families and friends visit and celebrate the lives of their loved ones."

The $65,000 donation didn't come a moment too soon for Bacca and the Dawson New Mexico Association, a nonprofit organization that maintains the cemetery and runs the biennial reunions on the old townsite. Bacca was worried about the future of the graveyard, given the damage caused over the years by wandering cattle and elk, flooding from heavy rains, and other factors. "I'm glad something finally got done because it was deteriorating fast," he said that day. "If we wouldn't have got that fence up, I don't know . . ."

Bacca had never lived in Dawson, but his family's ties to the community stretch back generations. His great-grandparents, Alex and Margarita Bacca, are buried here. His grandfather, Joe Bacca, was at work when the final car of coal was dumped on April, 28, 1950. His father, Fred, was born in Dawson and graduated from the town's high school. Given that pedigree, Bacca was a natural choice to become chairman of the association in 2012, a position he held until turning the reins over to his daughter in 2022. Over the years, he and his family have volunteered countless hours maintaining the cemetery, including every few years repainting the 383 white iron crosses that mark the graves of the miners who lost their lives in the 1913 and 1923 explosions.

✦

At the entrance to Dawson Cemetery—situated among the large survey map, plaques, and other memorial donations—is a black mailbox. Inside, visitors find a small notebook and pen to record any thoughts they choose to leave behind. Since its installation many years ago, more than 250 people from across the country have taken pen in hand, some to just jot down their names, others their observations. The solemnity of the occasion is not lost on those who walk these burial grounds.

Wrote one Illinois couple: "What a beautiful reminder of those who came before!"

CHAPTER 18

DOWN MEMORY LANE

The near ghost town of Dawson, once a thriving northern New Mexico city, came
briefly to life again last week when 65 of its residents gathered in Pasadena, Cal., for
the "Dawson Picnic."
—Albuquerque Journal
August 7, 1954

✦

Dawson's closing in 1950 touched off a spirited debate over what had *really* prompted the Phelps Dodge Corporation to shut it down. On one side? Repeated labor strife. On the other? Changing market conditions. Both played key roles, but they weren't the only reasons.

In 1975, Jackson M. Langton, chief geologist for Phelps Dodge in Morenci, Arizona, was tasked with ending speculation over how much coal the company had left behind when it closed its last mine. Langton found that previous estimates contained in a 1955 study were flawed, in part because they included eight million tons buried in mined areas that were no longer accessible. Conversely, he admitted that his own estimate of 10.9 million tons was "too conservative," leading him to recommend new drilling and further study.

Of even greater interest, however, is what was contained in the introduction to the nine-page report: five factors that persuaded Phelps Dodge to close the mine. The list was based on information provided to Langton by Gilbert Davis, who was general manager of the Dawson mines in the 1930s before transferring to Morenci.

Here, word for word, are the reasons cited in Langton's report:

- The 1948 drilling program, which was designed to find new reserves of clean coal, was unsuccessful.
- In 1949, the proportion of waste rock in the mine production was 36 percent of the total tonnage mined.
- The long distance (3 to 4 miles) from the mine portal to the coal beds.

- The unsatisfactory labor conditions in the coal industry.
- The fact that the Southern Pacific Railroad, which in the years 1945–1950 had been the outlet for 65 percent of the coal, decided to use diesel engines and abandon their coal-burning locomotives.

So while it is true that repeated labor strikes and changing market conditions influenced Phelps Dodge's decision, those weren't the only reasons.

✦

End of story? Hardly. Dawson lives on today in the hearts and minds of those who once lived and worked there, called it home, and dutifully passed down their memories to their children and grandchildren.

The first sign came in 1954, four years after the closing, when dozens of former residents gathered for a reunion one thousand miles away in Pasadena, California. While a few traveled from New Mexico—including former Central School principal Hannah McGarvey—most of the attendees had relocated to Greater Los Angeles. Among those who, no doubt, had stories to share were George and Nick Skandale, the two sons of 1923 mine disaster survivor Charles Skandale.

California would host more Dawson reunions around the state, including Marsh Creek outside of Stockton in 1959 and Micke Grove in Lodi in the 1970s. Soon they began popping up closer to home, usually in Albuquerque. The first reunion on the old Dawson townsite took place in 1980, where they have taken place on Labor Day weekend every two years since, with the exception of 2020 because of COVID-19 restrictions.

During the 1980s and 1990s, it was common for between 1,200 and 1,800 people from across the country—and occasionally the world—to attend the reunions. Even in 2018, nearly three-quarters of a century after the town's closing, about 450 people showed up for the festivities, which included a special exhibit at the Raton Museum and a Saturday night social at the Elks Lodge in Raton.

To be sure, Dawson isn't the only American mining town that has refused to be relegated to the dustbin of American history. Reunions can be found today in old mining towns scattered around the country. Nor can Dawson lay claim to hosting the oldest. A prime contender for that title is the ghost town of Central, Michigan, an Upper Peninsula community in Keweenaw County founded by the Central Mining Company in 1854. In 1907, a decade after the copper mine closed for good, the Central Mine Methodist Church began hosting a reunion service each July. The 2022 reunion was the church's 116th. Still, one would be hard-pressed to find a coal town reunion that has attracted as many attendees as Dawson since the first California reunion in 1954.

✦

So why do people return to Dawson? What is it about this old coal town that inspires such devotion after all these years? Perhaps it's to ensure that the town is remembered for more than the deadly twin disasters of 1913 and 1923. Perhaps it's to help soothe any lingering sores from the town's abrupt closing in 1950. Or perhaps it's as simple as this: Dawson was a wonderful place to live—at least for a coal town of that era—a tight-knit, cosmopolitan community of many customs, foods, and languages where the friendships forged above ground ran as deep as the coal seams below.

That "good old days" sentiment may be why it's not unusual to find references to Dawson and its reunions in the obituaries of those born or raised there: Joseph (Bob) McClary "returned biennially to Dawson for a reunion of former residents of this northern New Mexico ghost town." Frank Marcelli Sr. attended the reunions every two years, "where he enjoyed those visits with old friends, classmates and relatives." Beatrice Andazola McSweeney "never missed the Dawson picnics, staying in touch with friends and sharing memories." Frank V. Padilla "loved to travel and attend reunions of the coal-mining ghost town where he grew up." Clorinda Lucero "frequently entertained family and friends with letters and colorful stories of her childhood in Dawson."

For the living, you can see it in their eyes, hear it in their voices . . .

✦

Dolores Clara Fernandez Huerta is no stranger to American history. But before she began organizing farm workers, before she found herself standing behind Robert F. Kennedy minutes before he was assassinated, before her own life almost ended prematurely after suffering four broken ribs and a ruptured spleen at a protest courtesy of a police officer's baton, before becoming a fierce advocate for women's rights, before municipalities began naming public schools and streets after her, before President Barack Obama awarded her the Presidential Medal of Freedom, and before she formed the Dolores Huerta Foundation to push for social justice . . . she was a little girl in Dawson.

Huerta was born in 1930, the daughter of a coal miner and a homemaker, at house No. 1534 on Capitan Hill. Juan and Alicia Fernández, both New Mexico natives, married young—he was twenty, she seventeen—and they had a son, Johnny Xavier, before Dolores was born. A second boy, Marshall, was born a year after Dolores.

The family did not stay together long. Halfway through her second-grade year—between Christmas and New Year's Day, she remembers—Huerta's parents separated and she moved with her mother and two brothers to Stockton, California. Her father, who had been active in the early labor movement in Dawson, moved one hundred miles south to Las Vegas, where he was elected as a Democrat to the New Mexico House of Representatives in 1938.

Huerta and her family returned twice to visit friends in Dawson during her childhood—roughly 1941 and 1946—and remembers it as a "quaint little town" with nice houses and a theater. "People had a lot of loyalty to the place," she said. "People talked about Dawson with a lot of affection."

Years later, she would witness that affection again while attending her second reunion in 2002. That trip proved memorable on several counts, starting with the car she was in breaking down just before her arrival. ("One of the belts in the engine broke, so they had to come and rescue us. It was quite an adventure.")

Once there, she was touched by how far people had traveled to attend a reunion of a coal town that hadn't existed for more than half a century.

"There were people from all over," she said. "I mean, there was a family that came from England, and people came from the East Coast. It was really interesting that people had that much devotion to that place."

Huerta made another trip to Dawson in 2021, this time to the historic cemetery. There, she visited the graves of her paternal grandfather, Desiderio Fernández, a coal miner who died four years before she was born, and an uncle, Marcial Chavez, who was killed in the 1913 mine disaster.

What would she tell someone today if asked to describe life in Dawson?

"What I remember [is] it was a good community, I think, because everybody knew each other . . . and that people seemed really happy. That sounds kind of idyllic and Pollyannaish, but that's kind of what I remember. I'm sure the work in the coal mine was really, really hard . . . but in terms of the community itself, it seemed like a very close and just a pleasant place."

✦

Pietro "Pete" Scarafiotti is a big-time collector. Not baseball cards, not comic books, not old coins, but mining memorabilia, much of it specific to Dawson, much of it prominently on display in his home. A pick ax. An auger hand drill.

A miner's head lamp. A lunch pail. Wooden boxes marked "Phelps Dodge Merc. Co. / Dawson, N. Mex." and "Hercules Powder / High Explosives, Dangerous." A United Mine Workers of America plaque given to his great-grandfather of the same name when he left the Eagleville Mine in Trinidad, Colorado, to come to Dawson in 1916—the first in a long line of Scarafiottis to call Dawson home. Six of his sons would work at the mines, several right up to the final day.

Pete wasn't one of them. He was not born until three years after the town's closing, though he did work for a few years prior to entering college at a Phelps Dodge copper mine in Arizona. Nevertheless, he has become perhaps the most prominent disciple of Dawson's history, a walking encyclopedia of information, supplementing his home mining mementos with countless documents, maps, and photographs in what may be the largest personal collection of Dawson materials today.

In 2016, Scarafiotti started a Dawson Facebook page, which he began populating with photographs and stories drawn from his extensive collection of historical records and his own independent research. Among his numerous contributions: a detailed listing by name, nationality, cause, and location of all 521 miners who died of work-related injuries between 1902 and 1949; a firsthand account by his grandfather about his and his brother's participation in rescue efforts after the 1923 explosion; and a Dawson "cheat sheet" explaining what was where, accompanied by an aerial photograph of the town taken in 1942. He has been a longtime fixture at Dawson's every-other-year reunions, lugging enough memorabilia with him to stage show-and-tells with curious visitors.

Scarafiotti's immersion in Dawson began at a young age. He remembers accompanying his grandmother on many trips to Raton to visit with family and friends who had relocated there after the town closed. "[I]n those days, many former residents were still living, and I literally sat at the feet of these folks and listened to their stories," he said. "Of course, my family had a huge collection of Dawson memorabilia, which my grandmother passed along to me, and I added to it over the years."

Keeping all this history to himself never crossed his mind.

"I 'protect' Dawson today in memory of the great love those old folks had for their home," he said, explaining that they all "longed to return to the simpler times and the comfort they got from old friends and family. My family hoped I would carry on protecting Dawson's legacy, and I've always been so proud to bear that responsibility."

✦

Fred Becchetti, whose grandfather and father worked in the Dawson mines, has been one of Dawson's leading ambassadors, as unlikely as that might seem for someone who only lived there five years and didn't return until the working coal town was a distant memory.

Much happened to him in between: Graduation from Albuquerque High School months after the Japanese bombed Pearl Harbor. Enlistment in the Army Air Corps. Thirty-five missions as a navigator/bombardier aboard a B-24 Liberator with the 445th Bomb Group of the Eighth Air Force. Earning the Distinguished Flying Cross and other medals. Marriage to the former Vivienne Fleissner after his discharge from the military. College degrees under the GI Bill. A dozen years as a high-school Spanish and English teacher in Benson, Arizona, where he also served four years as mayor after winning a write-in campaign. Twenty-seven years as a US foreign service officer with assignments that took him to Chile, the Dominican Republic, Grenada, Honduras, Mexico, Panama, and Venezuela.

Prior to his retirement in 1989, after more than fifty years away, Becchetti made a return visit "home," even though he knew the old townsite was private property and off limits without the owner's permission. Still, despite his many years as a law-abiding citizen—"I obey red traffic lights at three-thirty in the morning with no cars in sight"—Becchetti couldn't resist stepping over a ditch and into what was left of the hometown of his youth.

"Our home in Number Seven Camp with a garage for my dad's Dodge had been there," he reminisced about house No. 641 in a first-person account published in the *Raton Range* the weekend of the 1988 reunion. "And right nearby, there had been a hill of red ants where I first learned that Mother Nature is not all sweetness and pretty flowers. The square fence pole where I laid a gash on my four-year-old forehead was on the street where we lived. I have the scar of it to this day."

Becchetti went to the Dawson reunion that weekend, the first of a dozen he would attend over the next twenty years. He became active in the town's afterlife, sharing his written stories, poems, watercolors—he painted five hundred landscapes after taking it up as a hobby in 1991—and other items.

"As for Dawson's children and grand-children, let them be proud of the men and women who worked in Dawson," he wrote in 2014, the year he turned ninety and wasn't able to attend that year's reunion. "They were proud, hard-working people who entered the mines every morning and faced the dangers for only one reason: To make a better life for their children. They were our heroes!"

✦

Nat Norris may not have lived in Dawson long, but to hear him tell it, he made quite the impression. The youngest of ten children, he and his family moved to Dawson in 1944. His father was the section foreman for the Southern Pacific between Dawson and French when he wasn't playing fiddle at the Snake saloon.

A self-described "scrawny little runt" ("Many afternoons I would be challenged to a fight because the other kid knew he could whip me"), he remembers sneaking out of school at recess to buy a bottle of Big Red soda at the company store. He also tried his luck a few times at boosting bananas. "The mercantile always had a big stalk of bananas, and I tried several times to swipe one but always got caught," he said. "They would just put it on my mother's bill, and she would find out about my thievery at the end of the month. Then I got another tanning."

Young Nat wasn't a good patient, either. A visiting dentist from Raton once had to physically hold him down before yanking "a rotten molar." But that experience paled in comparison to when he was a first-grader and had to get his shots to guard against diphtheria, pertussis, and tetanus. "I had never been vaccinated but knew what was coming," he said. "I started screaming bloody murder before we went upstairs and kept it up until [principal Hannah] McGarvey practically throttled me. My outburst set the first-grade kids to screaming, and the whole town heard what happened."

Norris had just completed fifth grade when the town closed and his family moved to Springer, where he graduated from high school in the Class of 1957. After that, he attended and graduated from New Mexico State University, earned his master's degree in education at the University of Arizona, and spent forty years as an educator and administrator in programs for the hearing impaired in Alaska, Arizona, Washington State, and Washington, DC, before retiring to Arizona.

✦

Joseph Padilla was three years old when his family moved from Springer to Dawson, where his father got a job as the town plumber. Some of his favorite memories go back to his days as an altar boy at the Catholic church, St. John the Baptist, even if not all of them had the best outcomes.

"Whoever got to the church first got to be the 'First Altar Boy,'" he recalled. "That meant you got to ring the bell at the consecration of the bread and wine. I was frequently the first one there, so the priest hired me to lock the church in the evening and unlock it in the morning. He paid me one dollar a week." All was good until he inadvertently left his dog, Peewee, in the church overnight. "He had shredded the drapes over the door to the sacristy and scratched the door badly," he said. "I was very embarrassed, but the priest was kind about it."

That wasn't his only embarrassing moment. The summer after the town closed, while visiting with relatives working at the power plant, he and a male friend decided to go for a swim in the Vermejo River. Neither had swimming trunks, so they stripped down to their birthday suits and entered the water. "Pretty soon a woman and her daughter showed up on the bank, and it felt like they would never leave," he said. "By the time they did we were very cold, and we were finally able to get out of the river and get dressed."

When Dawson closed, Padilla and his family moved back to Springer, where he graduated from high school along with Nat Norris in 1957. He later earned a degree at the University of New Mexico, moved to Oregon, and taught for thirty-four years at the high school and community college level.

+

Mary Frances García Reza, a Dawson native whose mother worked at the company store until its closure, has vivid memories of those last days. "Witnessing the exodus of truck after truck and cars loaded with their belongings leaving town was heartbreaking," she recalled. "The forlorn look in their eyes spoke volumes."

Reza, who grew up in Capitan, said she wasn't all that surprised by the closing of the town because her father, José Marcos García, had predicted it. "He would get in trouble because he'd say, 'If you continue the strikes, you're not going to make it,'" she said. "And he said this strike is going to prove deadly. . . . But I think for a lot of people, it was a tremendous shock."

These aren't her only memories of Dawson. She has plenty of happy ones, too. Walking to school in the snow. Climbing the nearby mountains. Picnics with friends.

But if there was one institution that defined her childhood, it was St. John the Baptist Church, a magnificent structure that opened in 1917 after years of negotiations between Phelps Dodge and the Archdiocese of Santa Fe. Reza remembers walking with her grandmother to the 6:00 a.m. daily Mass before heading off to school for the day.

"The church was central to my life," she said.

Little wonder. When her mother, Amelia Lopez García, wasn't working at the company store, she was an active participant in the parish, serving for many years as its organist and choir director. Her devotion to the church and its liturgical music inspired her daughter, who took piano lessons at an early age. "By the fifth or sixth grade," she said, "I was playing the pipe organ for Benediction."

That became her introduction into a life of music ministry and composing Spanish liturgical music. After receiving an undergraduate degree in music and a master's in education, she turned her attention to bilingual education and served as director of music for the Archdiocese of Santa Fe. Her music, recorded and published by the Oregon Catholic Press, earned her recognition as one of the "grande dames" of Hispanic music and ministry in the country.

"I could not have had a better childhood," she said, looking back at her early years in Dawson. "I wish every child would have [had] an opportunity to live there."

✦

Petra Tovar Sánchez was the youngest of nine children born in Dawson to her Mexican immigrant parents. Her father was a coal miner; her mother died when she was ten. As a teenager, she remembers rising at 5:30 a.m. and, along with her siblings, helping the family get ready for work: lighting the fire, making breakfast, packing lunches. After school, before the miners in the family got home, she would help prepare supper and heat the water for the nightly baths to wash away the day's coal dust.

Sánchez has fond memories of her two-bedroom home, which was located in the Five Hill section of Dawson: "We had a . . . place where my brothers played marbles and everything else. And we had a chicken coop, a plum tree, and peach tree, and an apple tree. One of my older brothers used to plant a garden. And we had shade trees."

She also speaks highly of the Dawson school system; when she graduated in 1947, Dawson High School was the only accredited high school in a New Mexico coal town. She was introduced to theater and music at a young age—"if you can imagine fourth- and fifth-graders doing an operetta"—and recalls, in particular, the experiential learning provided by one of her teachers, Florence Upton, a Massachusetts native. For a history lesson on the original thirteen colonies, she ordered from her home state "maple syrup cakes" and "Boston baked beans."

Sánchez, who taught for many years in New Mexico, has no doubt that growing up in Dawson gave her a strong foundation upon which to build her life. "At the time you don't know what you're missing," she said. "We didn't have money. Nobody was rich. But we didn't know we were poor."

✦

Patty Trujillo first visited Dawson in 1972, more than two decades after its closing, when she accompanied her father, Jesse Trujillo, to the cemetery to visit a family grave.

"It was the first time he'd ever remembered seeing his dad's grave," she said. "In 1972, there wasn't much left in Dawson. There was a caretaker's house and there were sidewalks, and the coke ovens were still there. But other than that, it was as desolate as it is today."

Finding a gravesite in those days was no easy task. The cemetery was overgrown and untended, she recalled, overrun with six-foot-high sunflowers—not to mention snakes. "We weren't able to get in the main gate, so we carefully walked around the side of the fence to a spot where we could easily get through," she said. "We walked down one row of graves and unbelievably went right to his grave—Alfredo Trujillo. Looking up at the many rows of graves and the hill behind, it just seemed impossible that we'd walked right to it."

Alfredo, twenty-nine, was one of the miners who perished in the 1923 mine explosion. He was buried next to his older brother, Anselmo, age thirty-six, who also lost his life in that blast.

Trujillo has no personal memories about Dawson, but she has the next best thing: photo albums handed down by her grandmother. Amalia Palmer moved to Dawson from Trinidad, Colorado, with her sister, Avelina, to work as nurses at Dawson Hospital.

Given her profession, many of the photos depict Amalia and her fellow nurses in uniform: posing in a field; holding an outstretched American flag; all lined up in a patriotic salute; even enjoying a picnic lunch. On a sadder note, there is also a photo of a document signed by the Rev. Joseph A. Couturier, confirming that Amalia and Alfredo were still married at the time of the 1923 mine disaster, presumably to clear the way for her to receive death benefits from his employer. Shortly after the explosion, when Jesse was three years old, Amalia left Dawson with her two sons.

The 1972 visit was Trujillo's first trip to Dawson, but it would not be her last. She and her father returned years later to attend three of the biennial reunions before his death in 2004.

"Truly, those are cherished memories for me," she said.

✦

Frank Turner never lived in Dawson, but it became a big part of his childhood just the same. Born in Tucumcari, he was the son of a brakeman/conductor who made the Dawson-to-Tucumcari run for the El Paso & Southwestern Railroad and later the Southern Pacific. His trips on the Polly, starting when he was seven or eight years old, were the first things to come to mind when he was contacted for this book decades later.

"That's without question my finest childhood memory: riding the Polly with my dad," he said. "It stopped for lunch in Roy, New Mexico. My dad was a pretty cool guy . . . and orders me a chocolate malt, and a cheeseburger, and fries, and all that. My mother was a little more strict about how we ate."

It was on the Polly that he was introduced to his first cup of hot coffee—"it burned the heck out of me"—and saw his father wield a crowbar to kill "a great, big old rattlesnake" that had crawled up against the rail during a stop at Campana. And he will never forget the seven-hour trip aboard a special train from Tucumcari to Dawson to attend a big high-school football game between the two schools in 1948. Both teams were undefeated, and 550 Tucumcari fans rode the train to the game, in which Tucumcari rallied from behind to win, 13–6, before more than three thousand fans. The contest was such a big deal that the Dawson and Tucumcari bands were joined by their counterparts from Las Vegas, Mosquero, Raton, and Springer. Turner recalled: "It was really cold . . . and the train was filled. I mean, it sold out. I remember a guy offering me a drink out of a flask. I wisely turned it down."

Turner chose to follow in his father's footsteps. He got his first railroad job with the Norfolk & Western Railway in Virginia and later served as president of the American Short Line and Regional Railroad Association. In 2014, he founded the Tucumcari Railroad Museum at the old Union Station depot building.

✦

Edward Zavala and his wife, Betty, are fixtures at both the cemetery and the reunions. Several times a year—Memorial Day, Labor Day, and the birthdays of Edward's father and brother—the Raton couple visit the cemetery to pay their respects and swap out the colorful artificial flower arrangements that fade quickly under the New Mexico sun. Edward's father, Jesus, is believed to have been the last miner buried in the cemetery; Edward's older brother, Raoul, was a twenty-one-year-old radio operator when his B-29 was downed by a kamikaze pilot over Manchuria during World War II. Edward and Betty have missed only one Dawson reunion since 1974.

Edward was born in Dawson, graduated from Dawson High School, and was nineteen when the town closed. He remembers, as a teen, getting up early in the morning to cut weeds in the cemetery. "There were three of us. . . . We used to work a couple of hours and then go to school," he said.

Unlike his father, Zavala never worked in a coal mine, although he came close. After moving to Raton when Dawson closed—"the only job I could get was driving a taxi"—a friend told him he would get him a mining job. "So he tells me, 'Next week, I got you in. Next week you're going to go in the mine.'" But when his sister, who was visiting from California, heard the news, she put the kibosh on that. "'No, you're not going in the mine,'" he remembers her saying, "'you're going with me to California.'"

Once there, Zavala found more than a steady job: he met his future wife, Betty. After retiring from his position with the state of California, the couple moved to Raton, where they have helped to keep the memory of Dawson alive.

"I had no idea what was on the outside. . . . If I had never known it, I would have been real satisfied with this," he said. "See, that's how I felt because this was a beautiful place to live."

✦

If there is one thing that keeps Dawsonites up at night, it's whether the biennial picnic reunion is sustainable. In 2018, the committee charged with running it consisted of fifteen people; four years later, there were seven, five from the same family.

Add to that uneasiness the future of the old townsite, now occupied by the Dawson Elk Valley Ranch. In early 2020, the fifty-thousand-acre ranch was put up for sale by owner Brad Kelley, one of the nation's largest private landowners. For years, Kelley has allowed the Dawson New Mexico Association to host its reunions on the private ranch, near the original site of the old Dawson Hotel. Should the next owner be less accommodating, a new location would become necessary.

Joe Bacca, the longtime chairman of the association, believes the reunions will continue to attract hundreds of attendees as long as they remain on the old townsite. "If that changes," he said, "I believe the numbers that attend will drop off." Still, he is optimistic that even if the ranch ownership should change hands, the new owners will be willing to accommodate them for one day every two years.

While Bacca acknowledges it has been difficult over the past several years to find people interested to serve on the reunion committee, he is blessed to have the strong support of his family. In 2022, he stepped down from the chairman's post he had held for fourteen years, though he made it clear he wasn't going anywhere.

"My daughter Bobbie Jo Bacca is now the chairman of the committee, and there are new members, all family," he said months before that year's reunion. "And I am still involved until she gets more comfortable with the position—and I will always be there to help her and the committee as much as I can."

+

If the reunions are to remain sustainable, it will be up to a new generation.

Enter Carlos Tenorio. The 19-year-old Albuquerque resident is the great-nephew of Angelo Muñoz—affectionately known as the "unofficial" mayor of Dawson—who was a familiar face at the reunions right up until his death on October 2, 2018, one month to the day after attending that year's event.

Despite his youth, Tenorio has already been to numerous reunions with his family: as an infant in 2004 and again in 2010, 2012, 2014, and 2022. He was introduced to Dawson's history by his great-grandfather, Frank Muñoz, who used to tell him stories about his childhood. "I'm sure many of them were over-exaggerated because that's who he was as a person," he said of the man he called "Popeye" because they used to watch "Popeye the Sailor" cartoons together. "But those stories fascinated me from a young age. He was not a miner. He actually was a junior in high school [in 1950] when Dawson actually closed."

Muñoz described this event to his great-nephew as "one of the worst days of his life." Tenorio said. "It always stuck with him that he never really got to live out his life in Dawson like his father, and them before, that were actually coal miners. And pretty much everyone who lived there was going to be a coal miner."

If there were any doubts about Tenorio's devotion to his family's home-town, they were put to rest early. Seven minutes into our interview outside an Old Town coffee shop in Albuquerque, he paused to pull up old photographs on his cellphone of his great-grandfather and his brothers growing up in Dawson, as well as more recent reunion photos. Also on his phone? Sheet music of the old Dawson High School song. The name of the family dog? Dawson.

For Tenorio, keeping the memory of Dawson alive is not based on senti-ment alone. "When Uncle Angelo died, one of the last things he told me was . . . 'When I'm gone, you better go to Dawson and keep it up for me,'" he recalls. "And I said, 'You know it, Uncle, you know it, but it won't be for a few years.' He's like, 'I know, but keep it up for me.'"

Tenorio promised to do his part.

"They say Tombstone's the town too tough to die, but, really, Dawson's the town too tough to die," declares Tenorio, whose generation is key to the long-term future of the biennial reunions. "People always will, as long as someone's alive for these stories . . . talk about Dawson."

EPILOGUE

I attended my first Dawson reunion during Labor Day weekend 2022, weeks before my deadline to submit the completed manuscript of this book. Up to that point, I had read the stories. I had seen the photographs. I had watched the videos. And I had spoken to dozens of Dawson folks who tried their best to explain what these biennial picnics were all about.

None did them justice.

I checked into a Raton hotel late Friday afternoon. I had arrived a few days early because the Dawson New Mexico Association and the Raton Museum had invited me to speak on Saturday afternoon, even though this book's release was a year away. Nevertheless, roughly seventy-five people crowded into the museum's upstairs conference room—many standing along the walls—to hear what this native New Englander had to say about their beloved Dawson. Since I suspected many of these folks knew more about the town's history than I did, I focused my remarks on how I first heard of Dawson, my initial trip to the historic cemetery, and the key things I learned during my four years of research into this old coal town. The talk was well received, no doubt more a reflection of the message than the messenger.

The next morning, I arrived at the old townsite shortly after 8:30. White tents, tables, and chairs had already been assembled for the reunion at what was once the site of the old Dawson Hotel. Soon a steady stream of cars and trucks was approaching the adjacent grass parking area. By the end of the day, nearly six hundred people would attend the 2022 reunion, some coming from as far as Alaska, California, Illinois, and Pennsylvania.

Coincidentally, the first person I encountered was George Cruz, whose family was the last to leave Dawson—not in 1950 when the town closed, but in 1968 when Phelps Dodge shut down its last surviving operation, the Dawson Ranch, and leased it to an outside company. George, the fourth of twelve children born to Joe and Cornelia Cruz, was a young boy in 1950 but remembers seeing Dawson houses loaded onto trucks and hauled to new destinations. When we spoke that morning, he was holding a three-ring binder containing 8" × 10" photographs depicting some of the places his family had lived in town. Joe Cruz was in charge of the ranch when Phelps Dodge decided to lease it out, but he was offered and accepted a job 450 miles away at the company's copper mine in Tyrone, New Mexico.

✦

While I enjoyed meeting new people during the weekend, it was comforting to put a face on those individuals with whom I had communicated only by email or phone.

Bob Grubesic was one of them. He contacted me in the spring of 2021 to tell me about his father, Anthony, the son of Croatian immigrants, who began working in the Dawson mines when he was twelve years old. Bob described his father as a hard worker who loved to hunt and fish, drink, and dance, and "did not suffer fools gladly." He also shared some letters his father had written to his mother while she was away in 1939–1940, covering such topics as sweltering in the mines ("Have to hang my underwear behind the stove . . . when I come home") and being rousted out of bed early one morning by the sounds of a skunk after his chickens ("I woke up and the chickens were raising H—)."

Gloria Atler Garcia was another. I interviewed her by telephone early in my research after she reached out upon seeing a story that I had written for the *Albuquerque Journal* about the renovations to Dawson Cemetery. Her father, Albert Atler, was born and raised in Dawson, and her grandmother lost two brothers in the 1923 explosion, Alfredo and Anselmo Trujillo. Gloria never lived in Dawson but remembers attending a family baptism as a child in the late 1940s. ("The church was beautiful," she said.) She also has a few Dawson family heirlooms, including the wedding certificates of her grandparents and parents, as well as her father's high-school diploma. Like me, this was her first reunion.

Roberta Hernandez Perez was there, too. I had spoken to the California resident a few months earlier about her father, Augustine Hernandez, who composed and sang "¡Adiós a Dawson!" at the opera house a month before the town's closing. Also in attendance was Marlene Hancock Kotchou, whose father ran the movie projector at the opera house and stayed on for a few years after the town closed as an employee of the power plant. Another attendee, geologist Amy Boyle, a retired Wyoming mine inspector, invited me and several others on a hike across the Vermejo River that day to view the remains of the old J. B. Dawson homestead and the family burial grounds.

On Sunday afternoon, during a short program, Dawson native Dolores Huerta spoke about what made this coal town such a special place and why so many people remain enamored with it. Her remarks punctuated all that I had learned during the preceding four years.

"There's something about Dawson, New Mexico, that brought all of us here today because it was a place where there was so much harmony, where people were together," she told the crowd. "We had people that came from different parts of Europe, people that came from Mexico, people that were born here in New Mexico. They all came together to work in the mines, although it was very dangerous. But in the town of Dawson, they all managed to live together and to get along in the peace and harmony that we know the world needs today . . . And I think this is why people keep coming back here to this very beautiful site."

✦

Two weeks later, I was sitting with my wife, Susan, at Chicago Midway International Airport. We were awaiting a connecting flight that would bring us home to Albuquerque from Massachusetts after attending my Lowell High School fifty-year reunion. To pass the time, I decided to show her the iPhone photographs I had taken during Dawson reunion weekend: the remains of the J. B. Dawson homestead and family cemetery; musician Rick Landers performing a ballad he wrote as a tribute to the Dawson miners killed in the explosions of 1913 and 1923; George Cruz holding his binder of Dawson memories. Suddenly, my eyes began to moisten, causing me to reach for the handkerchief in my back pocket.

I shouldn't have been surprised. Long before Dolores Huerta delivered her poignant remarks on that Sunday afternoon, I knew this project would be no academic exercise. Yes, there would be a detailed recounting of the two horrific mine disasters that shook the town, but in short order I came to understand that the story of Dawson was one of life, not death. Of sweet memories, not bitter remembrances. Of friendship, not grievances. Of seeking out common bonds, not exploiting cultural differences. Of love, not hate. That is why almost six hundred people gathered in that remarkable spot over Labor Day weekend.

Nearly three-quarters of a century after Dawson was no more.

ACKNOWLEDGMENTS

I first learned about Dawson in October of 2013, four months after Susan and I left our home in southern New Hampshire so I could accept an assistant editor job at the *Albuquerque Journal* and be closer to our two (now five) grandchildren. That month, the *Journal* published a story by staff reporter Charles D. Brunt commemorating the one-hundred-year anniversary of the 1913 Dawson mine explosion.

To this day, I'm not sure why Charles's story struck such a chord. Before I knew it, I was rummaging around the internet in my spare time for anything I could find on the mine disaster and a second ten years later. Perhaps it was the proximity of Dawson to my new Albuquerque home, at 230 miles a three-and-a-quarter-hour car ride away. Perhaps it was because three dozen of the men who died in the first explosion were recent immigrants from Greece, much like my father, who came to the United States a few years later at the age of seventeen and found work in the steel mills of Gary, Indiana. Perhaps it was my surprise—no, make that astonishment—that seventy years after the closing of the town, the Dawson community was very much alive.

Looking back, I suspect that the seeds for *Crosses of Iron* were planted right then and there. Any lingering doubts were laid to rest when I first visited Dawson Cemetery, two months after my retirement, on a chilly January morning in 2019. The white crosses. The engraved names. The hidden stories. They were all here, disturbed only by this stranger's presence, in this remote corner of New Mexico, five and a half miles from the nearest paved roadway.

None of what you read here would have been possible, of course, without the cooperation and contributions of countless people who were kind enough to take my hand and guide me through this unforgettable journey. Archivists. Geologists. Historians. Librarians. Private collection custodians. And, perhaps most of all, the folks who once lived in Dawson or whose ancestors did before them. I will be forever grateful to them for opening up their homes, their private collections, their very hearts, to help me understand the story of Dawson.

First and foremost, I would like to thank the University of New Mexico Press for partnering with me on this nearly forgotten chapter of American history. Editor Michael Millman couldn't have been more accommodating, ushering this first-time author through the intricacies of book publishing. Likewise, I am indebted to the UNM Press's editorial and design teams for transforming my spartan manuscript into the professional product you hold in your hands today. And I couldn't have asked for a better—or more meticulous—copy editor than Katherine Harper, whose "red pencil" and margin notations not only improved the prose but saved me from some embarrassing mistakes. Responsibility for any other errors lies with me and me alone.

Every first-time book author needs a mentor, and I was blessed with two: Richard Melzer, a retired University of New Mexico history professor, and Pietro "Pete" Scarafiotti, a descendant of multiple generations of Dawson residents and owner of perhaps the largest private collection of Dawson documents and memorabilia outside of Freeport-McMoRan. Richard, the author or coauthor of more than two dozen books about New Mexico history, was kind enough to meet with me numerous times over coffee, read an early draft of my manuscript, and write the foreword for this book. Likewise, Pete treated me like a member of his family, meeting with me several times at his Arizona home and regaling me with stories about Dawson's rich history. The Facebook page he started in 2016—a virtual clearinghouse of Dawson documents, maps, stories, and photographs—became a valued resource.

I am grateful to the Office of the State Historian and the Historical Society of New Mexico for awarding me a History Scholars research grant in 2020. While COVID-19 restrictions prevented an in-person presentation of my findings, the society's Henrietta M. Christmas recorded my Dawson presentation on Zoom and gave it a home on the organization's YouTube channel.

Speaking of research assistance, some came from unexpected sources. I first reached out to Manlio Badiali in October of 2020 after I saw his online post about the numerous Italians who lost their lives in the 1913 disaster, many from his home province of Modena in northern Italy. Manlio's interest wasn't purely academic—his grandfather lost two cousins in that explosion—and he went above and beyond in helping me recount this part of the story. He sent images and translations of Italian telegrams and newspapers. He visited research institutions in Fiumalbo, Modena, Serramazzoni, and once, while on vacation, Provence, France. He created Excel data files and family trees. And he took the photographs of the cenotaph and plaque memorializing the lost miners of Fiumalbo that appear in this book.

Likewise, the extended family of Maria Caputo, Tina Leslie, Constantine Makris, George Makris, Emmanuel Vozos, and Fannie Vozos were instrumental in helping me chronicle the story of the lost Karpathian miners, especially their relatives Constantine and Georgios Makris. The family also shared and translated Georgios' four letters to his wife from the original Greek, an embarrassing admission given my seven years in a K–6 Massachusetts elementary school where we were taught half the day in Greek and half the day in English. Emanuel Cassotis, author of *The Karpathian Presence in America (1872–2012)*, also was gracious with his time and shared his findings into the plight of the Karpathian miners.

I also would like to recognize two people who helped me relate the stories of their late grandparents: Bob Sexton, the grandson of 1913 disaster victim Lloyd Peter Upton, and Elizabeth Skandale, the granddaughter of 1923 explosion survivor Charles Skandale. Bob worked with me throughout my research to detail his grandfather's life before and after his arrival in New Mexico, while Elizabeth provided me with a college paper that she wrote years ago based on a conversation she had with her grandfather about that fateful day.

The more traditional custodians of New Mexico history also are deserving of my heartfelt gratitude. They included Gail Packard and Marcus Flores at the New Mexico State Records Center and Archives in Santa Fe; Katherine Wolf at the Fray Angélico Chávez History Library in Santa Fe; Gretchen Brock and Steven Moffson at the New Mexico Historic Preservation Division; Bernadette Lucero and Celine Baca Radigan at the Archdiocese of Santa Fe; Nancy Brown-Martinez at the Center for Southwest Research and Special Collections at the University of New Mexico in Albuquerque; Dennis Daily at the New Mexico State University Library Archives and Special Collections in Las Cruces; Kathryn Seidel at the Albuquerque Special Collections Library; Erica Weingartner at the Albuquerque Publishing Company (*Albuquerque Journal*); Thayla Wright and staff at the Arthur Johnson Memorial Library in Raton; and Dawn Bliss at the Manchester City Library in New Hampshire. I would be remiss if I didn't mention Gretchen Hoffman, principal senior coal geologist emeritus for the New Mexico Bureau of Geology and Mineral Resources, who agreed to meet with me early in my research at the New Mexico Institute of Mining and Technology in Socorro. She also provided me with an indispensable tool: a searchable database of New Mexico mine inspector reports covering the period between 1895 and 1951.

Throughout this book, I've tried wherever possible to rely on primary documents. That commitment was enhanced greatly by the cooperation of Freeport-McMoRan, which acquired the Phelps Dodge Corporation in 2007. As such, the Phoenix-based international mining company is the rights holder to the original documents, maps, and photographs once held by its predecessor. With the kind assistance of Michele Hughes, Freeport-McMoRan's manager for legal administration, I was given the opportunity to spend nearly a full day at corporate headquarters, digging through boxes crammed with original documents dating to the early 1900s. A thick folder containing papers related to the 1913 explosion—hundreds of pages of letters, reports, telegrams, and the like—had never before been accessed by the public since coming under Freeport-McMoRan's stewardship.

On a more personal level, I would like to thank two former *Albuquerque Journal* colleagues: photographer Roberto Rosales for the images taken at the 2022 Dawson reunion—including the book's cover—and Jim Frost for the map depicting Colfax County circa 1912 at the front of the book. I'm also indebted to my good friend DJ Nickles for building my website (nickpappasbooks.com), his wife, Margaret Nickles, for transcribing my far-too-often rambling interviews, and my daughter, Melanie Pappas, for lending her expertise to the design of my website and for her guidance in establishing a cohesive online presence. And, of course, my wife, Susan, for her patience and support throughout this project.

Two other individuals are deserving of recognition for their assistance at both ends of this project. Marty Levine, an online instructor with Creative Nonfiction, taught me the basics of storytelling as a student in his 2019 historical narratives class. Richard W. Etulain, a New Mexico historian and author, provided much-appreciated suggestions after reading an early draft of my manuscript. I owe a huge debt to both.

In closing, I'd like to single out a few Dawson folks who helped steer me through this project: Joe Bacca, the longtime chairman of the Dawson New Mexico Association; Vivien Pick, who tutored me several times over coffee on the history of Dawson Cemetery; Chuck Speed, the association's webmaster, who supplied me with a CD containing every issue of *The Dawson News*; Edward and Betty Zavala, who met with me in their home, at the cemetery, and on the old townsite; and Jeremy Smith, manager of the private Dawson Elk Valley Ranch, who agreed to open the gates for one day so I could get a firsthand look at what was once the old coal town of Dawson.

✦

As a small token of my appreciation to the many Dawsonites who made it possible for me to tell this story, 10 percent of the author's share of royalties from sales of this book will be donated to the Dawson New Mexico Association.

The nonprofit organization is dedicated to raising the necessary funds to run the reunions every other Labor Day weekend and to maintain historic Dawson Cemetery. If you would like to help, private and corporate tax-deductible donations can be mailed to:

Dawson New Mexico Association
528 N. First St.
Raton, NM 87740

May the memory of Dawson and its lost miners be kept alive for generations to come . . .

KILLED IN THE EXPLOSION OF
OCTOBER 22, 1913

Amargiotu, John	Greek
Anastasakis, John	Greek
Andres, John	Greek
Andres, Pavlo	Greek
Andrios, Thelfano	Greek
Anezakis, Makis	Greek
Anezakis, Stilen	Greek
Angela, Michele	Italian
Angelone, Pete	Italian
Arhondakis, Nick	Greek
Arkotas, Nick	Greek
Armeda, Rocco	Italian
Ballastrocci, Battista	Italian
Bediali, Antonio	Italian
Bediali, Celeste	Italian
Bella, Angelo	Italian
Berger, Jerry	American
Biagi, Giovanni	Italian
Biagio, Silvestre	Italian
Bianchi, Gugliemo	Italian
Biondi, Luigi	Italian
Boggio, Pietro	Italian
Bonnio, Dom	Italian
Bono, Anton	Italian
Bouzakis, Nick	Greek
Bravieri, Guiseppi	Italian
Bright, Willis	Negro
Brooks, J. M.	Negro
Brown, Frank	Negro
Brugione, Domenic	Italian
Brugione, Federico	Italian
Brugione, Listo	Italian

Brugione, Vanni	Italian
Brunos, Joe	Italian
Butte, Edward	Italian
Comacho, Antonio	Mexican
Candido, Demaretio	Italian
Carapello, Guiseppi	Italian
Carapellucci, B.	Italian
Carapellucci, D.	Italian
Careto, Guiseppi	Italian
Carleso, Carlo	Italian
Carleso, John	Italian
Carrole, Antonio	Italian
Castelli, Ermenegildo	Italian
Castenagus, Magus	Greek
Cavaiani, Giovanni	Italian
Cecconi, Pietro	Italian
Cericola, John	Italian
Cerillo, Mazoli	Italian
Champa, R.	Austrian
Chavez, Luis	Mexican
Chavez, Marcial	Mexican
Ciecarelli, Ubaldo	Italian
Colonintes, John	Greek
Conti, A.	Italian
Coral, Mike	Slav
Cotrules, Geo.	Greek
Cotrules, Mak	Greek
Cruz, F.	Mexican
Curioroni, Giovanni	Italian
Daen, A.	American
Dalzotto, Pietro	Italian
Davis, C. N.	American
Davis, J. F.	Negro
Dellaca, Giocomo	Italian
DeMichelli, Joe	Italian
Dianna, Luigi	Italian
DiCicco, Niclo	Italian
DiPaulo, Guiseppe	Italian

Duica, Romono	Italian
Edgar, Ed	Mexican
English, Arthur	American
Enrico, B.	Italian
Evans, Chas.	Negro
Fabba, Nicolo	Italian
Fanarakis, Michael	Greek
Farriano, Chas	Italian
Farrina, John	Italian
Fauri, Geo.	Italian
Fideli, A.	Italian
Foglia, Bart	Italian
Gabrelli, Anselmo	Italian
Gallegos, Dan	Mexican
Ganotti, Gio	Italian
Garcia, Felipe	Mexican
Garzanillo, Attilio	Italian
Gatti, Killo	Italian
Gelas, Geo.	Greek
Gianerelli, Ernest	Italian
Giganti, Camello	Italian
Giordani, Umberto	Italian
Giovanni, Antonio	Italian
Giovanni, Frederico	Italian
Grimaldo, Pietro	Italian
Gubelick, Gabriel	Bohemian
Guiatto, Luigi	Italian
Gulvas, Mihaly	Slav
Gunnoe, J. C.	American
Hicks, C. I.	Negro
Huerena, A.	Mexican
Iconome, Demetrius	Greek
Jan, John B.	French
Janos, John	Hungarian
Jessor, John	Russian
Johnson, Walter	Negro
Katis, Gust	Greek
Kiefer, Jacob	Hungarian

Kinter, Joe	Slav
Kriner, S. J.	American
Kluckinsky, Wm.	Russian
Ladis, Vassilias	Greek
Ladurini, Guiseppe	Italian
Laird, James	American
Lardi, Tony	Italian
Lindsay, Jas.	American
Littlejohn, Robt.	American
Locci, Atilio	Italian
Loger, Ben	American
Lolli, Gaetano	Italian
Lopakis, Magus	Greek
Lopez, B.	Mexican
Lori, Guiseppe (#335)	Italian
Lori, Guiseppe (#399)	Italian
Luccini, Paulo	Italian
Mafiola, Chas.	Italian
Magglis, Vassos	Greek
Mahoney, C. E.	American
Makris, Cost.	Greek
Makris, Geo.	Greek
Mandato, Francisco	Italian
Marchetti, Baldo	Italian
Marez, Fidencio	Mexican
Marinucci, Luigi	Italian
Martinelli, John	Italian
Martinelli, Victor	Italian
Mascognon, Angelo	Italian
Mascognon, Giacomo	Italian
Mati, Frank	Italian
Maxey, J. W.	American
Mazzoli, Aurelia	Italian
Mazzoni, Adamo	Italian
McCutcheon, Iva	Scotch
McDermott, Wm.	Irish
McDonald, Alex	American
McGraw, J. W.	American

McLennon, Thos.	American
McShane, H. P.	American
Melone, Aristede	Italian
Menopace, Allino	Italian
Mercer, Jas.	American
Merlotti, Frank	Italian
Merner, Harry	American
Mesini, Ermete	Italian
Mesini, Marino	Italian
Michael, Alex	Greek
Micheletti, Agostnio	Italian
Mifinigaun, Tones	Greek
Mijares, Pedro	Mexican
Miklovcic, Jno.	Slav
Minotaties, Emm	Greek
Montanez, Marcos	Mexican
Montman, Luigi	Italian
Montorsi, Silvio	Italian
Montoya, Felix	Mexican
Montoya, Nestor	Mexican
Montoya, Porfirio	Mexican
Montoya, Val	Mexican
Morgan, Wm.	American
Nardini, O.	Italian
Natali, Antonio	Italian
Nava, Guiseppe	Italian
Negrete, Jose	Mexican
Nicolocchi, Nick	Greek
Nizzi, Giovanni	Italian
Ola, Andy	Hungarian
Papas, Cost	Greek
Papas, Makis	Greek
Papas, Strat	Greek
Paperi, Mike	Greek
Parashas, Manon	Greek
Pascetta, Giacomo	Italian
Pascetta, Niclo	Italian
Pascetta, Selvino	Italian

Pascoe, J. J.	American
Pastore, Louis	Italian
Pattison, Thos.	American
Pearce, Joshua	American
Pellegrini, P.	Italian
Pensato, Stefano	Italian
Perez, Lucciano	Mexican
Passetto, Dominic	Italian
Pessetto, Tom	Italian
Pino, Kros	Greek
Piros, Giovanni	Italian
Pland, Joe	Italian
Poretti, Egildo	Italian
Poyser, William	British
Prevost, Sidnev	Italian
Prussing, Herbert	American
Ramuno, Carlo	Italian
Redlich, Frank	American
Redpath, Wm.	American
Reyes, Jesus	Mexican
Ribera, Juan	Mexican
Rifosco, A.	Italian
Rodriguez, Pedro	Mexican
Rojc, Val	Austrian
Romero, Daniel	Mexican
Romero, Marcelino	Mexican
Romolo, Saturno	Italian
Rounds, John	American
Santi, Angelo	Italian
Santi, Benianio	Italian
Santi, Carlo	Italian
Santi, Dom	Italian
Santi, Egisto	Italian
Santi, Geriomine	Italian
Santi, Luigi	Italian
Santi, Petro	Italian
Santi, Pit Della	Italian
Santi, Raymondo	Italian

Santisteven, M.	Mexican
Saturno, Nick	Italian
Saucedo, Higinio	Mexican
Serafini, Anselmo	Italian
Serrano, Joe	Mexican
Sexot, John	Greek
Short, McKinley	American
Silvio, Monfredino	Italian
Simoncini, Enrico	Italian
Sitko, Fritz	American
Sporer, Pete	Slav
Sporer, Sebastian	Slav
Stafford, Frank	American
Stark, Joe	Pole
Stavakis, Polikronis	Greek
Subart, Jakob	Slav
Tassi, Dom	Italian
Tollerc, Guiseppi	Italian
Tomasi, Giacomo	Italian
Tomasi, Pietro	Italian
Torok, Frank	Hungarian
Trujillo, Juan	Mexican
Tumen, Wm.	Slav
Tunney, Peter	American
Ulibarri, Patricio	Mexican
Upton, L.P.	American
Vallette, Ernest	Italian
Vegniti, Cesare	Italian
Velasco, Vic	Mexican
Vidalakis, Antonios	Greek
Wesley, Henry	Negro
Williams, Geo. H.	Negro
Williams, J.	American
Wilmoth, Frank	American
Wright, J. H.	American
Zacayinno, Camillo	Italian
Zamboni, Alcide	Italian
Zamboni, Duile	Italian

Zamboni, Narcisco	Italian
Zandi, Andre	Italian
Zefferini, B.	Italian

Note: The names above are listed exactly as they appeared in the second annual *Report of the State Mine Inspector of New Mexico* in 1913 but with three additions: Greek miner Nick Arhondakis and the two rescue men, James Laird and William Poyser. In some cases, the spelling of the names differs from elsewhere in the book.

Source: *Report of the State Mine Inspector of New Mexico*, 1913.

KILLED IN THE EXPLOSION OF
FEBRUARY 8, 1923

Aguilar, Alex	American
Alamillo, Anacledo	American
Alamillo, Marcial	Mexican
Archuleta, Julian	American
Arvis, Nick	Greek
Barranco, Jesus	Mexican
Bonaventura, Frenche	Italian
Briselli, Luigi	Italian
Capen, Louis	Montenegro
Cartazar, Alonzo	Mexican
Cassai, Luigi	Italian
Cenotto, Burley	American
Charette, George	American
Chavez, Pat	American
Cordova, Panfilo	Mexican
Cortez, Joe	Mexican
Costa, Christ P.	Italian
Cruz, Juan	Mexican
Cursi, Nazzarene	Italian
Dallas, John	Greek
Davies, William S.	American
De Abila, Felix	Mexican
DeLaLus, Manuel	Mexican
Delost, Joe	Austrian
Dominguez, Julian	American
Duke, Carl	American
Duran, Gregorio	Mexican
English, Albert	American
English, Albert E.	American
Estes, Clifton C.	American
Fipel, E. C.	American
Galderian, Gabino	Mexican

Gallegos, Fermin	Mexican
Gardea, Feliz	Mexican
Gasparac, Matt	Austrian
Gatti, Gennarion	Italian
Gatti, Oderino	Italian
Geromino, Antonio	Italian
Ghiboukis, Evagelos P.	Greek
Gomez, Cruz	Mexican
Gomez, Isadora	Mexican
Gomez, Santiago	Mexican
Gonzales, Andrey	Mexican
Gonzales, Leandro	American
Graves, Earl	American
Green, J. Austin	American
Gsyowich, Mike	Montenegro
Guesseppe, Tomasi	Unknown
Herrerra, Higinio	Mexican
Holmes, W. R.	American
Howard, James	American
Janakas, John	Greek
Kallas, Georgia	Greek
Kapich, Mike	Montenegro
Kapisch, Pete	Austrian
Karamougis, John	Greek
Kemp, Martin	Austrian
Kerr, Alex	American
Kobano, Anton	Russian
Lawson, William H.	American
Leeming, George W.	American
Liguzos, George	Greek
Lira, Anton	Italian
Litchford, Claud	American
Lorenzo, Jim	Italian
Marachino, Gios	American
Marez, Jesus	American
Maricich, Rode	Austrian
Markis, Geo.	Greek
Marlar, Ben	American

Masetas, Jose Anastacio	American
Masiar, Weneslado	Mexican
McNeish, Thomas	American
Mondregon, J. A.	Mexican
Montoya, Antonio	American
Morrison, Harry	American
Mullins, Ben H.	American
Nardini, Frank	Italian
Neca, Carlo	American
Oblock, Tony	American
Palumbo, Angelo	Italian
Papas, Floryan	Austrian
Papas, Nick	Greek
Payhas, George K.	American
Pelligrini, Baldo	American
Perovich, Nick	American
Pinedo, Juan	Mexican
Pokorn, Jozef	Austrian
Retsias, Nick J.	Greek
Rodriguez, Cruz	Mexican
Romero, Franicisco	Mexican
Rosales, Miguel	Mexican
Rounika, Frank	Austrian
Santa, Pacifico	Italian
Santilla, Pete	American
Scantillis, Antonios	Greek
Scopolitis, Criss	Greek
Scopolitis, Gust	Greek
Sena, Ben	American
Simpson, Aaron	American
Stamos, Paul	Greek
Stevovich, Mike	Montenegro
Stoynoff, John	American
Tomasino, Frank	Italian
Torres, Martio	Mexican
Tossi, Ernesto	Italian
Trujillo, Al	American
Trujillo, Fred	American

Trujillo, Roy	American
Valesquez, Marselino	Mexican
Valpando, Fileberto	American
Volanis, Nick	Greek
Volanovich, Ellis	Montenegro
Vucinich, Pete	Montenegro
Wislon, John	American
Ybarra, Manuel	Mexican
Ybarra, Manuel R.	Mexican
Ybarra, Secundino	Mexican
Zanoni, Tony	Italian
Zoani, Alesandro	Italian

Source: *Twelfth Annual Report of the State Inspector of Coal Mines to the Governor of New Mexico*, 1923.

Chapter 1

It was the impossible: "Death List in Stag Canon Mine Disaster Reaches an Appalling Total," *Albuquerque Morning Journal*, October 24, 1913, 1.

High-capacity fans: *Report of the Mine Inspector for the Territory of New Mexico* (annual: Washington, DC: GPO, 1899–1911) 1909, 17; *Report of the Mine Inspector, 1910*, 22.

Such was the reputation: *Report of the Mine Inspector*, 1905, 17; "Southwestern Buys Northeastern," *El Paso Herald*, May 19, 1905, 1.

On the afternoon: "Thomas H. O'Brien, Mining Leader, Dies," *Arizona Republic*, June 26, 1947, 1.

Around 3:00 p.m.: "Death Gathers Rich Harvest at Dawson," *Raton Range*, October 24, 1913, 1.

O'Brien activated: "Death List in Stag Canon," 1.

Undeterred, O'Brien: "Death List in Stag Canon," 1, 4.

Time was not on their side: "Explosion in Dawson Coal Mine Entombs Two Hundred and Eighty Men," *Albuquerque Morning Journal*, October 23, 1913, 1.

O'Brien was a beacon of hope: "Death List in Stag Canon," 4.

James "J. C." Roberts: "Explosion," 1.

Rushing to a mine disaster: *Fourteenth Biennial Report of the State Coal Mine Inspector* (Denver: Smith-Brooks Printing Co., 1909–1910), 154; J. C. Roberts, "Cokedale Explosion" report, February 9, 1911, 1, https://usminedisasters.miningquiz. com/saxsewell/cokedale_1911.pdf; *Annual Report of the State Coal Mine Inspector of Wyoming* (Cheyenne: Wyoming Labor Journal, 1912), 8.

Roberts and his team: "Death List in Stag Canon," 1, 4.

For some families: "Death List in Stag Canon," 1, 4.

Dr. James Douglas: "Death List in Stag Canon," 1, 4.

Douglas was no bean-counting figurehead: Carlos A. Schwantes, *Vision & Enterprise: Exploring the History of Phelps Dodge Corporation* (Tucson: University of Arizona Press, 2000), 10–12.

Still, the long train ride: "Death List Expected to be 263 at Dawson Mine—23 are Rescued Alive," *Santa Fe New Mexican*, October 24, 1913, 1, 4.

This wasn't the first visit: "Dawson Death Toll Stands at 263 with 61 Bodies Recovered," *Albuquerque Morning Journal*, October 25, 1913, 1.

Both arrived just in time: "Death List Expected," 1.

Town Supervisor Thaddeus "T. L." Kinney: "Explosion," 1; "Refuse to Allow Union Official to Stay in Dawson," *Waco Morning News*, October 25, 1913, 6.

That's precisely what happened: "Refuse," 6.

Later, the *United*: "Property Laws and Human Rights," *United Mine Workers Journal* 25, no. 33 (December 24, 1914): 4.

Rees H. Beddow: *Report of the State Mine Inspector of New Mexico* (annual: Gallup, NM, 1912–1950), 1913, 34.

The fifty-four-year-old inspector: *Report of the State Mine Inspector*, 1913, 7.

Beddow did flag: *Report of the State Mine Inspector*, 1913, 7.

Beddow was a hundred miles away: "Near Three Hundred Men Meet Death in Flaming Mine at Dawson," *Albuquerque Evening Herald*, October 23, 1913, 1; "Coroner's Inquest Report," November 15, 1913, 4, Freeport-McMoRan collection.

Governor William C. McDonald: "William Calhoun McDonald," *National Governors Association*, https://www.nga.org/governor/william-calhoun-mcdonald; "New Mexico Will Render Whatever Aid Is Necessary," *Albuquerque Morning Journal*, October 24, 1913, 1.

The American Red Cross: "New Mexico Will Render," 1; "Death List in Stag Canon," 1.

Both offers were appreciated: Letter from Walter Douglas to Italian Consul General Oreste da Vella, December 21, 1913, Freeport-McMoRan collection; letter from Walter Douglas to Austro-Hungarian consul Dr. John Schwegel, November 1, 1913.

Mine Superintendent William McDermott: S. Tellier, *Blood and Coal*, June 7, 2007, 4.

McDermott was still in the mine: "Bodies of McDermott, M'Shane Recovered," *Albuquerque Morning Journal*, October 27, 1913, 1.

Ultimately, the official death toll: "Fire Adds Horror and Checks Work of Rescue in Dawson Mine," *Albuquerque Morning Journal*, October 26, 1913, 1; *Report of the State Mine Inspector*, 1913, 5, 13–15.

Three weeks after: "Coroner's Inquest Report," 1.

To determine: "Coroner's Inquest Report," 2.

Chapter 2

I went sometimes: Delphine Dawson Wilson, *John Barkley Dawson: Pioneer, Cattleman, Rancher* (Self-published, 1997), 148.

J. B. Dawson was born: Wilson, *John Barkley Dawson*, 1; Carol Ruth (Anderson) Dawson, *Dawsons in the Revolutionary War (and Their Descendants)*, Volume 2 (Eau Claire, WI: Genealogical Department of the Church of Jesus Christ of Latter-Day Saints, 1983), 300.

As recounted by his granddaughter: Wilson, *John Barkley Dawson*, 2.

After spending six years: Wilson, *John Barkley Dawson*, 3.

Near the end of the decade: Patricia A. Etter, "Effect of the California Gold Rush," *Encyclopedia of Arkansas*, last updated December 21, 2021, https://encyclopediaofarkansas.net/entries/effect-of-the-california-gold-rush-4211.

These prospectors: Wilson, *John Barkley Dawson*, 4.

That turned out to be Rough and Ready: Wilson, *John Barkley Dawson*, 5; Keri Brenner, "The Great Republic of Rough and Ready Rejoins Union after 3-Month 'Secession' in 1850," *Union* (Grass Valley, CA), September 21, 2014, https://www.theunion.com/news/local-news/the-great-republic-of-rough-and-ready-rejoins-union-after-3-month-secession-in-1850; "The Great Republic," webpage, Rough and Ready Chamber of Commerce, https://www.roughandreadychamber.com/our-history/the-great-republic.html.

The Dawson family's stay: Wilson, *John Barkley Dawson*, 9.

The California Gold Rush: Wilson, *John Barkley Dawson*, 5.

Few details exist: Wilson, *John Barkley Dawson*, 9, 145.

That the trip was a financial success: Wilson, *John Barkley Dawson*, 15–16.

By this time: Wilson, *John Barkley Dawson*, 18–19.

That cattle drive: Gene Lamm, "Dawson, Goodnight and the Great American Cattle Drives," November 2017, 3, Village of Cimarron, http://www.cimarronnm.com/uploads/2/3/9/7/23975243/dawson-goodnight_nov_2017.pdf.

Dawson met the woman: Wilson, *John Barkley Dawson*, 25.

John was thirty years old: Wilson, *John Barkley Dawson*, 26.

In the aftermath: Wilson, *John Barkley Dawson*, 26–27.

The only record of his service: Wilson, *John Barkley Dawson*, 28–29.

Based on Sumners's published account: Wilson, *John Barkley Dawson*, 28–29.

Sumners's account: Wilson, *John Barkley Dawson*, 29.

Shortly after partnering: Wilson, *John Barkley Dawson*, 41–42, 48.

The search for wife No. 3: Wilson, *John Barkley Dawson*, 51.

Dawson picked up a Baptist magazine: Wilson, *John Barkley Dawson*, 51–52.

No doubt many women: Jeanne Wilkins Wilde, *Lavinia* (Lincoln, NE: iUniverse, 2005), 13; Wilson, *John Barkley Dawson*, 52.

Still, they corresponded: Wilson, *John Barkley Dawson*, 54. The station agent was mistaken when referring to Lavinia's "mother," who had died when Lavinia was young.

The pair's morning visit: Wilson, *John Barkley Dawson*, 54.

'I went as did Rebecca of old': Wilson, *John Barkley Dawson*, 54.

Once Lavinia reached the Dawson ranch: Wilson, *John Barkley Dawson*, 57–58.

Lavinia not only stayed: Wilde, *Lavinia*, 43, 45, 47, 52, 59, 61.

But Lavinia did much more: Wilson, *John Barkley Dawson*, 58–59.

Dawson was just a boy: William A. Keleher, *The Maxwell Land Grant* (Albuquerque: University of New Mexico Press, 1984), 13, 18–20, 42–43.

Enter Dawson: Keleher, *Maxwell Land Grant*, 143–44; Wilson, *John Barkley Dawson*, 41.

Fifteen months later: Keleher, *Maxwell Land Grant*, 83–84, 115, 118.

By this time: Keleher, *Maxwell Land Grant*, 143; *Maxwell Land Grant Co. v. Dawson*, 151 U.S. 586 (1894).

The company had no issue: Wilson, *John Barkley Dawson*, 82.

In 1892: Keleher, *Maxwell Land Grant*, 143–45; *Maxwell Land Grant Co. v. Dawson*; "Court Cases," *Las Vegas Daily Optic*, May 27, 1896, 4.

Dawson retained ownership: Keleher, *Maxwell Land Grant*, 145.

For Dawson and his family: Wilson, *John Barkley Dawson*, 110–11, 118–19.

Ironically, Dawson soon realized: Wilson, *John Barkley Dawson*, 142.

John and Lavinia: "Former Owner Unnerved. Lives at Ocean Park," *Los Angeles Times*, October 30, 1913, 9.

I have been greatly distressed: "Former Owner Unnerved."

On December 27, 1918: Wilson, *John Barkley Dawson*, 143; Wilde, *Lavinia*, 231.

Chapter 3

This property at Dawson: "New Mexico Coal Mines Working Full Capacity," *Albuquerque Morning Journal*, March 14, 1904, 5.

Even before Phelps, Dodge: New Mexico Secretary of State, Corporations and Business Services, Dawson Fuel Company, incorporation papers, June 12, 1901, https://portal.sos.state.nm.us/BFS/online/corporationbusinesssearch/CorporationBusinessInformation, s.v. "Dawson Fuel Company."

Dawson Fuel dumped its first: *Report of the Mine Inspector for the Territory of New Mexico to the Secretary of the Interior* (annual: Washington, DC: GPO, 1899–1911), 1903, 58–59 ; Vernon J. Glover, *El Paso and Southwestern Railroad System* (Upland, CA: Southern Pacific Historical & Technical Society, 2021), 80–82.

Something else was taking root: *Report of the Mine Inspector*, 1905, 18.

Sheridan may have missed: *Report of the Mine Inspector*, 1905, 19.

By 1905, 125 ovens: *Report of the Mine Inspector*, 1905, 17–18, 57, 61–62; Carlos A. Schwantes, *Vision & Enterprise: Exploring the History of Phelps Dodge Corporation* (Tucson: University of Arizona Press, 2000), 101.

On September 4, 1903: *Report of the Mine Inspector*, 1904, 13.

For the next twelve hours: "Coal Mine Fire," *Albuquerque Weekly Citizen,* September 12, 1903, 8.

After the explosion: *Report of the Mine Inspector,* 1904, 13.

W. R. Martin: "No Lives Were Lost," *El Paso Daily Times,* September 11, 1903, 5.

On September 17: *Report of the Mine Inspector,* 1904, 14–15.

The next morning: *Report of the Mine Inspector,* 1904, 15.

By the time Sheridan: *Report of the Mine Inspector,* 1904, 15; "Joe [sic] Sheridan to Investigate Coal Mine Fire at Dawson," *Albuquerque Weekly Citizen,* September 12, 1903, 5; "Disastrous Mine Fire at Dawson," *Albuquerque Morning Journal,* September 12, 1903, 3.

Sheridan didn't buy: *Report of the Mine Inspector,* 1904, 13.

Dawson Fuel's emergence: Paige W. Christiansen, *The Story of Mining in New Mexico* (Socorro: New Mexico Bureau of Mines & Mineral Resources, 1974), 26, 39.

But it wasn't until the expansion: Richard W. Kimball, "Uncle Dick Wootton's Toll Road to Raton Pass," *Territorial News,* October 17, 2018, 1, 10.

In 1865, Wootton: Kimball, "Uncle Dick Wootton's," 1, 4, 10, 16; Howard Bryan, "Off the Beaten Path," *Albuquerque Tribune,* July 13, 1959, A-10; Milton W. Callan, "Las Vegas, New Mexico—The Town That Wouldn't Gamble," *Las Vegas Daily Optic,* April 5, 1962, 8.

Instead, he asked for and received: Kimball, "Uncle Dick Wootton's," 4; Bob Wiedrich, "A Lesson from Uncle Dick," *Chicago Tribune,* January 13, 1982, Section 1, 15; "Funeral Services for Miss Wootton," *Las Vegas Daily Optic,* March 9, 1957, 1.

The AT&SF: David F. Myrick, *New Mexico's Railroads: A Historical Survey* (Albuquerque: University of New Mexico Press, Revised Edition, 1990).

For some, hauling coal: *Report of the Mine Inspector,* 1907, 16.

Charles B. Eddy's: Glover, *El Paso and Southwestern,* 62; Vernon J. Glover, *Logging Railroads of the Lincoln National Forest, New Mexico* (Albuquerque: Windy Point Press, 1984), 10–11.

While Eddy had better luck: Glover, *El Paso and Southwestern,* 67–68; *Report of the Mine Inspector,* 1904, 56.

Enter Phelps, Dodge & Co.: Schwantes, *Vision & Enterprise,* 100–1, 139.

When Charles Eddy approached: Myrick, *New Mexico's Railroads,* 95; "E.P-N.E. System Sold," *Alamogordo Daily News,* May 20, 1905, 1.

When the sale closed: Schwantes, *Vision & Enterprise,* 101.

Phelps Dodge could not: Robert Glass Cleland, *A History of Phelps Dodge, 1834–1950* (New York: Alfred A. Knopf, 1952), 149.

Three years later: Schwantes, *Vision & Enterprise,* xxi.

Chapter 4

Dawson now has a splendid hotel: "$25,000 Theatre for People of Dawson Camp," *Albuquerque Morning Journal*, December 23, 1906, 2.

To call Dawson a "coal camp": D. R. Lane, "Dawson, New Mexico: Stag Canyon Fuel Company," in *New Mexico: The Land of Opportunity: Official Data on the Resources and Industries of New Mexico—the Sunshine State* (Albuquerque: Press of the Albuquerque Morning Journal, 1915), Part Two, 50–58, 50; Stephen Zimmer and Gene Lamb, *Images of America: Colfax County* (Charleston, SC: Arcadia, 2015), 101; "Briefly Told," *Dodge City Journal*, August 25, 1921, 4.

None of this was by accident: James B. Allen, *The Company Town in the American West* (Norman: University of Oklahoma Press, 1966), 4.

While Phelps Dodge knew little: Carlos A. Schwantes, *Vision & Enterprise: Exploring the History of Phelps Dodge Corporation* (Tucson: University of Arizona Press, 2000), 39–40.

Still, it would be a dozen: Robert Glass Cleland, *A History of Phelps Dodge, 1834–1950* (New York: Alfred A. Knopf, 1952), 91–97; Thomas Sterry Hunt, James Douglas, and James Oscar Stewart, *The Hunt and Douglas Process for Extracting Copper from Its Ores* (Boston: A. A. Kingman, 1876), 33.

At that time, William E. Dodge Jr.: Schwantes, *Vision & Enterprise*, 10–11.

Coincidentally, shortly before: Schwantes, *Vision & Enterprise*, 10–11; Roberta Watt, "History of Morenci, Arizona," (PhD diss., University of Arizona, 1956), 24–25.

The company's introduction: Dwight E. Woodbridge, "Arizona and Sonora: The Clifton-Morenci-Metcalf District," *Engineering and Mining Journal*, 82, no. 2 (July 14, 1906): 50; Watt, "History of Morenci," 48; Watt, citing Jennie Parks Ringgold, *Frontier Days in the Southwest* (San Antonio: The Naylor Co., 1952), 50.

Not long after Phelps Dodge: Woodbridge, "Arizona and Sonora," 50. Mills would step away briefly to fight alongside Teddy Roosevelt and the Rough Riders in Cuba during the Spanish-American War.

Embellished? Perhaps: Watt, "History of Morenci," 49–52.

Phelps Dodge adhered: Schwantes, *Vision & Enterprise*, 115.

Phelps Dodge didn't have to wait: Ralph Emerson Twitchell, ed., *Leading Facts of New Mexican History*, Volume 3 (Cedar Rapids, IA: Torch Press, 1917), 93.

Perhaps nowhere was this: "$25,000 Theatre," 2; "Dawson's New Theater Ready," *Albuquerque Morning Journal*, August 5, 1907, 5.

On September 28, 1907: "Pretty New Theater at Dawson Opened," *Santa Fe New Mexican*, September 30, 1907, 3.

Phelps Dodge didn't move as quickly: *Report of the Mine Inspector*, 1903, 12; *1912 Annual Report* (New York: Phelps, Dodge & Company, 1912), 8.

Two years later: Advertisement, *Dawson News*, January 24, 1924, 5; advertisement, *Dawson News*, September 6, 1923, 7.

For Amelia Lopez García: Amelia Lopez García, unpublished manuscript, 1987, typescript.

One of the first things: Schwantes, *Vision & Enterprise*, 131; *Report of the Mine Inspector for the Territory of New Mexico to the Secretary of the Interior* (annual: Washington, DC: GPO, 1899–1911), 1906, 17; *Report of the Mine Inspector*, 1909, 23.

Under the direction: Twitchell, *Leading Facts*, 95.

Little of this would have mattered: *Report of the Mine Inspector*, 1909, 23.

None of this would have been possible: [*Second Annual*] *Report of the State Mine Inspector of New Mexico* (annual: Gallup, NM, 1912–1950), 1913, 26.

One other development: *Report of the Mine Inspector*, 1910, 21–22.

Word of the rescue station and training: "Producers See Explosion of Mine," *Pittsburgh Post-Gazette*, October 31, 1911, 6; Charles L. Wright, "The First National Mine-Safety Demonstration: Study of a Real Mine Explosion." *Scientific American*, December 2, 1911, https://www.scientificamerican.com/article/the-first-national-mine-safety-demo.

Chapter 5

So and so: Henry Pratt Fairchild, *Greek Immigration to the United States*. (New Haven: Yale University Press, 1911), 224, as cited in Peter C. Moskos and Charles C. Moskos, *Greek Americans: Struggle and Success* (New York: Routledge, 2017), 11.

Eugene Santi must have been: Ship manifest, Ellis Island Foundation, https://heritage.statueofliberty.org/passenger-details/czoxMzoiOTAxMjMyMDAyNTMyMCI7/czo4OiJtYW5pZmVzdCI7.

What is known is that: Manlio Badiali, email correspondence with author, January 17, 2021; *Report of the Mine Inspector for the Territory of New Mexico to the Secretary of the Interior* (annual: Washington, DC: GPO, 1899–1911), 1910, 18.

Italian immigrants in search of work: Vincenza Scarpaci, *The Journey of Italians in America* (Gretna, LA: Pelican, 2008), 13.

The Santis of Fiumalbo: Badiali, email correspondence with author.

In Italy, the unification: Scarpaci, *Journey of Italians in America*, 11–13, 27; *The 1908 Messina Earthquake: 100-Year Retrospective*, Risk Management Solutions, 2008, 3–7.

Like its European neighbor: Moskos and Moskos, *Greek Americans*, 11.

Two thousand Greeks: Moskos and Moskos, *Greek Americans*, 11, 15; Giula Meloni and Johan F. M. Swinnen, *Standards, Tariffs and Trade: The Rise and Fall of the Raisin Trade between Greece and France in the Late 19th Century and the Definition of Wine*,

Center for Institutions and Economic Performance & Department of Economics, LICOS Discussion Paper No. 386, University of Leuven, Belgium, January 2017, 5–6, https://papers.ssrn.com/sol3/papers.cfm?abstract_id=2919311.

Seraphim G. Canoutas: Moskos and Moskos, *Greek Americans*, 16.

While each European nation: "Immigration to the United States, 1851–1900," timeline, Library of Congress, https://www.loc.gov/classroom-materials/united-states-history-primary-source-timeline/rise-of-industrial-america-1876-1900/immigration-to-united-states-1851-1900; Vaclav Smil, "Crossing the Atlantic," *IEEE Spectrum*, April 2018, 23.

The long ocean voyage: Ronald H. Bayor, *Encountering Ellis Island: How European Immigrants Entered America* (Baltimore: Johns Hopkins University Press, 2014), 20–25.

Morris Abraham Schneider: "Oral History of Morris Schneider Remembering Being on the Steamship *Rotterdam*," Ellis Island Oral History Collection, October 14, 2020, https://www.nps.gov/elis/learn/education/oral-history-ei-116.htm.

Stories such as these: US Congress, Senate, US Immigration Commission, *Steerage Conditions; Importation and Harboring of Women for Immoral Purposes; Immigrant Homes and Aid Societies; Immigrant Banks*, 61st Cong., 3rd sess., December 13, 1909, 2, 23.

While conditions varied: US Congress, *Steerage Conditions*, 23.

Georgios V. Makris was one: Ship manifest, Ellis Island Foundation, https://heritage.statueofliberty.org/passenger-details/czoxMjoiMTAxNTg1MTMwMTgxIjs=/czo4OiJtYW5pZmVzdCI7.

The Makris brothers: Emanuel G. Cassotis, *The Karpathian Presence in America (1872–2012)* (Rhodes, Greece: Stegi Grammaton ke Technon Dodecanesou, 2012), 23.

What we know about Georgios's trip: Georgios Makris to Stamatina Makris, January 19, 1913; January 24, 1913. All letters in this group are from the family collection and have been translated from Greek.

Stamatina didn't hear from her husband: Georgios Makris to Stamatina Makris, March 7, 1913.

Georgios's fourth and final letter: Georgios Makris to Stamatina Makris, September 18, 1913.

There were other Karpathians: Cassotis, *Karpathian Presence*, 91–95.

Phelps Dodge depended heavily: *Annual Report, Territory*, 1910, 18.

Perhaps no American: Graduate records, Brown University, 1906; *Brown Alumni Monthly*, October 1914, 81.

Upton, the second-oldest: *Brown Alumni Monthly*, October 1914, 81; "Hiram D. Upton: Found Dead in His Room at Home Today," *Daily Mirror and American*, December 1, 1900.

Three years later: "Hiram D. Upton."

By the time his forty-one-year-old father: Graduation program, Manchester High School Class of 1902, 3, Manchester Historic Association, Manchester, New Hampshire; Brown University Yearbook, *Liber Brunensis*, 1906, 129.

But a whiff of phosgene gas: D. Bradley Upton, *Homestead Daze in Burro Canyon* (Self-published, 1986), 6; *Brown Alumni Monthly*, October 1914, 81.

When Upton arrived: *Brown Alumni Monthly*, October 1914, 81.

As at Brown: Graduate records, Brown University, 1906.

Life out West: Upton, *Homestead Daze*, 66.

A different encounter: Bob Sexton, email correspondence with author, June 3, 2019; *Brown Alumni Monthly*, October 1914, 81.

Chapter 6

The first recorded fatal mine accident: Karen Stein Daniel, *New Mexico Mining Fatalities and Accidents, 1894–1925* (Albuquerque: New Mexico Genealogical Society, 2001), 21.

The White Ash Mine: "White Ash Mine Horror," *Santa Fe Daily New Mexican*, February 28, 1895, 1.

Newspaper reports sketched: "Killed!" *Albuquerque Morning Journal*, February 28, 1895, 1.

Coincidentally, John W. Fleming: *Report of the United States Coal Mine Inspector for the Territory of New Mexico to the Secretary of the Interior for the Fiscal Year Ending June 30, 1895* (Washington, DC: GPO, 1895), 24.

Before Duggan returned: *Report of the United States Coal Mine Inspector*, 24.

Fleming wasted little time: *Report of the United States Coal Mine Inspector*, 24.

While mine explosions would: Albert H. Fay, *Coal Mine Fatalities in the United States, 1870–1914* (Washington, DC: GPO, 1916), 14–15.

First and foremost: Daniel, *New Mexico Mining Fatalities*, 22–24.

Did all these men have to die?: Joseph A. Holmes, "Report of the Director of Bureau of Mines," *Mining and Engineering World* 42, no. 3 (January 16, 1915), 137.

That sentiment was shared: US Congress, Senate, *A Federal Mining Commission Address by John Randolph Haynes, M.D. before the Joint Session of the American Economic Association and the Association for Labor Legislation at Washington, D.C., December 30, 1911*, 62nd Cong., 2nd sess. (Washington, DC: GPO, 1912), 3.

To make his point: US Congress, *Federal Mining Commission Address*, 3–5.

Haynes called upon Congress: US Congress, *Federal Mining Commission Address*, 10–12.

The federal government: US Department of the Interior, Bureau of Mines,

United States Mining Statutes Annotated: Part I, Sections and Statutes Relating to Metalliferous and Coal Mining, by J. W. Thompson, Bulletin 94 (Washington, DC: GPO, 1915), 802–803.

What the law did not do: James Whiteside, *Regulating Danger: The Struggle for Mine Safety in the Rocky Mountain Coal Industry* (Lincoln: University of Nebraska Press, 1990), 64.

Nearly two decades would pass: "Mine Disasters in the United States," United States Mine Rescue Association, https://usminedisasters.miningquiz.com/saxsewell/historical.htm; Whiteside, *Regulating Danger*, 99.

The New Mexico territory's: Whiteside, *Regulating Danger*, 62.

These two and a half pages: Whiteside, *Regulating Danger*, 110–11.

Perhaps the biggest obstacle: US Coal Commission, *Report of the United States Coal Commission, Vol. 3: Bituminous Coal: Detailed Labor and Engineering Studies* (Washington, DC: GPO, 1925), 1312.

Of these tasks: Fay, *Coal Mine Fatalities*, 14–15.

By all measures: "Mine Disasters in the United States."

Horrific incidents such as these: "Coal Fatalities for 1900 through 2020," Mine Safety and Health Administration, https://arlweb.msha.gov/stats/centurystats/coalstats.asp.

In December 1907: "A Modern Day Miracle: 1907 Monongah, West Virginia," Saint Nicholas Center, https://www.stnicholascenter.org/who-is-st-nicholas/stories-legends/modern-miracles/miracles-united-states/monongah.

My dad was supposed to be in the mine: Tara Tuckwiller, "Monongah Disaster: 100 Years Later," *Charleston Gazette Mail*, December 7, 2007, https://www.wvgazettemail.com/news/special_reports/monongah-disaster-100-years-later/article_dac7e886-fbd7-560e-b2ee-c3a8803120fb.html.

Two weeks after Monongah: John R. Ball, "Explosion in Pittsburgh Coal Company's Mine at Jacob's Creek, Westmoreland County, Kills Nearly 200 Men and Imprisons Scores of Others behind Impassable Burning Barriers; Open Lamp Reported Cause; Rescue Parties Hard at Work; Harrowing Scenes Witnessed," *Pittsburgh Post*, December 20, 1907, 1–2.

Although the days: "Julian Calendar," *Encyclopedia Britannica*, https://www.britannica.com/science/Julian-calendar.

That to-day's disaster: Ball, "Explosion in Pittsburgh," 1–2.

During a December 2007 service: "Centennial of the Miracle of St. Nicholas: Jacobs Creek," Saint Nicholas Center, https://www.stnicholascenter.org/who-is-st-nicholas/stories-legends/modern-miracles/miracles-united-states/modern-miracle/centennial.

Two years later: US Congress, Senate, *A Resolution Designating December 6, 2009, as National Miners Day*, S. Res. 337, 111th Cong., 1st sess, introduced December 3, 2009, https://www.congress.gov/bill/111th-congress/senate-resolution/337/text.

Chapter 7

The scenes around the mine: "Two Thousand Heroic Men," 1.

From the moment: "Black Damp is Believed to Have Caused Horror; Little Probability of Rescuing Any of the Victims," *Albuquerque Morning Journal*, October 23, 1913, 1; "Two Thousand Heroic Men Work Desperately in Effort to Save Possible Survivors in Gas Filled Depths 3,000 Feet from Surface," *Albuquerque Evening Herald*, October 23, 1913, 1.

The sound of the explosion: "Death List in Stag Canon," 1.

There is every reason to believe: "Hope to Take Out Entombed Men Alive," *Albuquerque Morning Journal*, October 23, 1913, 1.

Searle's optimism was echoed: "Wrecked Mine Regarded as Model in Every Way," *Albuquerque Morning Journal*, October 23, 1913, 1.

The first men to arrive: "Explosion in Dawson Coal Mine Entombs Two Hundred and Eighty Men," *Albuquerque Morning Journal*, October 23, 1913, 1.

While the fallen debris: US Department of the Interior, Bureau of Mines, *Black Damp in Mines*, by G. A. Burrell, I. W. Robertson, and G. G. Oberfell, Bulletin 105 (Washington, DC: GPO, 1916), 78; US Department of Commerce, Bureau of Mines, *Gases That Occur in Metal Mines*, by D. Harrington and E. H. Denny, Bulletin 347 (Washington, DC: GPO, 1931), 11.

Adding to the urgency: "Near Three Hundred Men Meet Death in Flaming Mine at Dawson," *Albuquerque Evening Herald*, October 23, 1913, 1; *Report of the Mine Inspector for the Territory of New Mexico* (annual: Washington, DC: GPO, 1899–1911), 1910, 23.

The ventilating fan did not stop: *Report of the State Mine Inspector of New Mexico* (annual: Gallup, NM, 1912–1950), 1913, 6.

Beddow's estimate: "Near Three Hundred," 1.

For the rescuers: US Department of the Interior, Bureau of Mines, *Loss of Life among Wearers of Oxygen Breathing Apparatus*, by G. W. Grove, Information Circular 7279 (Washington, DC, April 1944), 1, 3.

The Dawson-based rescuers: *Report of the Mine Inspector*, 1910, 21–22.

By 2:00 a.m.: "14 Bodies Removed and Seven Miners Found Alive at 2 A.M. Today; Death List Sure to be Appalling," *Albuquerque Morning Journal*, October 23, 1913, 1; "Near Three Hundred," 1; *Report of the State Mine Inspector*, 1913, 6.

While helmeted rescue teams: "Near Three Hundred," 1.

At 3:00 p.m.: "Two Thousand Heroic Men," 1.

It will be two days: "Two Thousand Heroic Men," 1.

Shortly after 5:00 p.m.: "Rescuers Penetrate Far into Mine Which They Find Strewn with Dead; No More Living Men in Workings," *Albuquerque Morning Journal*, October 24, 1913, 1.

An hour later: "Rescuers Penetrate," 1.

If Fernandez ever spoke: "Rescuers Lose Lives in Fruitless Search of Mine," *Lincoln Daily News*, October 24, 1913, 1.

Though they tried: "Refuse to Allow Union Official to Stay in Dawson," *Waco Morning News*, October 25, 1913, 6; Zeese Papanikolas, *Buried Unsung: Louis Tikas and the Ludlow Massacre* (Lincoln: University of Nebraska Press, 1991), 96–98.

Unlike Doyle: Papanikolas, *Buried Unsung*, 96–98.

I was working when there came: "Rescuers Dying in Stag Canon Mine," *Omaha Daily News*, October 24, 1913, 2.

Six months later: Papanikolas, *Buried Unsung*, xvii, 235; Mark Walker, "The Ludlow Massacre: Class, Warfare, and Historical Memory in Southern Colorado," *Historical Archaeology* 37, no. 3 (2003): 69.

Under a smiling October sun: "Death Gathers Rich Harvest at Dawson," *Raton Range*, October 24, 1913, 1.

The savvy wordsmith: "Death Gathers Rich Harvest," 1.

While many newspapers: "Death Gathers Rich Harvest," 1.

Like Fernandez: "Rescuers Dying," 2.

Less is known: "Rescuers Dying," 2.

Marco Nizzi's good fortune: Vivien A. Andrews, *Dawson Coal Mine Cemetery Inscriptions, Dawson, Colfax County, NM*, booklet, 1998.

At 8:00 p.m.: "Death List Expected to be 263 at Dawson Mine—23 are Rescued Alive," *Santa Fe New Mexican*, October 24, 1913, 1.

It was here: *Report of the State Mine Inspector*, 1913, 6.

A government report: *Report of the State Mine Inspector*, 1913, 6; US Department of the Interior, *Loss of Life*, 7.

Neither of these official reports: "Rescuers Lose Lives," 1.

News of the accident: "Death List Expected," 1.

The second government rescue car: "Death List Expected," 1; "History of the Mining Program," National Institute for Occupational Safety and Health, https://www.cdc.gov/niosh/mining/content/history.html.

After being briefed: "Dawson Death Toll Stands at 263 with 61 Bodies Recovered," *Albuquerque Morning Journal*, October 25, 1913, 1.

Both young men were well known: "Death Gathers," 1.

Laird, a month shy: *Report of the Mine Inspector*, 1903, 62.

Later that morning: "Doctors and Nurses Hurry from El Paso to Dawson," *El Paso Herald*, October 23, 1913, 1.

By midafternoon: Western Union telegram from Walter Douglas to A. V. Dye, October 24, 1913, Freeport-McMoRan Collection.

Five days would pass: Walter Douglas to company headquarters, October 29, 1913, Freeport-McMoRan Collection.

The difficulty of bringing out: Walter Douglas to company headquarters, October 29, 1913.

For rescue men still reeling: "Danger is Grave in Dawson Mine," *Albuquerque Evening Herald*, October 25, 1913, 1.

Despite these interruptions: "Dawson Mine's Dead List 263," *Washington Times*, October 25, 1913, 2.

While recovery teams battled: "Fire Adds Horror and Checks Work of Rescue in Dawson Mine," *Albuquerque Morning Journal*, October 26, 1913, 1.

By four days after the explosion: "Dawson Explosion Most Violent in History of Country," *Albuquerque Morning Journal*, October 27, 1913, 1.

On this day: "Dawson Explosion Most Violent," 1.

Coincidentally, the unnamed AP correspondent: "Dawson Explosion Most Violent," 1.

Among those found with him: "M'Shane a Mine Victim," *Baltimore Sun*, October 24, 1913, 16.

Chapter 8

And all through the service: "Dawson Death Toll Stands at 263 with 61 Bodies Recovered," *Albuquerque Morning Journal*, October 25, 1913, 1.

That was the stark response: "Santa Fe Is All Sympathy and Mourning, but Can Do Nothing," *Santa Fe New Mexican*, October 24, 1913, 1.

The first plea went out: "Near Three Hundred Men Meet Death in Flaming Mine at Dawson," *Albuquerque Evening Herald*, October 23, 1913, 1; "Rescuers Lose Lives in Fruitless Search of Mine," *Lincoln Daily News*, October 24, 1913, 1.

Then there was the matter of embalmers: "Hard Work for the Local Undertakers," *Raton Range*, October 31, 1913, 1.

With a steady supply of coffins: *Representative New Mexicans: The National Newspaper Reference Book of the New State Containing Photographs and Biographies of Over Four Hundred Men Residents of New Mexico*, Volume 1 (London: Forgotten Books, 2019 [1912]), 333; *North American Family Histories, 1500–2000* (Provo, Utah: Ancestry. com Operations Inc., 2016), 217–18.

Two days after the explosion: "Dawson Death Toll," 1.

Afterward, the black coffins: "Dawson Death Toll," 1.

George Thomas had a bird's-eye view: "Closing Scenes of Dawson Disaster," *Raton Range*, October 31, 1913; *Report of the Mine Inspector for the Territory of New Mexico* (annual: Washington, DC: GPO, 1899–1911), 1911, 18.

As each body is recovered: "Closing Scenes."

Not all of the dead: "Closing Scenes"; Nathan Dennies, "Green Mount Cemetery," *Baltimore Heritage*, https://explore.baltimoreheritage.org/items/show/80.

Phelps Dodge needed only a few days: Federal Mine Safety and Health Act of 1977, Pub. L. No. 91–173, Section 317 (p), https://arlweb.msha.gov/REGS/ACT/ACT2.HTM#1; Jo. E. Sheridan, "The Conditions at Dawson and Possible Causes of the Appalling Disaster," *Albuquerque Evening Herald*, October 27, 1913, 3.

By October 27: Untitled document, October 27, 1913, Freeport-McMoRan collection.

While small in number: "The African-American Experience in Dawson," Pietro Scarafiotti, January 6, 2018, https://www.facebook.com/groups/556793837833040/search/?q=African-Americans (members-only group); US Census, 1910, 1920, 1950.

Phelps Dodge was eager: Walter Douglas to company headquarters, October 29, 1913, Freeport-McMoRan collection.

While Douglas believed the company's offer: Walter Douglas to company headquarters, October 29, 1913.

That was not the only: T. H. O'Brien to E. E. Ellingwood, December 4, 1913, Freeport-McMoRan collection.

Two months later: Walter Douglas to T. H O'Brien, February 12, 1914, Freeport-McMoRan collection.

Not all settlements: Dr. James Douglas to George Notman, April 28, 1914, Freeport-McMoRan collection.

Despite the challenge: Untitled document, November 13, 1913, Freeport-McMoRan collection.

While settlement talks: T. H. O'Brien to Walter Douglas, January 20, 1915, Freeport-McMoRan collection.

Through it all: Western Union telegram from H. J. Simmons to Walter Douglas, October 22, 1913, Freeport-McMoRan collection.

Chapter 9

She would just keep repeating: Fannie Vozos, author interview, June 11, 2020.

The bodies of Carlo: "Death Toll at Dawson is 263," *Albuquerque Evening Herald*, October 24, 1913, 1; "Identified Dead," *Albuquerque Morning Journal*, October 26, 1913, 1.

For Frank Santi: Walter Santi to Jerry Scanlon, February 28, 2001, Dawson New Mexico Association collection.

Angelo was the youngest: Ship manifest, Ellis Island Foundation, https:// heritage.statueofliberty.org/passenger-details/czoxMjoiMTAwNzQ4MDIwMjE2Ijs= /czo5OiJwYXNzZW5nZXIiOw==; *Report of the State Mine Inspector of New Mexico* (Gallup, NM, 1912–1950), 1913, 15; Manlio Badiali, email correspondence with author, October 25, December 31, 2020.

All told, 133 Italians: Badiali, email correspondence with author; Manlio Badiali, email correspondence with Chuck Speed, Dawson New Mexico Association, March 31, 2014.

It took only a few days: "Twenty one from Modena Died, Dawson Mining Disaster," *Gazzetta dell'Emilia*, October 31, 1913.

Once news of the mine disaster: "Dawson, the Tragedy of the Mine: Modenese Victims in an Explosion Almost a Hundred Years Ago," *Legislative Assembly of the Emilia-Romagna Region*, https://www.assemblea.emr.it/ emilianoromagnolinelmondo/la-consulta/storia-emigrazione/casa-della-memoria-dellemigrazione/sezioni/il-salotto/storie%20di%20emigrazione/stati-uniti/ dawson-la-tragedia-della-miniera.

Villagers rallied around the stricken families: "The Story of the People of Modena Involved in the Tragedy of the Dawson Mine," *Emilia-Romagna Council in the World*, https://www-migrer-org.translate.goog/storie/la-storia-dei-modenesi-coinvolti-nella-tragedia-della-miniera-di-dawson/?_x_tr_sl=it&_x_tr_tl=en&_x_tr_hl=en&_x_tr_pto=sc.

After the explosion: Frank Santi to T. H. O'Brien, May 26, 1914, Freeport-McMoRan collection.

Citing the extreme: Frank Santi to T. H. O'Brien, May 26, 1914.

O'Brien forwarded a copy: T. H. O'Brien to Walter Douglas, June 11, 1914, Freeport-McMoRan collection.

Douglas notified O'Brien: Walter Douglas to T. H O'Brien, June 14, 1914, Freeport-McMoRan collection; Dr. James Douglas to T. H. O'Brien, June 17, 1914, Freeport-McMoRan collection.

The great American mining tragedies: Manlio Badiali, email correspondence with author, December 18, 2020.

Frank Santi would return: Walter Santi, author interview, July 22, 2020.

For Frank, it would get worse: Walter Santi, author interview; Ana Pacheco, "A

Much Maligned Symbol," History in Santa Fe New Mexico, https://historyinsantafe.com/a-much-maligned-symbol/.

Frank visited Dawson one more time: Walter Santi, author interview; Walter Santi to Dawson New Mexico Association, Dawson New Mexico Association collection, February 28, 2001.

In one account: Minas Minaidis, *Reminiscing* (Athens, Greece, 1978), 49–53.

A second version: Emanuel G. Cassotis, *The Karpathian Presence in America (1872–2012)* (Rhodes, Greece: Stegi Grammaton ke Technon Dodecanesou, 2012), 582–83.

Cries and wails: Fannie Vozos, author interview.

So that's [the churchyard] where they went: Fannie Vozos, author interview.

A century later: Transcript, 27th Pan-Karpathian memorial service, Pan-Karpathian Foundation, August 3, 2014.

Because it was summertime: Maria Makris Caputo, author interview, June 15, 2020.

Afterward, Maria's grandmother: Maria Makris Caputo, author interview.

Vasilios G. Makris: "Vasilio G. Vaso Makris," *Star-Ledger*, September 16, 2008; George Makris, author interview, April 9, 2019.

George Makris, his son: George Makris, author interview.

George and his wife: George Makris, author interview.

Lloyd Peter Upton: D. Bradley Upton, *Bradley Upton's Roads & Trails* (Solano, NM: D. B. Upton, 1989), 36.

Given his birth: "Lloyd Upton is Mine Victim," *Manchester Union*, October 30, 1913; "Manchester Boy Killed in Mine," *Manchester Leader*, October 29, 1913.

The original source: "Lloyd Upton is Mine Victim."

Mr. Upton is well remembered here: "Lloyd Upton is Mine Victim." The actual wedding date was January 7, 1913, his graduation year from Brown, 1906.

One final clue: Edward W. Holmes to Louise Prosser Bates, Brown University, June 17, 1914.

Dorothy Lloyd Upton: "Society," *El Reno Daily Democrat*, June 2, 1914, 2; "Solano," *Spanish-American*, October 20, 1917, 4.

Alice remained in California: "Obituaries," *Fresno Bee*, February 4, 1996, B4.

Chapter 10

The mine itself is wrecked: "Declares Somebody Slipped When the Mine Blew Up," *Albuquerque Evening Herald*, October 25, 1913, 1.

Simply put, there are two: Centers for Disease Control and Prevention, National Institute for Occupational Safety and Health, "Coal Mine Explosion

Prevention," CDC website, December 9, 2011, https://www.cdc.gov/niosh/mining/features/coalmineexplosion.html; Denise Chow, "Why Do Coal Mines Explode?" LiveScience website, April 6, 2010. http://www.livescience.com/environment/coal-mines-explosion-100406.html.

This is why the role: *Report of the Mine Inspector for the Territory of New Mexico* (annual: Washington, DC: GPO, 1899–1911), 1909, 25–26.

One of the first recorded: US Department of the Interior, Bureau of Mines, "January 12, 1886; Almy No. 4 Mine, Almy, Wyo.; 13 Killed," in *Historical Summary of Coal-Mine Explosions in the United States, 1810–1958*, by H. B. Humphrey, Bulletin 586 (Washington, DC: GPO, 1960): 13, https://usminedisasters.miningquiz.com/saxsewell/almy_1886.pdf; Phil Roberts, "The Most Dangerous Occupation: The Quest for Safety in Wyoming's Coal Mines," WyoHistory.org, https://www.wyohistory.org/encyclopedia/most-dangerous-occupation-quest-safety-wyomings-coal-mines; Carl Miller, "Miners' Superstitions Are Eventually Overcome," *Herald Democrat* (Leadville, CO), June 19, 2013, https://www.leadvilleherald.com/leadville_life/article_cc23cfa2-d92b-11e2-b29d-001a4bcf6878.html.

Like methane: "Universal Colliery Explosion—Senghenydd—1913," *Northern Mine Research Society*, https://www.nmrs.org.uk/mines-map/accidents-disasters/glamorganshire/universal-colliery-explosion-senghenydd-1913/.

Methane and coal dust: CDC, "Coal Mine Explosion Prevention"; "The World's Worst Coal Mining Disasters," *Mining Technology*, updated October 25, 2021, https://www.mining-technology.com/analysis/feature-world-worst-coal-mining-disasters-china/.

In Dawson: "Dawson Death Toll Stands at 263 with 61 Bodies Recovered," *Albuquerque Morning Journal*, October 25, 1913, 1.

Not everyone bought into: "Declares Somebody Slipped," 1.

Hanraty was no pencil-pushing: Fred W. Dunbar, "Hanraty, Peter (1864–1932)," Oklahoma Historical Society, https://www.okhistory.org/publications/enc/entry.php?entry=HA018; Fred W. Dunbar, "Coal-Mining Strikes," Oklahoma Historical Society, https://www.okhistory.org/publications/enc/entry.php?entry=CO005; Ethan D. Beck, "The Rise and Fall of the Knights of Labor: A Gilded Age Tale," *The Idea of an Essay*, Volume 3, Article 34, 2016, available at: https://digitalcommons.cedarville.edu/idea_of_an_essay/vol3/iss1/34.

There is nothing to this theory: "Declares Somebody Slipped," 1.

Hanraty wasn't the only: *Report of the State Mine Inspector of New Mexico* (annual: Gallup, NM, 1912–1950), 1913, 5, 34.

By the time Beddow: "Dust Was Cause of the Dawson Horror," *Las Vegas Optic*, November 4, 1913, 1.

Three days later: "Miner Who Fired Shot Responsible for Explosion at Dawson," *Albuquerque Morning Journal*, November 8, 1913, 1.

In essence, the miner: "Miner Who Fired Shot."

But all these precautions: "Miner Who Fired Shot."

Not everyone thought: William G. Shepherd, "Eyewitness at the Triangle," *Milwaukee Journal*, March 27, 1911, as cited in Leon Stein, *Out of the Sweatshop: The Struggle for Industrial Democracy* (New York: Quadrangle/New York Times Books, 1977, 188–93).

When Shepherd arrived: "About the Day Book," Library of Congress, https://chroniclingamerica.loc.gov/lccn/sn83045487/.

Writing under the eye-catching: William G. Shepherd, "Was Stag Canon Mine Horror Just Out-and-Out Murder?" *The Day Book*, October 27, 1913, 4–5.

Second, since McDermott: Shepherd, "Was Stag Canon."

Based on his conversations: Shepherd, "Was Stag Canon," 5.

A labor-friendly journalist: John C. Schwegel to Walter Douglas, November 22, 1913, Freeport-McMoRan collection.

Schwegel wrote that McDermott: Schwegel to Douglas.

For his part: T. H. O'Brien to Walter Douglas, December 3, 1913, Freeport-McMoRan collection.

Some theories were a bit: Carl Scholz to H. U. Mudge, November 3, 1913, Freeport-McMoRan collection.

This sensational scheme: Walter Douglas to T. H. O'Brien, November 10, 1913, Freeport-McMoRan collection.

That coal dust was suspected: US Department of the Interior, United States Geological Society, *The Explosibility of Coal Dust*, by George S. Rice, Bulletin 425 (Washington, DC: GPO, 1910), 11.

Still, it would be another eighty years: USDI, "Explosibility," 17.

The road toward enlightenment: USDI, "Explosibility," 24.

In New Mexico: "Mine Disaster at Gallup," *Albuquerque Weekly Citizen*, April 6, 1901.

Jo E. Sheridan: *Report of the Mine Inspector*, 1901, 20.

Sheridan did not stop: *Report of the Mine Inspector*, 1901, 20.

Sheridan was an early believer: *Report of the Mine Inspector*, 1901, 20; *Report of the Mine Inspector*, 1911.

In Dawson: Rees H. Beddow to T. H. O'Brien, December 23, 1912, University of New Mexico, Center for Southwest Research and Special Collections.

Chapter 11

Note: Unless otherwise specified, material in this chapter is based on the coroner's inquest report, November 15, 1913, Freeport-McMoRan collection.

Only rarely did coroners' juries: James Whiteside, *Regulating Danger: The Struggle for Mine Safety in the Rocky Mountain Coal Industry* (Lincoln: University of Nebraska Press, 1990), 85.

The coroner's inquest: "T. L. Kinney Laid to Rest in Trinidad Cemetery," *Dawson News*, April 3, 1924, 1.

Kinney would become: "T. L. Kinney Laid to Rest"; "Judge Kinney Wins Prize," *Dawson News*, July 5, 1923, 1; "Judge T. L, Kinney," Dawson New Mexico Association, https://chuckspeed.com/Dawson_Association/Kinney.html.

R. H. Worcester: "Geo. Remley Dies; Longtime Lawyer," *Albuquerque Journal*, May 23, 1946, 3.

That same night: *Report of the State Mine Inspector of New Mexico* (annual: Gallup, NM, 1912–1950), 1913, 36.

The statement was signed: "Blame Fixed for Dawson Mine Explosion," *Albuquerque Morning Journal*, November 18, 1913, 2.

While the jury's verdict: Whiteside, *Regulating Danger*, 85; "More Lessons from History," Spokane County, Washington, https://www.spokanecounty.org/3073/More-Lessons-From-History.

Between 1904 and 1914: Whiteside, *Regulating Danger*, 22, 85–86.

In Dawson: John C. Schwegel to Walter Douglas, November 22, 1913, Freeport-McMoRan collection.

Similarly, coziness between: "Dawson Disaster," *Albuquerque Morning Journal*, November 5, 1913, 6; "State Mine Inspector Issues Formal Statement on Dawson Disaster," *Albuquerque Evening Herald*, November 7, 1913, 3.

Yet, on November 5: Western Union telegram, T. H. O'Brien to Walter Douglas, November 5, 1913, Freeport-McMoRan collection.

Like many of the telegrams: Undated document, Freeport-McMoRan collection.

Beddow's "special report": Rees H, Beddow to Gov. William C. McDonald, November 10, 1913, University of New Mexico, Center for Southwest Research and Special Collections.

A century later: John C. Schwegel to Walter Douglas, November 22, 1913, Freeport-McMoRan collection; T. H. O'Brien to Walter Douglas, December 3, 1913, Freeport-McMoRan collection.

So who was Thomas Pattison?: US Census Bureau, 1900, 1910; US Army

Quartermaster Corps, *Applications for Headstones for U.S. Military Veterans, 1925–1941*, comp. Claire Prechtel-Kluskens (Washington, DC: National Archives and Records Administration, 2005), 1,018.

Pattison's body wasn't found: "Pennsylvania Paragraphs," *Pittsburgh Post*, October 28, 1913, 3.

To be fair: J. J. Ruttledge, "The Use and Misuse of Explosives in Coal Mining," US Bureau of Mines, Miners' Circular 7, 1916, 17, 30.

Chapter 12

Dawson and the industry: Ralph Emerson Twitchell, ed., *Leading Facts of New Mexican History*, Volume 3 (Cedar Rapids, IA: Torch Press, 1917), 92.

If Rees H. Beddow: *Report of the State Mine Inspector of New Mexico* (annual: Gallup, NM, 1912–1950), 1914, 32–33

Beddow also took note: *Report of the State Mine Inspector*, 1914, 31.

But those weren't the only things: *Report of the State Mine Inspector*, 1914, 31.

Beddow was back: *Report of the State Mine Inspector of New Mexico*, 1915, 25–121.

Phelps Dodge made several: *1914 Annual Report* (New York: Phelps, Dodge & Company, 1914), 42.

The company also ended: *1914 Annual Report*, 43.

In the spring of 1914: "Colorado Needs Spirit of New Mexico Coal Camps, Says," *Santa Fe New Mexican*, May 29, 1914, 3.

Dawson, the biggest coal mining camp: R. G. Gill Jr., "Dawson Coal Camp Pays Honor to Victims of Tragedy in the Mine," *Denver Post*, May 27, 1914.

Phelps Dodge spent months: Dr. James Douglas to T. H. O'Brien, February 20, 1914; April 15, 1914, Freeport-McMoRan collection.

As conveyed in the *Denver Post*: T. H. O'Brien to Dr. James Douglas, May 30, 1914, Freeport-McMoRan collection.

No less impressed: "Colorado Needs Spirit," 3.

While the explosion prompted: *Report of the State Mine Inspector*, 1914, 22–23.

For Dawson, it only would get better: *1916 Annual Report* (New York: Phelps, Dodge & Company, 1916), 37–39; "Dawson Mines Production and Employment," Freeport-McMoRan collection.

Dawson's coming of age: Twitchell, *Leading Facts*, 92.

Phelps Dodge would never achieve: *Annual Report*, (New York: Phelps Dodge): 1916, 39; 1917, 27–28; 1918, 31; 1919, 26; William Notz, "The World's Coal Situation during the War," *Journal of Political Economy* 26 (1918): 567–611.

Phelps Dodge was also active: *Annual Report*, 1916, 40; 1917, 29; 1920, 24; 1921, 13; 1922, 13.

But the company had much more: Richard Melzer, "Phelps Dodge Knows Best: Welfare Capitalism in a New Mexico Camp, Dawson, 1920–1929," *Southwest Economy & Society* 6, no. 1 (1982): 12–34.

The Welfare Department: Melzer, "Phelps Dodge Knows Best," 22; "Welfare Committee Meets," *Dawson News*, February 17, 1921.

A key component: "Clean-Up Week," *Dawson News*, April 21, 1921, 3; "Welfare Committee Meets," *Dawson News*, August 11, 1921, 2; "Welfare Committee Meets," *Dawson News*, December 22, 1921, 4.

Perhaps the most visible: "A Foreword," *Dawson News*, February 3, 1921, 1.

Conway's front-page news: "Dedication of New High School Building," *Dawson News*, February 3, 1921, 1; "Dawson's Sanitary Dairy," February 3, 1921, 1; "The Dawson News Suspends Publication," *Dawson News*, October 31, 1929, 1.

In 1917, New Mexico: *Annual Report*, 1918, 33; "New Mexico is Placed in 'Dry' Column by Vote of Two to One," *Albuquerque Journal*, November 7, 1917, 1.

President Woodrow Wilson's decision: Pietro Scarafiotti, "Dawsonites in the Military (1898-1950), Dawson New Mexico Facebook page, August 14, 2017, https://www.facebook.com/groups/556793837833040/search/?q=World War II (members-only resource).

Five Dawson soldiers: "New Mexico, US World War I Records, 1917–1919."; US War Department, *Commissioned and Enlisted Personnel of the Army Who Entered Service from the State of New Mexico and Died while Members of the American Expeditionary Forces* (Washington, DC: Adjutant General's Office, 1920), 3, 5.

Roughly 150 Dawson men: Pietro Scarafiotti, "Dawsonites in the Military (1898–1950), Dawson New Mexico Facebook page, August 14, 2017, https://www.facebook.com/groups/556793837833040/search/?q=World War II. (members-only resource).

Robert Lucero nearly joined them: "The Miner's Pick," Dawson New Mexico Association, March 2006, 1–2.

During the 1996 Dawson reunion: Toby Smith, "Laughter Fills Ghost Town," *Albuquerque Journal*, August 18, 1996, 31.

Chapter 13

Nearly everyone in town: Enes Federici Caraglio Covert, *Dawson, the Town That Was* (Albuquerque: Far West & Associates, 1984), 26–27.

May Dee Lunsford: Cee Savvy, "Disasters at Dawson," *Enchantment Magazine*, June 1980; "Scot [sic] Dupont injured," *Dawson News*, February 15, 1923, 1.

This wasn't the only similarity: US Department of Labor, *Report on No. 1 Mine Explosion, Dawson, New Mexico, February 8, 1923*, by D. Harrington (Washington,

DC, April 1923), 20; "Explosion in No. 1 Mine," *Dawson News*, February 15, 1923, 1; "Rescue Work is Hurried to Relieve Dawson Men," *El Paso Herald*, February 9, 1923, 1.

The bakery made the bread: Savvy, "Disasters at Dawson."

As soon as they heard: "Rescue Work," 1.

Enes Covert was there, too: Covert, *Dawson*, 6, 26.

It wasn't until: Covert, *Dawson*, 26.

Covert watched as rescue crews: Covert, *Dawson*, 26–37.

Superintendent Daniel Harrington: USDL, *Report on No. 1 Mine*, 19.

While Dawson officials welcomed: *Report of the State Mine Inspector of New Mexico* (annual: Gallup, NM, 1912–1950), 1923, 89; US Department of the Interior, Bureau of Mines, *Self-Contained Oxygen Breathing Apparatus: A Handbook for Miners*, by D. J. Parker, G. S. McCaa, and E. H. Denny (Washington, DC: GPO, 1934), 34.

Technically, this was not: *Report of the State Mine Inspector*, 1920, 12–15.

That night: *Report of the State Mine Inspector*, 1920, 13.

Everything was in order: *Report of the State Mine Inspector*, 1920, 12.

Unbeknownst to the electrician: *Report of the State Mine Inspector*, 1920, 13.

In his report: *Report of the State Mine Inspector*, 1920, 13.

The five men left three widows: *Report of the State Mine Inspector*, 1920, 10.

Not much is known: Stephen Reed, email correspondence with author, October 16, 2020; Certificate of Death, New Mexico Department of Health, April 16, 1920.

On the morning of February 8: "100 Miners Entombed by Dawson Explosion," *Santa Fe New Mexican*, February 9, 1923, 1, 6; "125 Buried in Mine Explosion," *Houston Post*, February 9, 1923, 1; "Rescue Work is Hurried," 1.

The work of entering the mine: "100 Miners Entombed," 1, 6.

By the next morning: "100 Miners Entombed," 1, 6; US Census Bureau, 1920; Pietro Scarafiotti, "Stories of Dawson Families: The English Family," Dawson New Mexico Facebook page, May 24, 2016, https://www.facebook.com/groups/556793837833040/search/?q=%20STORIES%20OF%20DAWSON%20FAMILIES%3A%20The%20English%20Family (members-only resource); Find a Grave, https://www.findagrave.com/memorial/72440345/albert-edward-english.

A temporary morgue: "100 Miners Entombed," 1, 6; "Stricken Dawson Searches for Dead under Thick Blanket of Snow," *Santa Fe New Mexican*, February 10, 1923, 1.

Unlike ten years earlier: "100 Miners Entombed," 1, 6.

Guerino "Shorty" Scarafiotti: Pietro Scarafiotti, "Explosion of Mine #1—first-person account," Dawson New Mexico Facebook page, February 19, 2020, https://www.facebook.com/groups/556793837833040/search/?q=Guerino (members-only resource).

In Guerino's words: Scarafiotti, "Explosion of Mine #1."

As I shined my light on them: Scarafiotti, "Explosion of Mine #1."

W. W. Risdon was no stranger: US Bureau of Mine Safety, *State Mine Inspector's 2016 Report to the Governor* (Socorro, NM: New Mexico Tech, 2016), 17; New Mexico Bureau of Mines & Mineral Resources, *One Hundred Years of Coal Mining in the San Juan Basin, New Mexico*, by Howard B. Nickelson, Bulletin 111 (Socorro, NM, 1988), 15.

Risdon had visited: *Report of the State Mine Inspector*, 1922, 64–65; *Report of the State Mine Inspector*, 1918, 95–97.

Upon his arrival: *Report of the State Mine Inspector*, 1918, 95.

On February 26: *Report of the State Mine Inspector*, 1918, 95–96.

Unable to carry them: *Report of the State Mine Inspector*, 1918, 97.

One possible explanation: US Department of the Interior, Bureau of Mines, *Loss of Life among Wearers of Oxygen Breathing Apparatus*, by G. W. Grove, Information Circular 7279 (Washington, DC, April 1944), 13–14.

Risdon had great respect: *Report of the State Mine Inspector*, 1918, 97.

Murphy, the son of an Irish miner: USDI, *Loss of Life*, 13–14.

Just minutes after the 1923: *Report of the State Mine Inspector*, 1923, 89.

Risdon's first stop: *Report of the State Mine Inspector*, 1923, 89.

Charles George Skandale: Elizabeth Skandale, "A Mine Explosion," unpublished manuscript, 1981, 2.

Skandale found something else: Skandale, "A Mine Explosion," 3.

Like many miners' wives: Skandale, "A Mine Explosion," 4.

Filomeno diMartino was already: Mark DiVecchio, "Filomeno diMartino," http://www.silogic.com/genealogy/Filomeno diMartino.html; US Census Bureau, 1910.

DiMartino returned: DiVecchio, "Filomeno diMartino"; US Census Bureau, 1920.

On that day: Skandale, "A Mine Explosion," 3–5.

The mine lights were out: Frank H. Bartholemew, United Press Staff Correspondent, "Two Men Out of 122 Walk in Safety out of 5,000-Foot Tomb," *Hastings Daily Tribune*, February 10, 1923, 1.

They waited not years: Skandale, "A Mine Explosion," 8–9.

The next morning: Skandale, "A Mine Explosion," 9–10; Bartholemew, "Two Men," 1.

They continued stumbling: Skandale, "A Mine Explosion," 10.

We ain't hurt: "Two Kept Calm and Lived," *Kansas City Times*, February 10, 1923, 1.

Reporters on the scene: Bartholemew, "Two Men," 1.

Despite his death-defying escape: Certificate of Death, New Mexico Department of Health, February 9, 1923.

Charles Skandale did not hesitate: Elizabeth Skandale, author interview, March 28, 2019.

He was a quiet man: Skandale, author interview.

Until his death in 1979: Skandale, "A Mine Explosion," 10.

Less is known about: DiVecchio, "Filomeno diMartino."

Unlike the 1913 mine disaster: *Report of the State Mine Inspector*, 1923, 47–49.

Chapter 14

[T]he mine was very dry: *Report of the State Mine Inspector of New Mexico* (annual: Gallup, NM, 1912–1950), 1923, 79.

After the euphoria: "Find 34 Dead, 2 Alive in Mine," *El Paso Times*, February 10, 1923, 1.

Getting to the other remains: "Find 34 Dead."

Huddled in little groups: "Find 34 Dead," 2.

While rescue crews: "Fifty Miners Remain in Depths of Mine Damaged by Explosion at Dawson," *Albuquerque Morning Journal*, February 12, 1923, 1.

Meanwhile, the first set: "70 Victims of Blast Taken from Mine at Dawson," *El Paso Times*, February 12, 1923, 1.

On February 12: US Department of Labor, *Report on No. 1 Mine Explosion, Dawson, New Mexico, February 8, 1923*, by D. Harrington (Washington, DC, April 1923), 23–24.

That afternoon, an Associated: "Utter Devastation is Wrought by Explosion in Dawson Coal Mine," *Albuquerque Morning Journal*, February 13, 1923, 1.

In the meantime: "Utter Devastation."

Justice of the Peace: *Report of the State Mine Inspector*, 64.

W. D. Brennan: *Report of the State Mine Inspector*, 65.

Henry "Scott" Dupont: *Report of the State Mine Inspector*, 69.

Edmond Thomas brought: *Report of the State Mine Inspector*, 72–73.

The final two witnesses: *Report of the State Mine Inspector*, 79.

Before the day was out: USDL, *Report on No. 1 Mine*, 28.

The official finding: USDL, *Report on No. 1 Mine*, 28.

I have been told: *Report of the State Mine Inspector*, 1923, 61.

Risdon concluded: *Report of the State Mine Inspector*, 62.

Two months later: USDL, *Report on No. 1 Mine*, 29–45.

Harrington acknowledged: USDL, *Report on No. 1 Mine*, 29.

Like Risdon, Harrington: USDL, *Report on No. 1 Mine*, 38.

Two weeks later: "Sweeping Legislative Probe Proposed," *Santa Fe New Mexican*, February 24, 1923, 1.

Phelps Dodge wasted little time: "Passage of Mine Probe Bill Expected Tonight," *Santa Fe New Mexican*, February 26, 1923, 6.

Company Makes Explanation: "Company Makes Explanation of Mine Explosion," *Albuquerque Morning Journal*, February 26, 1923, 1.

The House passed the bill: "Senate Would Have Experts Probe Mine," *Santa Fe New Mexican*, February 27, 1923, 1; "Third Effort Made to Rush Dawson Mine Investigation," *Santa Fe New Mexican*, February 28, 1923, 3; "Third Effort for a Quick Probe Fails," *Santa Fe New Mexican*, March 1, 1923, 3; "New Mexico Legislature Was Adjourned Fri.," *Deming Headlight*, March 16, 1923, 1.

Neither Brennan nor Dupont: US Census Bureau, 1910, 1920; Pietro Scarafiotti, untitled, Dawson New Mexico Facebook page, July 7, 2018, https://www.facebook.com/groups/556793837833040/search/?q=Scott%20Dupont (members-only resource).

Dupont remained as superintendent: Richard Stanley to Phelps Dodge, September 30, 1926, Freeport-McMoRan collection.

Perhaps to his surprise: Walter Douglas to Richard Stanley, October 11, 1926, Freeport-McMoRan collection.

Several years later: Anonymous letter to Phelps Dodge, January 16, 1928, Freeport-McMoRan collection.

In this instance: C. E. Dodge to P. G. Beckett, January 19, 1928, Freeport-McMoRan collection.

Whether or not the complaints: "Henry Scott Dupont," Find a Grave, https://www.findagrave.com/memorial/125971235/henry-scott-dupont.

Chapter 15

[S]igns of Dawson's dying: Richard Melzer, "A Death in Dawson: The Demise of a Southwestern Company Town," *New Mexico Historical Review* 55, no. 4 (October 1, 1980): 314–15.

Dawson recovered: "100 Years with Coal Age," *Coal Age*, September 14, 2012, https://www.coalage.com/features/100-years-with-coal-age/3/; *1923 Annual Report* (New York: Phelps Dodge, 1923), 13–14.

The Great Depression's impact: *1928 Annual Report*, 13–14; *Report of the State Mine Inspector of New Mexico* (annual: Gallup, NM, 1912–1950), 1932, 13–14.

Dawson's quality of life: Melzer, "A Death in Dawson," 311.

The economic downturn: Melzer, "A Death in Dawson," 312–13.

To its credit: *1923 Annual Report*, 14.

The use of rock dust: US Bureau of Mines, *Mining Practice at Harmony Mines Co., Baker, Idaho*, by R. Duncan Gardner, Information Circular 6240 (Washington, March 1930), 27; C. K. Man and K. A. Teacoach, "How Does Limestone Rock Dust Prevent Coal Dust Explosions in Coal Mines?" *Mining Engineering* 61, no. 9 (2009): 69–73, https://www.cdc.gov/niosh/mining/userfiles/works/pdfs/hdlrdp.pdf; US Department of Health and Human Services, *One Hundred Years of Federal Mining Safety and Health Research*, by John A. Breslin, DHHS (NIOSH) Publication No. 2010-128, Information Circular 9520 (Pittsburgh, 2010), 22, https://www.cdc.gov/niosh/mining/userfiles/works/pdfs/2010-128.pdf.

State mine inspector: *Report of the State Mine Inspector*, 1932, 99.

Phelps Dodge's renewed commitment: *1924 Annual Report*, 13.

Denny's report: Excerpt from report of E. H. Denny, February 21, 1925, Freeport-McMoRan collection.

The writer considers: Report of E. H. Denny, February 21, 1925.

This is not to say: "Dawson Post Master Accidentally Killed," *Dawson News*, December 15, 1927, 1.

This was a tragic end: "Popular Dawson Couple Married at Raton," *Dawson News*, October 15, 1925, 1; "New Acting Postmaster," *Dawson News*, October 13, 1927, 1; P. G. Beckett to W. D. Brennan, December 13, 1927, Freeport-McMoRan collection.

On the night of the shooting: "Dawson Post Master," 1.

A coroner's jury: "Dawson Post Master," 1; Beckett to Brennan, December 13, 1927.

Justice of the Peace: "Mrs. Frazzini Is Freed after Hearing in Raton," *Dawson News*, March 1, 1928, 1; Charles F. Coan, *A History of New Mexico*, Volume 2 (Chicago: American Historical Society, 1925), 445.

Besides newspaper accounts: W. D. Brennan to P. G. Beckett, December 13, 1927, Freeport-McMoRan collection.

In the second: Brennan to Beckett, December 21, 1927.

Given Dupont's position: Pietro Scarafiotti, "Death of a Postmaster—Angelo Frazzini," Dawson New Mexico Facebook page, September 9, 2019, https://www.facebook.com/groups/556793837833040/search/?q=Death%20of%20a%20Postmaster (members-only resource); Mark DiVecchio, "Angelo Frazzini," email correspondence from Marilou Moschetti, http://www.silogic.com/genealogy/Angelo Frazzini.html; "In Memoriam," *Dawson News*, December 13, 1928, 4.

Even before the Great Depression: *1925 Annual Report*, 12–13; *1926 Annual Report*, 13; *1927 Annual Report*, 13; Melzer, "A Death in Dawson," 311.

Phelps Dodge did not sit idly: *1928 Annual Report*, 13; *Report of the State Mine Inspector*, 1928, 15.

Nevertheless, despite its best efforts: *1929 Annual Report*, 11; *Report of the State Mine Inspector*, 1915, 19; *Report of the State Mine Inspector*, 1932, 13.

Phelps Dodge had little tolerance: Mitchell Abidor, *I'll Forget it When I Die!: The Bisbee Deportation of 1917* (Chico, CA: AK Press, 2021), 37, 103, 160–62, 173.

This intolerance resurfaced: "New Truce to End Nation-Wide Coal Strike," *Albuquerque Journal*, September 27, 1935, 1; National Labor Relations Act of 1935, Pub. L. No. 74–198, National Archives and Records Administration, https://www.archives.gov/milestone-documents/national-labor-relations-act.

The new contract: "New Truce," 1.

For its part: "Contract Demanded at Dawson," *Albuquerque Journal*, October 2, 1935, 1.

Unbeknownst to Davis: "Contract Demanded at Dawson," 1.

Phelps Dodge waited: "To Close Mine, Manager Says," *Albuquerque Tribune*, October 10, 1935, 1.

This was not the first time: "250 Phelps-Dodge Miners at Dawson Fail to Go to Work," *Albuquerque Journal*, October, 3, 1933, 1; "Miners to Return to Pits Tomorrow under a New Code," *Clovis Evening News-Journal*, October 31, 1933, 1.

This time, when the striking: "Abandonment of Dawson Mine Starts," *Santa Fe New Mexican*, October 14, 1935, 2.

The company's threat: Western Union Telegram from Frank Hefferly to John L. Lewis, Penn State University Libraries, October 15, 1935, https://digital.libraries.psu.edu/digital/collection/umwac/id/211291/rec/1.

State Labor Commissioner: "Dawson Parley On: Way Sought to Avert Mine Closing," *Albuquerque Journal*, October 17, 1935, 1.

If Phelps Dodge officials: "Miners Must Act Quickly Says Notice," *Santa Fe New Mexican*, October 19, 1935, 6.

That decision came: "Strikers Will Work at Dawson," *Albuquerque Journal*, October 24, 1935, 1; "National Coal Board of Arbitration Dockets, 1935–1938," Penn State University Libraries, https://aspace.libraries.psu.edu/repositories/3/resources/1472.

The next fifteen years: "Mines Seized by US," *Pittsburgh Press*, May 1, 1943, 1; *1943 Annual Report*; *1944 Annual Report*.

For Dawson, 1943 was memorable: Carlos J. Craig, "The Unionization of the Mines in Dawson, New Mexico," master's thesis, New Mexico Highlands University, 1970, 63.

On May 8, 1945: Frank Hefferly to John L. Lewis, Penn State University Libraries, Digital Collections, United Mine Workers of America, President's Office Correspondence with Districts, May 8, 1945.

The labor peace: "Coal Walkout Will Hit Reconversion," *Albuquerque Journal*, April 1, 1946, 1; "Soft Coal Strike is Settled; Senate Kills Draft of Strikers," *Pittsburgh Post-Gazette*, May 30, 1946, 1; "Lewis Gives Up Coal Strike," *Pittsburgh Press*, December 8, 1946, 1.

The two shutdowns: *1946 Annual Report; 1947 Annual Report.*

Dawson miners joined: "160,000 Miners on Strike," *Pittsburgh Press*, March 15, 1948, 1; "Striking Miners Load Coal for State Hospitals," *Albuquerque Journal*, April 3, 1948, 5; "Lewis Calls Off Strike," *Pittsburgh Press*, April 12, 1948, 1.

Indications are that operations: *1948 Annual Report.*

Chapter 16

They have a Marshall plan: "Dawson Residents Start Exodus, Victims of Dying Industry," *Albuquerque Journal*, May 21, 1950, 19.

Phelps Dodge's downbeat assessment: US Department of Labor, Bureau of Labor Statistics, *Analysis of Work Stoppages during 1949*, by Don Q. Crowther and Ann J. Herlihy, Bulletin 1003 (Washington, DC: GPO, 1950), 14; *1949 Annual Report*, (New York: Phelps Dodge, 1949); "Area Miners Beginning to Walk Out," *Pittsburgh Post-Gazette*, September 19, 1949, 1; "Lewis Ends Strike for 3 Weeks," *Pittsburgh Post-Gazette*, November 10, 1949, 1; "Miners Go Back on 3-Day Week," *Pittsburgh Post-Gazette*, December 2, 1949, 1.

The new arrangement: "President Asks 70-Day Coal Truce," *Pittsburgh Post-Gazette*, February 1, 1950, 1; "Coal Pact is Signed," *Pittsburgh Post-Gazette*, March 6, 1950, 1.

Gerald O. Arnold was the author: "Dawson, New Mexico, 1904–1950, The Last Hurrah," *Cimarron News*, September 16, 1988, 1–4; "Mine to Lay Off 90," *Albuquerque Journal*, December 2, 1948, 8; "Dawson Mine Closing April 30; Notice Posted by Company at Noon; 1,200 Persons at Camp," *Raton Range*, February 25, 1950, 1.

The announcement received: "Phelps Dodge to Shut Mine at Dawson," *Santa Fe New Mexican*, February 26, 1950, 1; "Raton Coal Mine Closes April 30; 300 Workers Hit," *Albuquerque Journal*, February 26, 1950, 4.

While the shutdown: "Dawson Faces Death; Phelps Dodge's Town to Give Up April 28," *Santa Fe New Mexican*, April 11, 1950, 5.

To all residents of Dawson: Pietro Scarafiotti, Dawson New Mexico Facebook page, untitled, June 1, 2017, https://www.facebook.com/groups/556793837833040/search/?q=%22This%20is%20the%20notice%22 (members-only resource).

Meanwhile, jobs at other coal camps: Scarafiotti, Dawson New Mexico Facebook page, untitled, June 1, 2017; "'Uncrowded' Raton Offers Dawson Aid," *Albuquerque Journal*, April 14, 1950, 17; "Dawson Residents Start Exodus," 19.

It will be hardest: "Take a Bow, John L.," *El Paso Herald-Post*, April 12, 1950, 14.

Karl F. Guthmann: "In New Mexico," *Albuquerque Journal*, May 10, 1950, 6.

Faced with these obstacles: "Dawson Residents Ask Stay of Town Death Sentence," *Albuquerque Journal*, April 12, 1950, 1.

US Rep. Antonio M. Fernández: "New Vermejo Project is Introduced in Congress," *Clovis News-Journal*, May 2, 1950, 1.

Truman signed off: "Truman Signs Vermejo Bill," *Santa Fe New Mexican*, September 27, 1950, 1; "Contract on Vermejo Project Signed," *Albuquerque Tribune*, August 8, 1952, 1; Jedediah S. Rogers, "Vermejo Project: Historic Reclamation Projects," US Bureau of Reclamation, 2009, 10.

Phelps Dodge had a different idea: "Dawson on Block," *Santa Fe New Mexican*, June 7, 1950, 6.

Miner Fred Bergamo: Richard Melzer, "A Death in Dawson: The Demise of a Southwestern Company Town," *New Mexico Historical Review* 55, no. 4 (October 1, 1980), 323.

Later that night: Roberta Hernandez Perez, author interview, August 2, 2022.

It was the last concert: Perez, author interview.

Two weeks later: *Clovis News-Journal*, "Doomed Town Graduates 20," May 14, 1950, 4; *Albuquerque Tribune*, "Miner Killed in Rock Fall," August 9, 1949, 11.

By this point: Guthmann, "In New Mexico," 6.

Samuel Shapiro: "Dawson on Block," 6; "Phoenix Junk Firm Deals in World Trade," *Arizona Republic*, July 2, 1950, Section 2, 3.

But those jobs paled: "Diesel Engineers Are Requiem for N.M. Coal Mining Town," *Arizona Daily Star*, July 18, 1950, Section B, 1.

Shapiro was no small-town: "Phoenix Junk Firm."

Shapiro didn't waste much time: "Local Firm Buys 400 Dawson Houses," *Albuquerque Tribune*, June 15, 1950, 10.

A prime beneficiary: "Clovis Man Moves Ghost Mining Town," *Amarillo Daily News*, July 5, 1950, 14; "House Movers" advertisement, *Clovis News-Journal*, July 30, 1950, 27; "Homer Bennett Moves the Town of Dawson," *Clovis News-Journal*, September 4, 1950, 3; "Homer Bennett to Move Another Whole Town," *Clovis News-Journal*, December 18, 1950, 3; "New Mine Activity Revitalizes Bisbee," *Tucson Daily Citizen*, June 19, 1951, 10.

The doleful dismantling: "Wreckers Take Dawson, Once-Thriving Coal

Camp," *Albuquerque Journal*, August 23, 1950, 5; "Nothing Is Left in Town of Dawson, Now Scattered over United States," *Albuquerque Journal*, October 6, 1951, 4.

It's a little sad: "Nothing Is Left," 4.

O'Neil spoke these words: "Nothing Is Left," 4.

Marlene Hancock Kotchou: "Phelps Dodge Sells Town to Salvage Firm," *Tucson Citizen*, June 6, 1950, 15.

Kotchou's maternal grandparents: Marlene Hancock Kotchou, author interview, July 7, 2020.

While it has been more than seventy years: Kotchou, author interview.

In October of 1950: "Spring Co-Op to Modernize Power Company Purchased," *Clovis News-Journal*, October 8, 1950, 12; *Albuquerque Journal*, "Utility Transfer," December 5, 1950, 6.

Kotchou and her family: Kotchou, author interview.

The editorial writer: "Railroads Ask to Quit Service to Dawson," *Albuquerque Journal*, August 30, 1950, 4; "ICC Examiner Must Decide Next Move on Closing Time," *Clovis News-Journal*, May 4, 1951, 14.

Ultimately, the State: "Recommends Dawson Line Be Abandoned," *Albuquerque Tribune*, August 24, 1951, 7; Railroad Serving Dawson Closed," *Albuquerque Journal*, March 19, 1952, 18.

The opponents' victory: "Rail Line Must Run, Is Ruling," *Albuquerque Journal*, August 3, 1956, 22.

The Southern Pacific: "Rail Line Closing in State Approved," *Albuquerque Tribune*, August 23, 1961, D-1.

The news came as a shock: "State Hits Move to Abandon 114 Miles of Railroad," *Albuquerque Journal*, August 26, 1961, B-3.

On that day: Marilyn Mullins, "Old 'Polly' Makes Last Run," *Albuquerque Journal*, November 9, 1962, A-8; "1 Dead; 2 Hurt; 1 Missing in Freight Wreck," *Albuquerque Journal*, October 27, 1922, 1.

Boswell was accompanied: Mullins, "Old 'Polly.'"

Joining them on this historic ride: "54 Years of Railroading Service Comes to an End in New Mexico," *Santa Fe New Mexican*, November 11, 1962, 10.

At one time: "54 Years," 10.

For Boswell, that final ride: "Tucumcari Born with a Railroad Boom," *Albuquerque Journal*, March 11, 1979, E-1, 3, 4.

Chapter 17

Dale Christian wasn't sure: Morrow Hall, "Forgotten Cemetery Lush with

History," *Roswell Daily Record*, August 27, 1999: A5; Laura Christian, author interview, September 30, 2019.

We were both shocked: Hall, "Forgotten Cemetery."

That didn't sit well: Hall, "Forgotten Cemetery."

When I gave them: Hall, "Forgotten Cemetery."

The Christian brothers: "Lloyd Christian," *Argus-Leader*, October 27, 1999, 4B; "Oriskany, CV-34," *Naval History and Heritage Command*, April 27, 2016, https://www.history.navy.mil/research/histories/ship-histories/danfs/o/oriskany.html; "Lloyd Arthur Christian," Find a Grave, https://www.findagrave.com/memorial/10825581/lloyd-arthur-christian.

If Lloyd was the carefree jokester: Christian, author interview; Robert Locke, "Solar One," *The Desert Sun*, November 2, 1982, 1.

To each of his activities: Christian, author interview.

Laura remembers: Christian, author interview.

He was pretty angry: Christian, author interview.

New Mexico Historic Preservation: Untitled document, New Mexico Historic Preservation Division collection, October 11, 1990.

For the next 18 months: New Mexico Historic Preservation Division collection: Dale Christian to Dr. Mary Ann Anders, November 13, 1990; Christian to Anders, January 19, 1991; Christian to Corrine Sze, April 2, 1991, April 5, 1991; Christian notes after visit to cemetery, June 3, 1991; Christian to Anders, November 13, 1990.

On February 18, 1992: National Register of Historic Places Registration Form, Dawson Cemetery cover sheet, National Park Service, February 18, 1992, https://npgallery.nps.gov/GetAsset/89541c8b-ea85-4959-85f7-85994e4caa28.

Acceptance was no slam dunk: "National Register of Historic Places: Criteria for Evaluation." *Code of Federal Regulations*, Title 36, Parks, Forest, and Public Property, Chapter I, Part 60, Section 60.4, https://www.ecfr.gov/current/title-36/chapter-I/part-60/section-60.4.

The completed nomination form cited: Registration Form, Dawson Cemetery, National Park Service, 192.

On April 9, 1992: "Dawson Cemetery Placed on National Register," *New Mexico Preservation* 10, no. 1 (Summer 1993), 1.

If Dale Christian helped: Vivien A. Andrews, *Dawson Coal Mine Cemetery Inscriptions, Dawson, Colfax County, NM*, booklet, 1998.

Four years later: Vivien Pick, author interview, January 30, 2019.

That Pick had a hand: Vivien Pick, author interview, August 12, 2019.

It was around this time: Pick, author interview, August 12, 2019.

In 1983, Pick: Pick, author interview, May 24, 2021.

I remember feeling: Pick, author interview, May 24, 2021.

While Pick is not related: Pick, author interview, May 24, 2021.

When they had to leave: Pick, author interview, May 24, 2021.

On October 20, 2013: Charles D. Brunt, "Dawson Disaster 100 Years Later," *Albuquerque Journal*, October 20, 2013, B1, 6.

Georgia Maryol: Tom Sharpe, "Santa Fe woman works to honor Dawson's victims," *Santa Fe New Mexican*, October 20, 1913, A-4.

Pam Thompson did not attend: Pam Thompson, author interview, August 22, 2021.

The photo prompted her: Thompson, author interview.

Davis was living with his parents: Chester NC Davis to his sister Pearl Davis, July 7, 1913, private collection.

Davis never made it home: *Toluca Star*, November 21, 1913.

Upon learning of the explosion: *Toluca Star*, November 21, 1913; Pam Thompson, email correspondence with author, September 2, 2021.

One hundred and eight years later: Thompson, author interview, August 22, 2021.

'It's just real now': Thompson, author interview, August 22, 2021.

Joe Bacca approaches: Nick Pappas, "'Beautiful Reminder of Those Who Came Before,'" *Albuquerque Journal*, September 2, 2019, A1, 5.

A year earlier: Bruno Ridolfi, email correspondence with author, May 23, 2022.

The historic Dawson Cemetery: Pappas, "Beautiful Reminder," A5.

The $65,000 donation: Pappas, "Beautiful Reminder," A5.

Bacca never lived in Dawson: Joe Bacca, author interview, August 14, 2019.

At the entrance to Dawson Cemetery: Pappas, "Beautiful Reminder," A5.

Chapter 18

In 1975, Jackson M. Langton: "The Dawson Ranch Coal Potential, Northeast of Cimarron, New Mexico," Jackson M. Langton, September 25, 1975, Freeport-McMoRan Collection, 1, 3, 5, 9.

Of even greater interest: Langton, "Dawson Ranch Coal Potential," 3.

Here, word for word, are the reasons: Langton, "Dawson Ranch Coal Potential," 3.

The first sign came in 1954: "Former Dawson Residents Attend California Picnic," *Albuquerque Journal*, August 7, 1954, 6.

California would host: "Dawson Reunion," *Sacramento Bee*, May 24, 1959, W4; Marian Padilla Aguirre, "When Was the First Dawson Picnic?" Dawson New Mexico Facebook page, January 26, 2021, https://www.facebook.com/groups/

556793837833040/search/?q=When%20was%20the%20first%20Dawson%20picnic (members-only resource).

During the 1980s and 1990s: "Coal Town is Dead, but Memories Live," *Albuquerque Journal*, *Journal North* edition, September 8, 1998, 3; Dawson New Mexico Association, https://www.chuckspeed.com/Dawson_Association/.

To be sure: Emily Bingham, "This U.P. Ghost Town Comes to Life One Day Each Year, Reuniting Copper Miners' Descendants," MLive.com, https://www.mlive.com/news/2021/07/this-up-ghost-town-comes-to-life-one-day-each-year-reuniting-copper-miners-descendants.html.

That "good old days" sentiment: "Joseph Robert McClary," *Albuquerque Journal*, April 10, 2011, D9; "Frank Marcelli, Sr.," *Albuquerque Journal*, February 15, 2012, D6; "Beatrice Andazola McSweeney," *Albuquerque Journal*, August 9, 2015, B4; "Frank V. Padilla," *Albuquerque Journal*, April 13, 2016, C8; "Clorinda Lucero," *Albuquerque Journal*, December 3, 2017, B3.

Dolores Clara Fernandez Huerta: "Dolores Huerta: The Feminist Seed is Planted," Dolores Huerta Foundation, https://doloreshuerta.org/doloreshuerta/.

Huerta was born in 1930: US Census Bureau, 1930; "Marshall Fernandez," *The Californian*, June 24, 2005, 4A.

The family did not stay: Dolores Huerta, author interview, March 23, 2022; "Democrats Gain Control of the Legislature," *Albuquerque Journal*, November 10, 1938, 1.

Huerta and her family returned: Huerta, author interview.

Years later: Huerta, author interview.

There were people from all over: Huerta, author interview.

What I remember: Huerta, author interview.

Pietro "Pete" Scarafiotti: Pietro "Pete" Scarafiotti, author interview, September 9, 2021.

[I]n those days: Scarafiotti, email correspondence with author, August 23, 2022.

I "protect" Dawson today: Scarafiotti, email correspondence with author, August 23, 2022.

Fred Becchetti: Fred Becchetti, author interview, October 20, 2020.

Prior to his retirement: Fred Becchetti, "Home Again to Dawson," *Raton Range*, September 2, 1988.

Our home in Number Seven Camp: Becchetti, "Home Again to Dawson."

Nat Norris: Nat Norris, email correspondence with author, August 7, 2020.

Joseph Padilla: Joseph Padilla, email correspondence with author, November 30, 2020.

Mary Frances García Reza: Mary Frances García Reza, author interview, August 8, 2021.

That became her introduction: Reza, author interview; "Mary Frances Reza," Oregon Catholic Press, https://www.ocp.org/en-us/artists/164/mary-frances-reza.

Petra Tovar Sánchez: Petro Tovar Sánchez, author interview, May 1, 2020.

Patty Trujillo: Patty Trujillo, email correspondence with author, November 20, 2020.

Frank Turner: Frank Turner, author interview, May 14, 2020.

It was on the Polly: Turner, author interview; "Tucumcari Beats Dawson, 13–6," *Albuquerque Journal*, November 21, 1948, 7.

Edward Zavala and his wife, Betty: Edward Zavala, author interview, August 14, 2019.

Unlike his father: Edward Zavala, author interview, September 1, 2021.

If there is one thing: Reunion newsletters, Dawson New Mexico Association, 2018, 2022, https://chuckspeed.com/Dawson_Association/Dawson_History2.html.

Add to that uneasiness: Nick Pappas, "Historic Site of Dawson Coal Town on the Market," *Albuquerque Journal*, April 19, 2020, A8.

Joe Bacca: Joe Bacca, email correspondence with author, April 8, 2022.

My daughter Bobbie Jo Bacca: Bacca, email correspondence with author.

Enter Carlos Tenorio: Carlos Tenorio, author interview, July 14, 2021.

Munoz described this event: Tenorio, author interview.

They say Tombstone: Tenorio, author interview.

BIBLIOGRAPHY

Books

Abidor, Mitchell. *I'll Forget It When I Die!: The Bisbee Deportation of 1917*. Chico, CA: AK Press, 2021.

Allen, James B. *The Company Town in the American West*. Norman: University of Oklahoma Press, 1966.

Ambrose, Stephen E. *Nothing Like It in the World: The Men Who Built the Transcontinental Railroad 1863–1869*. New York: Simon & Schuster, 2000.

Bayor, Ronald H. *Encountering Ellis Island: How European Immigrants Entered America*. Baltimore: Johns Hopkins University Press, 2014.

Beach, Horace Dougald, and Rex A. Lucas, eds. *Individual and Group Behavior in a Coal Mine Disaster*. Washington, DC: National Academy of Sciences–National Research Council, 1960.

Cassotis, Emanuel G. *The Karpathian Presence in America (1872–2012)*. Rhodes, Greece: Stegi Grammaton ke Technon Dodecanesou, 2012.

Christiansen, Paige W. *The Story of Mining in New Mexico*. Socorro: New Mexico Bureau of Mines & Mineral Resources, 1974.

Cleland, Robert Glass. *A History of Phelps Dodge, 1834–1950*. New York: Alfred A. Knopf, 1952.

Clyne, Rick J. *Coal People: Life in Southern Colorado's Company Towns 1890–1930*. Louisville, CO: University Press of Colorado, 1999.

Covert, Enes Federici Caraglio. *Dawson: The Town That Was: A Family Story*. Albuquerque: Far West & Associates, 1984.

Daniel, Karen Stein. *New Mexico Mining Fatalities and Accidents 1894–1925*. Albuquerque: New Mexico Genealogical Society, 2001.

Fox, Maier, B. *United We Stand: The United Mine Workers of America 1890–1990*. Washington, DC: United Mine Workers of America, 1990.

Freese, Barbara. *Coal: A Human History*. New York: Basic Books, 2016.

Galuszka, Peter A. *Thunder on the Mountain: Death at Massey and the Dirty Secrets behind Big Coal*. Morgantown: West Virginia University Press, 2014.

García, Ricardo L. *Coal Camp Days: A Boy's Remembrance*. Albuquerque: University of New Mexico Press, 2001.

Glover, Vernon J. *El Paso and Southwestern Railroad System*. Upland, CA: Southern Pacific Historical & Technical Society, 2021.

Green, James. *The Devil Is Here in These Hills: West Virginia's Coal Miners and their Battle for Freedom*. New York: Grove Press, 2015.

Hamby, Chris. *Soul Full of Coal Dust: A Fight for Breath and Justice in Appalachia*. New York: Little, Brown, 2020.

Keleher, William A. *The Maxwell Land Grant*. Albuquerque: University of New Mexico Press, 1984.

Kern, Robert, ed. *Labor in New Mexico: Unions, Strikes, and Social History since 1881*. Albuquerque: University of New Mexico Press, 1983.

Lane, D. R. "Dawson, New Mexico: Stag Canyon Fuel Company." In *New Mexico: The Land of Opportunity: Official Data on the Resources and Industries of New Mexico—the Sunshine State*. Albuquerque: Press of the Albuquerque Morning Journal, 1915, Part Two, 50–58.

McAteer, Davitt. *Monongah: The Tragic Story of the 1907 Monongah Mine Disaster*. Morgantown: West Virginia University Press, 2014.

Melzer, Richard. *Madrid Revisited: Life and Labor in a New Mexican Mining Camp in the Years of the Great Depression*. Santa Fe: Lightning Tree, 1976.

Moskos, Peter C., and Charles C. Moskos. *Greek Americans: Struggle and Success*. Abingdon: Routledge, 2014.

Myrick, David F. *New Mexico's Railroads: A Historical Survey*. Revised Edition. Albuquerque: University of New Mexico Press, 1990.

Olsen, Gregg. *The Deep Dark: Disaster and Redemption in America's Richest Silver Mine*. New York: Three Rivers Press, 2005.

Papanikolas, Zeese. *Buried Unsung: Louis Tikas and the Ludlow Massacre*. Lincoln: University of Nebraska Press, 1991.

Punke, Michael. *Fire and Brimstone: The North Butte Mining Disaster of 1917*. New York: Hachette Books, 2006.

Riskin, Marci L. *The Train Stops Here: New Mexico's Railway Legacy*. Albuquerque: University of New Mexico Press, 2005.

Scarpaci, Vincenza. *The Journey of the Italians in America*. Gretna, LA: Pelican, 2008.

Schwantes, Carlos A. *Vision & Enterprise: Exploring the History of Phelps Dodge Corporation*. Tucson: University of Arizona Press, 2000.

Smith, Toby. *Coal Town: The Life and Times of Dawson, New Mexico*. Santa Fe: Ancient City Press, 1993.

Stanley, F. *The Dawson, New Mexico Story*. Pantex, TX: F. Stanley, 1961.

Stanley, F. *The Dawson Tragedies*. Pep, TX: F. Stanley, 1964.

Tintori, Karen. *Trapped: The 1909 Cherry Mine Disaster*. New York: Atria, 2002.

Twitchell, Ralph Emerson, ed. *The Leading Facts of New Mexican History*, Volume 3. Cedar Rapids, IA: Torch Press, 1917.

Upton, D. Bradley. *Bradley Upton's Roads & Trails*. Solano, NM: D. B. Upton, 1989.

Upton, D. Bradley. *Homestead Daze in Burro Canyon: The Memoirs of D. Bradley Upton*. Self-published, 1986.

Upton, D. Bradley, and Janet Cates. *Homestead Daze in Burro Canyon: Part Two*. Self-published, 1991.

Whiteside, James. *Regulating Danger: The Struggle for Mine Safety in the Rocky Mountain Coal Industry*. Lincoln: University of Nebraska Press, 1990.

Wilde, Jeanne Wilkins. *Lavinia*. Lincoln, NE: iUniverse, 2005.

Wilson, Delphine Dawson. *John Barkley Dawson: Pioneer, Cattleman, Rancher*. Self-published, 1997.

Wolff, David A. *Industrializing the Rockies: Growth, Competition, and Turmoil in the Coalfields of Colorado and Wyoming, 1868–1914*. Boulder: University Press of Colorado, 2003.

Zimmer, Stephen, and Gene Lamm. *Images of America: Colfax County*. Charleston, SC: Arcadia Publishing, 2015.

Government Documents

Centers for Disease Control and Prevention. National Institute for Occupational Safety and Health. "Coal Mine Explosion Prevention." CDC website, last updated December 9, 2011. https://www.cdc.gov/niosh/mining/features/coalmineexplosion.html.

Centers for Disease Control and Prevention. National Institute for Occupational Safety and Health. "History of the Mining Program." CDC website, last updated September 19, 2012. https://www.cdc.gov/niosh/mining/content/history.html.

Fay, Albert H., comp. *Coal-Mine Fatalities in the United States, 1870–1914, with Statistics of Coal Production, Labor, and Mining Methods, by States and Calendar Years*. Washington, DC: Government Printing Office, 1916.

"National Register of Historic Places: Criteria for Evaluation." *Code of Federal Regulations*, Title 36, Parks, Forest, and Public Property, Chapter I, Part 60, Section 60.4.

National Register of Historic Places Registration Form: Dawson Cemetery. National Park Service. February 18, 1992. https://npgallery.nps.gov/GetAsset/89541c8b-ea85-4959-85f7-85994e4caa28.

New Mexico Bureau of Mines & Mineral Resources. *One Hundred Years of Coal Mining in the San Juan Basin, New Mexico*, by Howard B. Nickelson. Bulletin 111. Socorro, NM, 1988.

Report of the Mine Inspector for the Territory of New Mexico to the Secretary of the Interior (annual: Washington, DC: GPO, 1899–1911).

Report of the State Mine Inspector of New Mexico (annual: Gallup, NM, 1912–1950).

Report of the United States Coal Mine Inspector for the Territory of New Mexico to the Secretary of the Interior for the Fiscal Year Ending June 30, 1895. Washington, DC: GPO, 1895.

US Coal Commission. *Report of the United States Coal Commission*. Vol. 3: *Bituminous Coal: Detailed Labor and Engineering Studies*. Washington, DC: GPO, 1925.

US Congress. House. Subcommittee of the Committee of Mines and Mining. *Conditions in the Coal Mines of Colorado: Hearings before the Subcommittee of the Committee of Mines and Mining*. 63rd Cong., 2nd sess., February 9–12, 1914.

US Congress. Senate. *A Federal Mining Commission Address by John Randolph Haynes, M.D. before the Joint Session of the American Economic Association and the Association for Labor Legislation at Washington, D.C., December 30, 1911*. 62nd Cong., 2nd sess. Washington, DC: GPO, 1912.

US Congress. Senate. *A Resolution Designating December 6, 2009, as National Miners Day*. S. Res. 337. 111th Cong., 1st sess. Introduced December 3, 2009.

US Congress. Senate. US Immigration Commission. *Steerage Conditions; Importation and Harboring of Women for Immoral Purposes; Immigrant Homes and Aid Societies; Immigrant Banks*. 61st Cong., 3rd sess., December 13, 1909.

US Department of Commerce. Bureau of Mines. *Gases That Occur in Metal Mines*, by D. Harrington and E. H. Denny. Bulletin 347. Washington, DC: GPO, 1931.

US Department of Health and Human Services. *One Hundred Years of Federal Mining Safety and Health Research*, by John A. Breslin. DHHS (NIOSH) Publication No. 2010-128. Information Circular 9520. Pittsburgh, 2010.

US Department of Labor. Bureau of Labor Statistics. *Analysis of Work Stoppages during 1949*, by Don Q. Crowther and Ann J. Herlihy. Bulletin 1003. Washington, DC: GPO, 1950.

US Department of Labor. Mine Safety and Health Administration. *Coal Fatalities for 1900 through 2020*. Dataset. Accessed November 4, 2022 at https://arlweb.msha.gov/stats/centurystats/coalstats.asp.

US Department of Labor. *Report on No. 1 Mine Explosion, Dawson, New Mexico, February 8, 1923*, by D. Harrington. Washington, DC, April 1923.

US Department of the Interior. Bureau of Mines. *Black Damp in Mines*, by G. A. Burrell, I. W. Robertson, and G. G. Oberfell. Bulletin 105. Washington, DC: GPO, 1916.

US Department of the Interior. Bureau of Mines. *Loss of Life among Wearers of Oxygen Breathing Apparatus*, by G. W. Grove. Information Circular 7279. Washington, DC, April 1944.

US Department of the Interior. Bureau of Mines. *Self-Contained Oxygen Breathing*

Apparatus: A Handbook for Miners, by D. J. Parker, G. S. McCaa, and E. H. Denny. Washington, DC: GPO, 1934.

US Department of the Interior. Bureau of Mines. *United States Mining Statutes Annotated: Part I, Sections and Statutes Relating to Metalliferous and Coal Mining,* by J. W. Thompson. Bulletin 94. Washington, DC: GPO, 1915.

US Department of the Interior. *Coal-Mine Timbering: Technical Information for Use in Vocational Classes.* Vocational Education Bulletin No. 40. Trade and Industrial Series No. 10. Second revised edition. Washington, DC: GPO, 1935.

US Department of the Interior. United States Geological Society. *The Explosibility of Coal Dust,* by George S. Rice. Bulletin 425. Washington, DC: GPO, 1910.

Periodicals and Reports

Andrews, Vivien A. *Dawson Coal Mine Cemetery Inscriptions, Dawson, Colfax County, NM.* Booklet, 1998.

Becchetti, Fred. "Home Again to Dawson." *Raton Range* September 2, 1988.

Chow, Denise. "Why Do Mines Explode?" LiveScience website, April 6, 2010. http://www.livescience.com/environment/coal-mines-explosion-100406.html.

Hall, Morrow. "Forgotten Cemetery Lush with History." *Roswell Daily Record,* August 27, 1999: A5.

Holmes, Joseph A. "Report of the Director of Bureau of Mines." *Mining and Engineering World* 42, no. 3 (January 16, 1915): 137–38.

Langton, Jackson M. "The Dawson Ranch Coal Potential, Northeast of Cimarron, New Mexico." September 25, 1975. Freeport-McMoRan Collection.

Man, C. K., and K. A. Teacoach. "How Does Limestone Rock Dust Prevent Coal Dust Explosions in Coal Mines?" *Mining Engineering* 61, no. 9 (2009): 69–73.

Meloni, Giulia, and Johan F. M. Swinnen. "Standards, Tariffs and Trade: The Rise and Fall of the Raisin Trade between Greece and France in the Late 19th Century and the Definition of Wine." January 2017. LICOS Discussion Paper no. 386. https://papers.ssrn.com/sol3/papers.cfm?abstract_id=2919311.

Melzer, Richard. "A Death in Dawson: The Demise of a Southwestern Company Town." *New Mexico Historical Review* 55 no. 4 (October 1, 1980): 309–30.

Melzer, Richard. "Phelps Dodge Knows Best: Welfare Capitalism in a New Mexico Camp, Dawson, 1920–1929." *Southwest Economy & Society,* 6, no. 1 (Fall 1982): 12–34.

Pettit, R. F. Jr. "History of Mining in Colfax County." *New Mexico Geological Society 17th Annual Fall Field Office Guidebook.* Socorro, NM: NMGS, 1966.

Rogers, Jedediah S. "Vermejo Project: Historic Reclamation Projects." US Bureau of Reclamation, 2009. Edited and reprinted by Andrew H. Gahan, 2013. https://www.usbr.gov/history/ProjectHistories/Vermejo D2.pdf.

Savvy, Cee [Cecile Lunsford Crosthwaite]. "Disasters at Dawson." *Enchantment*, June 1980.

Skandale, Elizabeth. "A Mine Explosion." Unpublished manuscript, private collection.

Smil, Vaclav. "Crossing the Atlantic." *IEEE Spectrum*, April 2018: 23.

"The Story of the People of Modena Involved in the Tragedy of the Dawson Mine." MigrER, Council of Emilia-Romagna in the World. https://www.migrer. org/storie/la-storia-dei-modenesi-coinvolti-nella-tragedia-della-miniera-di-dawson/.

Tellier, S. "Blood and Coal." Unpublished manuscript. June 7, 2007.

Wright, Charles L. "The First National Mine-Safety Demonstration" *Scientific American* 105, no. 23 (December 1911): 498–99.

Zhu, Liping. "Claiming the Bloodiest Shaft: The 1913 Tragedy of the Stag Cañon Mine, Dawson, New Mexico." *Journal of the West*, 35, no. 4 (October 1996): 58–64.

Dissertations

Craig, Carlos J. "The Unionization of the Mines in Dawson, New Mexico." Master's thesis, New Mexico Highlands University, 1970.

Watt, Roberta. "History of Morenci, Arizona." Master's thesis, University of Arizona, 1956.

Newspapers

Alamogordo Daily News (NM)

Albuquerque Evening Herald (NM)

Albuquerque Journal (NM)

Albuquerque Morning Journal (NM)

Albuquerque Weekly Citizen (NM)

Amarillo Daily News (TX)

Arizona Daily Star

Arizona Republic

Baltimore Sun (MD)

Californian

Charleston Gazette-Mail (WV)

Chicago Tribune (IL)

Cimarron News (NM)

Clovis Evening News-Journal (NM)
Clovis News-Journal (NM)
Daily Mirror and American (NH)
Dawson News (NM)
Day Book (IL)
Denver Post (CO)
Desert Sun (CA)
Dodge City Journal (KS)
El Paso Herald (TX)
El Paso Herald-Post (TX)
El Paso Times (TX)
El Reno Daily Democrat (OK)
Engineering and Mining Journal
Gazetta dell'Emilia (Italy)
Hastings Daily Tribune (NE)
Kansas City Times (MO)
Lincoln Daily News (NE)
Los Angeles Times (CA)
Manchester Leader (NH)
Manchester Union (NH)
Milwaukee Journal (WI)
Omaha Daily News (NE)
Pittsburgh Post (PA)
Pittsburgh Post-Gazette (PA)
Pittsburgh Press (PA)
Raton Range (NM)
Roswell Daily Record (NM)
Sacramento Bee (CA)
Santa Fe Daily New Mexican (NM)
Santa Fe New Mexican (NM)
Star-Ledger (NJ)
Toluca Star (IL)
Tucson Citizen (AZ)
Tucson Daily Citizen (AZ)
Union (CA)
United Mine Workers Journal
Waco Morning News (TX)
Washington Times (DC)

INDEX

Afterdamp, 53

Alamogordo & Sacramento Mountain Railway, 21

Alamogordo Lumber Company, 21

American Hellenic Education and Progressive Association, 139

American Red Cross, 6, 28

Anders, Mary Ann, 136

Anderson, Clinton P., 127

Aragon, Alonzo, 91

Arkansas, 8–9

Arizona, 1, 3, 20, 22–24, 28, 40, 52, 57, 84, 95, 119–20, 128–31, 143, 147–49, 161

Arnold, G. O., 125–26

Atchison, Topeka and Santa Fe Railway, 19, 132

Atler, Albert, 158

Austria, xiv, 33–34, 39, 56, 59–60, 63, 72, 84, 104

Bacca, Bobbie Jo, 154

Bacca, Joe, 141, 154, 163

Badiali, Manlio, 61, 63, 161

Beaubien, Carlos, 13

Becchetti, Fred, 148

Beckett, P. G., 95, 106, 114, 118

Beddow, Rees H., 5, 46, 70–71, 75, 77–84, 86–87, 99

Bennett, Homer, 129

Bergamo, Fred, 128

Bisbee, Arizona, 25–27, 84, 131; Deportation, 119–20

Bituminous Coal Labor Board, 122

Black damp, 3, 45, 54

Blasting powder, 38, 70, 78, 147

Blossburg mine, New Mexico, 20, 52

Boswell, W. G., 133

Boyle, Amy, 158

Brennan, W. D., 95–96, 100, 107–8, 110, 113–14, 118

Brilliant mine, New Mexico, 20, 63, 91, 196

Brown, Thomas, 99–100

Brown University, 35, 67

California, 8–9, 15, 20, 39, 67, 115, 135, 144–46, 154, 157–58

Canoutas, Seraphim G., 29, 31

Caputo, Maria Makris, 65

Caraglio, John, 94

Carbon dioxide, 3, 45, 53

Carbon monoxide, 18, 69, 98, 100

Carson, Kit, 9, 19

Carthage Fuel Company fire, 99–100

Central Mining Company, Michigan 144

Cericola, Fred, 128

Cericola, Jay, 128

Cerrillos Coal Railroad Company, 37–38

Chávez, Dennis, 27

Chavez, Marcial, 146

Chemical Copper Company, Pennsylvania, 23

Cherry, Illinois, mine disaster, 42

Chicago, Rock Island & Pacific Railroad, 16, 19, 67, 73

Christian, Dale, 134–35, 137

Christian, Laura, 135

Christian, Lloyd, 134–35, 137

Church, William, 23–24

Coal Creek, Tennessee, mine disaster, 42

Coal cutting machines, 72, 89, 108, 112, 116, 119

Coal dust, 5, 15, 18, 28, 35, 38–39, 68–75, 79, 84–87, 105, 107, 109–13, 116–17, 151

Coal mine strikes, 120–24, 126, 143–44, 150

Cokedale, Colorado, mine disaster, 3

Colfax County War, 14

Collier, A. C., 57

Colorado, 1, 3–4, 6, 8–9, 13, 15, 19, 23, 30, 44, 48, 53, 56, 72, 76, 83, 96, 106, 118, 131, 147, 152

Colorado Fuel and Iron Company, 21, 48, 74, 95

Colorado School of Mines, 3, 141

Conger, Harry "Red," 141

Conway, Jay T., 90–91

Copper mining, 1, 3–4, 22–25, 28, 84, 129–31, 144, 147, 157

Courrières, France, mine disaster, 5

Couturier, J. A., 106, 152

Covert, Enes Federici Caraglio, 93–94

Cruz, Cornelia, 157

Cruz, George, 157, 159

Cruz, Joe, 157

Curtis, Joel, 13

Davis, Alvin, 138–39

Davis, Charles, 121–22

Davis, Chester NC, 140

Davis, Emily, 140

Davis, Gilbert, 120–21, 143

Davis, John Henry, 140

Davis, Pearl, 140

Dawson Cemetery, 58, 62, 92, 96, 134–42, 146, 152–53, 157–60, 163–64

Dawson coroner's inquest: 1913 mine disaster, 6, 76–84; 1923 mine disaster, 107–10

Dawson Elk Valley Ranch, 154

Dawson Facebook page, 147, 161

Dawson Fuel Company, 1, 15–18, 20–21

Dawson, Henrietta, 8

Dawson, John Barkley, 7–15, 158–59

Dawson, Lavinia, 12–13, 15

Dawson, New Mexico: founded, 16; funerals, 4, 57–59, 106; golf course, 22; hospital, 26–27; mercantile store, 25–26; mine disaster 1913, 1–6, 44–85; mine disaster 1923, 93–113; mine explosion 1920, 95–96; mine fire 1903, 17–18; opera house, 25; peak employment, 89; peak production, 89; ranch, 157; rescue station, 28; reunions, 64, 92, 138, 141, 144–48, 152–55, 157–59, 163–64; St. John the Baptist Church, 104, 106, 149–50; unionization, 122–23

Dawson New Mexico Association, 139, 141, 154, 157, 163–64

Dawson News, 90–91, 163

Dawson Railway Company, 16, 21, 114, 132–33

Delagua, Colorado, mine disaster, 3

Denver and Rio Grande Railroad Company, 19

Detroit Copper Mining Company, 22–23

Dillingham Commission, 32

DiLorenzo, David, 131

DiLorenzo, Fritzi, 131

DiMartino, Filomeno, 101–5, 109

DiVecchio, Mark, 101

Diver, Frank C., 27

Dodge, Cleveland E., 114

Dodge, Cleveland H., 45

Dodge, William E. Jr., 23

Douglas, James, 3–4, 21, 23, 52, 60, 63, 73–78, 88

Douglas, Walter, 3–4, 52, 59, 63, 69, 73, 84, 114, 116

Doyle, Edward L., 4

Dupont, Pearl, 93, 117–18

Dupont, Scott, 93, 97, 108, 113–14, 117–18

Eddy, Charles B., 15–16, 20–21

Ellis Island, 30, 100

El Paso & Northeastern Railroad, 16, 18–21

El Paso & Rock Island Railroad, 16, 19, 21, 67, 73

El Paso & Southwestern Railroad, 19, 28, 133, 152

English, Albert, 97–98

English, Albert Jr., 97–98, 107, 110

English, Arthur, 47, 58

English, Fred, 97

Evans, F. B., 82

Experimental Mine, Pennsylvania, 28, 75, 116

Federal Mine Safety & Health Act, 58

Fernández, Alicia, 145–46

Fernández, Antonio M., 127

Fernandez, Desiderio, 146

Fernández, Johnny Xavier, 146

Fernandez, Jose, 47–49

Fernández, Juan, 145–46

Fernández, Marshall, 146

Fire boss, 68–69, 109

Firedamp, 68

Fleming, John W., 37–38

Fort Craig, New Mexico, 18

Fort Smith, Arkansas, 8

France, xiv, 5, 31, 33–34, 39, 61, 91, 124, 161

Frazzini, Angelo, 117–18

Freeport-McMoRan, 141, 161–63

Freeport-McMoRan Foundation, 141

French, New Mexico, 132–33, 149

Frontier Power Company, 130–31

Gallup, New Mexico, mine disaster, 74–75

Garcia, Amelia Lopez, 26, 150–51

Garcia, Felipe, 47

Garcia, Gloria Atler, 158

Garcia, José Marcos, 150

Gardiner mine, New Mexico, 20, 91, 126

Germany, xiv, 33–34, 39, 63, 135

Glover, Vernon J., 20

Great Depression, 115

Greece, xiv, 6, 30–34, 43, 48, 56, 58, 60–61, 64–66, 91, 100–104, 106, 139, 160–62

Gonzalez, Nick, 127

Goodnight, Charles, 10

Grubesic, Anthony, 158

Grubesic, Bob, 158

Guest, Dugan, 129

Guthmann, Karl F., 127, 133

Hancock, William, 130–31

Haner, Ray C., 117–18

Hanraty, Peter, 68–70

Hall, Morrow, 134

Harrington, Daniel, 95, 111

Haynes, John Randolph, 37, 39–40

Hefferly, Frank, 121–22

Hernandez, Augustine, 128, 158

Hinkle, James F., 110

Holmes, Joseph A., 39, 51

Honkeiko, China, mine disaster, 69

Huerta, Dolores, xiv, 145–46, 158–59

Hungary, 33–34, 60, 72, 84

Iannacchione, Oliveta, 101, 104

Immigration, 29–34

Influenza pandemic of 1918, 91

Interstate Commerce Commission, 132

Italy, xiv, 6, 29–34, 38, 48, 58, 60–64, 72–73, 101, 104, 106, 118, 139, 161

Jacobs Creek, Pennsylvania, mine disaster, 42–43

Johnson, Walter, 47

Jones, D. P., 18

Karantzias, John, 91–92

Keating, Edward E., 4

Kelley, Brad, 154

Kemmerer, Wyoming, mine disaster, 3

Kerr, Walter, 51

Kinney, T. L., 4, 6, 76, 82–83, 107, 109

Knights of Labor, 70

Koelling, F. W., 124

Koehler mine, New Mexico, 20, 44, 50

Kotchou, Marlene Hancock, 130–31, 158

Kritikos, Alexis, 34

Ladis, Vasilios, 34

Laird, James, 50–53, 100

Landers, Rick, 159

Langton, Jackson M., 143

Larrazolo, Octaviano, 96

Lewis, John L., 120–25

Loger, Ben, 140

Lorenzo, Sylvester, 121

Lucero, Robert, 92

Lunsford, May Dee, 93–94

Maglis, Vasilios, 34

Makris, Constantine, 33–34, 65, 162

Makris, Georgios V., 33–34, 64–65, 162

Makris, Michael, 65

Makris, Vasilios G., 66

Manchester (NH) High School, 35

Martin, W. R., 18

Maryol, Georgia, 139

Maulding, Taylor, 13

Mavroidis, George, 48, 50

Maxwell Land Grant, 13

Maxwell Land Grant Company, 14, 19

Maxwell Land Grant and Railway Company, 14

Maxwell, Lucien, 13

McDermott, William, 6, 50, 52, 54–55, 58, 72–73, 77–78, 82–83

McDonald, William C., 6, 94, 98

McGarvey, Hannah, 144, 149

McShane, Emmeline P., 60

McShane, Henry P., 55, 58, 60

Melzer, Richard, foreword, xi–xii; 90, 115, 161

Mexico, 10, 13, 18, 20, 26, 33–34, 39, 47, 56, 58–59, 103–4, 128, 148, 151

Miles, John E., 127

Miller, Dick, 13

Mine check in/check out system, 58, 81–82, 84

Mine rock dust, 111, 116

Mine safety, 1, 27, 28, 41, 51, 68, 71, 86–87, 111, 116–17

Mine shot firing, 5, 70–71, 78–81, 83–85, 95–96, 111

Mine sprinklers, 1, 86, 112–13

Mine timbering, 41, 116

Mine ventilation, 1–3, 5, 17–18, 38, 40–41, 45–46, 70, 72–73, 77–78, 94–95, 97, 100, 102, 107, 111

Miranda, Guadalupe, 13

Monongah, West Virginia, mine disaster, 42–43

Montgomery, Robert, 121

Montoya, Ernest, 47

Morenci, Arizona, 22–27, 143

Morgan, William, 53

Munden, Ed, 121

Muñoz, Angelo, 155

Muñoz, Frank, 155

Murphy, David, 99–100

National Iron and Metal Company, 129–30

National Park Service, 136–37

New Hampshire, 34, 66–67, 160, 162

New Mexico Department of Cultural Affairs, 134

New Mexico Historic Preservation Division, 134, 136–37

New Mexico mine inspector, 5, 16, 18, 20, 39–41, 46, 50, 68–71, 73–74, 77, 79, 81, 83–84, 86, 95–96, 98–100, 110, 112, 116, 162

New Mexico Railway and Coal Company, 21

New Mexico Register of Cultural Properties, 137

New Mexico State Corporation Commission, 132

New York, 1, 4, 20–24, 26, 29, 31, 33, 45, 48, 52, 55, 58–59, 61, 66, 71, 88, 121

Nizzi, Giovanni, 50, 60

Nizzi, Marco, 49–50

Norris, Nat, 149

O'Brien, T. H., 1–2, 44–45, 52, 59, 62–63, 73–75, 81–84, 88, 93, 99

Oklahoma, 8, 40, 67–70, 114, 139

Padilla, Joseph, 149–50

Palmer, Amalia, 152

Palmer, Avelina, 152

Palumbo, Domenick, 109–10

Pattison, Thomas H., 82–85

Paul, James W., 78, 95

Perez, Roberta Hernandez, 128, 158

Phelps, Anson Green, 22–23

Phelps, Dodge & Company/Corporation: Arizona copper holdings, 20–24, 28, 119–20, 129; company founding, 22–23; Dawson mines acquisition, 1, 21; Dawson mines closing, 115, 125, 128; Dawson town closing, 124–31, 143–44, 150; hiring of salvage firm, 128; model company towns, 22–28; union relations, 48, 90, 119–23, 125–26

Pick, Vivien, 137–39, 163

Pit boss, 6, 17

Poland, xiv, 31, 33

Poyser, William, 50–53, 100

Prohibition, 91

Raton Coal and Coke Company, 39

Raton Museum, 139, 144, 157

Raton, New Mexico, 39, 49, 51–52, 56–58, 92, 96–97, 100, 117, 121, 125–26, 129, 136, 139, 141, 144, 147–49, 153–54, 157, 162, 164

Reed, Albert James, 96

Reed, Stephen, 96

Remley, George E., 6, 76–83

Rengal, Serapio, 18

Reza, Mary Frances, 150

Ridolfi, Bruno, 141

Risdon, W. W., 95, 98–100, 110–11, 116

Roberts, J. C., 1–3, 51, 69, 78

Rough and Ready, California, 8–9

Russell, J. S., 106

Salazar, Miguel M., 18

Sánchez, Petra Tovar, 151

Santi, Frank, 61–64

Santi, Walter, 63–64

Scanlon, Jerry, 64

Scarafiotti, Guerino, 97–98

Scarafiotti, Guido, 97–98

Scarafiotti, Pietro "Pete," 146–47, 161

Schwegel, John C., 60, 72–73, 84

Scofield, Utah, mine disaster, 42

Searle, F. C., 44–45

Shapiro, Samuel, 129

Shepherd, William G., 71–72

Sheridan, Jo E., 16–18, 74–75, 81, 96, 99

Shields, Harvey M., 56–57

Simpleman, Roy, 50–51

Skandale, Antonio, 103

Skandale, Charles George, 100–104, 144, 162

Skandale, Elizabeth, 101, 104, 162

Skandale, George, 104, 144

Skandale, Nick, 144

Slavs, 33–34, 43, 104

Smith, Joe, 72–73

Springer Electric Cooperative of New Mexico, 131

Southern Pacific Railroad, 19, 125, 132–33, 144, 149, 153

Southwestern Mercantile Company, 17, 25

St. Elias the Prophet Greek Orthodox Church, 139

St. George Greek Orthodox Church, 139

St. Louis, Rocky Mountain & Pacific Company, 19, 27

Stag Cañon Fuel Company, 1, 5, 27, 72, 83, 99, 122–23, 139

Stanley, Richard, 113–14

Stavrakis, Polichronis, 34

Stockton, Edwena, 10, 13

Stockton, Tom, 10–11

Stringer, Ambrose, 49–50

Subat, Jakob, 59–60

Sugarite mine, New Mexico, 44, 91, 126

Supreme Court, Territory of New Mexico, 14

Supreme Court, US, 7, 14

Swastika mine, New Mexico, 63

Sze, Corinne, 136

Tenorio, Carlos, 155

Texas, 4, 9–11, 13, 20, 45, 56, 129–30

Texas Rangers, 10

Thomas, Edmond, 108–9, 113

Thomas, George, 57–58

Thompson, Pam, 139–40

Tikas, Louis, xiv, 48

Tingley, Clyde, 121

Tinsley, Tim, 6, 78

Trujillo, Alfredo, 152, 158

Trujillo, Anselmo, 158

Trujillo, Jesse, 152

Trujillo, Juan, 47

Trujillo, Patty, 152

Tsakonas, Christos, 30

Tucumcari, New Mexico, 16, 66, 114, 125, 131–33, 152–53

Turner, Frank, 152–53

United Mine Workers of America, 120–25, 127, 147

United Mine Workers Journal, 4–5, 83

Ulibarri, Patricio, 47

Universal Colliery, South Wales, mine disaster, 69

Upton, Alice Estella, 36, 67

Upton, Dorothy Lloyd, 67

Upton, Florence, 151

Upton, Hiram D., 34–35

Upton, Lloyd Peter, 34–36, 66–67, 162

US Bureau of Mines, 1–2, 5, 28, 39–40, 45, 51, 69–70, 75, 78, 85, 95, 111, 116, 136

Utah, 30, 40, 42, 101

Utley, T. M., 117

Van Houten mine, New Mexico, 20, 44, 91, 111, 138

Vermejo River, 11, 13–14, 16–17, 127, 150, 158

Victor American Fuel Company, 15

Vozos, Fannie, 61, 65

Wallsend, England, mine disaster, 74

White Ash Mine, New Mexico, 37–38

White Oaks, New Mexico, 6, 20

Wilson, John, 131

Wilson, Nellie, 131

Wilson, Robert, 131

Wootton, Richens Lacy "Uncle Dick," 19

Worcester, R. H., 76–77

World War I, 35, 63, 89, 91–92

World War II, 92, 122, 131, 153

Wyoming, 3, 9, 30, 42, 69, 95, 115, 158

Yankee mine, New Mexico, 44, 91

Zavala, Edward, 153–54, 163